Australian Tales

Marcus Andrew Hislop Clarke

AUSTRALIAN TALES

BY THE LATE

MARCUS CLARKE

WITH A

BIOGRAPHY

BY

HAMILTON MACKINNON.

LORD ROSEBERY writes (1884) :—

"It is rare, I think, that so young a country has produced so great a literary force. I cannot but believe that the time must soon come when Australians will feel a melancholy pride in this true son of genius."

MELBOURNE :

A. & W. BRUCE, PRINTERS, 434 BOURKE STREET.

MDCCCXCVI.

"THREE CASTLES" *CIGARETTES*

MILD and FRAGRANT.

"CAPSTAN" *CIGARETTES (Navy Cut).*

Manufactured from the
Finest Selected Growth of Virginia.

"THREE CASTLES" *TOBACCO*

In 2 oz. square packets.

"CAPSTAN" *TOBACCO (Navy Cut).*

Three grades of strength—" Mild," " Medium," and
" Full" Flavor.   In 2 oz. and 4 oz. Patent Air-tight Tins.

Manufactured
by **W. D. & H. O. WILLS Ltd.,**

Bristol and London, U.K.

THE

Victoria Insurance Co. Ltd.

Authorised Capital, £1,000,000.

Subscribed Capital, £898,710.

Paid-up Capital, £50,000.

Reserve Fund, £50,000.

Chairman, HON. EDWARD MILLER.

Fire, Marine, and General Insurance Business Conducted.

W. LEE ARCHER, Secretary,

Market Street, Melbourne.

CONTENTS.

PRESBYTERIAN LADIES' COLLEGE,
EAST MELBOURNE.

Principal ... ... *Rev. S. G. M'Laren, M.A.*
Head Master ... *J. P. Wilson, Esq., M.A., LL.D.*

1. **THE EDUCATION IS UNSURPASSED.** Here the College stands at the head of all girls' schools—16 Exhibitions, 61 First Class Honors, and 48 Second Class Honors having been won in 15 years. At last examination 11 pupils passed, and 11 more were classed in Honors; 27 separate Honors were gained. The Exhibition in English and History was also won for the eighth time in 11 years. There is a Kindergarten for the little ones.

2. **ACCOMPLISHMENTS** are as thoroughly taught as ordinary branches. Mr. G. B. Fentum, Herr Hartung, and others, teach Music and Singing. Scholarships are awarded for Music and Singing. Senhor Loureiro teaches Drawing and Painting. Gymnastics, Elocution, Bookkeeping, &c., taught by the best specialists.

3. **THE DISCIPLINE IS GOOD.** The manners and morals of the pupils are alike attended to. Outside the round of study, all healthy interests, physical and social, are fostered, and bulk largely in the life of the College.

4. **WITH REGARD TO BOARDERS**, their education, health, training, and religious instruction are carefully attended to. Recreation is mingled with study, and opportunities for social intercourse are provided. The Council of the College recognise the keen competition there is now between schools, and they are determined that in **EVERY RESPECT** the Ladies' College shall be kept in the front rank. Delicate girls, girls laid aside by illness, and young girls receive special attention. Each boarder goes to her own church.

For Illustrated Handbook apply to the Principal.

Pupils may enter at any time, and are charged in proportion.

TO THE

AUSTRALIAN PUBLIC

THIS BOOK IS

DEDICATED

BY THE AUTHOR'S WIDOW.

"MARK TWAIN" ON MARCUS CLARKE.

LECTURE, MELBOURNE, OCT., 1895.

"I not only regret, but feel surprised that the 'Selected Works' of Australia's only literary genius—a genius such as you will not see again for many a long year—should be out of print. Through the courtesy of his widow I obtained a copy of the work after failing to buy one anywhere. And such a work, such reading, such power. It was just the sort of reading to banish from one's thoughts such pain as I have been suffering. The subjects so interesting, and their treatment so brilliant and fascinating. No works of such a man should be left unpublished. It is the *duty* of Australians to assist the widow of so great a writer in publishing his works. I may tell you that we think a deal more of Marcus Clarke in our country than I am sorry to think you do here." (Applause).

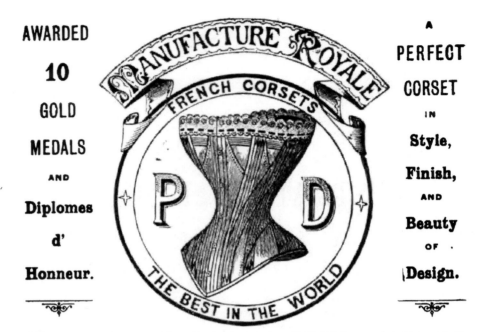

PREFACE.

IN placing this, the first volume of a cheap series of the miscellaneous works of the late MARCUS CLARKE before the Public of Australia, I venture to think that I am not only fulfilling my duty as his Literary Executor, but am removing a reproach which attaches to that Public in the eyes of such literary lights as Lord Rosebery, Sir Charles Dilke, " Mark Twain," the late Oliver Wendell Holmes and others who have spoken and written in no stinted phrases as to Marcus Clarke's position in the intellectual world, and expressed surprise at his works not being more popularly known among those on whom his genius has shed world-wide renown. To enable these works to come within the buying power of all classes, this series is being brought out at a price which no one should cavil about. It is therefore to be hoped that the people of these " new lands 'cross the seas " will give an emphatic denial to the old world saying—" a prophet hath no honour in his own country." In conclusion, grateful thanks are due to those who have rendered the publication of this book possible by assisting the author's widow in the very practical manner of advertising in it ; and of these let it be said :

" Cast thy bread upon the waters, for
Thou shalt find it after many days."

HAMILTON MACKINNON.

IS BOTTLED AND SHIPPED UNDER BOND

BY

ANDREW M'NAB & CO., LEITH.

The *Lancet* is the greatest Medical Journal in the World and it says:—

"GALLEY WHISKY is a thoroughly well matured spirit, exceptionally mellow to the taste, and, notwithstanding its excellent rich color, there is no residue, and mineral matter and fusel oil are absolutely nil."

" A THOROUGHLY HEALTHY STIMULANT."

Litthauer Stomach Bitters.

One Small Wineglassful on Rising.
One Small Wineglassful before Dinner.
Half Small Wineglassful before going to Bed.
Will be found to be

AN EXCELLENT TONIC,

And an

EFFICACIOUS STIMULANT TO EXCITE THE APETITE.

LLOYD'S MISSING FRIENDS, NEXT OF KIN,

Unclaimed Money and Secret Investigation Offices,

101 SWANSTON ST., MELBOURNE, AUSTRALIA.

Telegraphic Address—"*Subvolabus*" (Registered at Reuter's).   Telephone 1375.

Advances made on Legacies, Reversions, Life Annuities, Settlements, Interests under Wills, &c., and same promptly and cheaply Collected through guaranteed British and Foreign Agents.   Assistance rendered for the prosecution and recovery of claims in any part of the world.
Lloyd's Unclaimed Money Register of Chancery Heirs, Next of Kin, and persons advertised for to claim money for the past century.   Search and Particulars, 10/6.
Private Inquiry Branch—Confidential and Secret Investigations conducted in all parts of the World by Expert Detectives.

BIOGRAPHY.

MARCUS ANDREW HISLOP CLARKE was born at Kensington—the Old Court suburb of London—on the 24th April, 1846. His father, William Hislop Clarke, a barrister-at-law, was recognised as a man of ability, both professionally and as a *littérateur*, albeit eccentric to a degree. Of his mother little is known beyond that she was a beautiful woman, of whom her husband was so devotedly fond that when her death occurred some months after the birth of the subject of this biography, he isolated himself from the world, living afterwards the life of a recluse, holding of the world an opinion of cynical contempt. Besides his father, there were among other brothers of his two whose names belong to the history of the Australian colonies; the one is that of James Langton Clarke, once a County Court Judge in Victoria, and the other, Andrew Clarke, Governor of Western Australia, who died and was buried at Perth in 1849. The latter was the father of General Sir Andrew Clarke, K.C.M.G., formerly Minister of Public Works in India, and Governor of the Straits Settlements. To the colonists of Victoria he will be better known as Captain Clarke, the first Surveyor-General of the colony, the author of the Existing Municipal Act, and one of the few lucky drawers of a questionable pension from this colony.

The late Marcus Clarke claimed a distinguished genealogy for his family, which, though hailing as regards his immediate ancestors from the Green Isle, were English, having only betaken themselves to Ireland in the Cromwellian period. And among his papers were found the following notes referring to this matter :—

In 1612 William Clarke was made a burgess of Mountjoie, Co. Tyrone, and in 1658 Thurloe wrote to Henry Cromwell, desiring him to give Colonel Clarke land in Ireland for pay.

With an inherited delicate constitution, and without the love-watching care of a mother, or the attention of sisters, he passed his childhood. And that the absence of this supervision and guidance was felt by him in after years, we have but to read this pathetic passage from a sketch of his :—

To most men the golden time comes when the cares of a mother or the attention of sister aid to shield the young and eager soul from the blighting influences of wordly debaucheries. Truly fortunate is he among us who can look back on a youth spent in the innocent enjoyments of the country, or who possesses a mind moulded in its adolescence by the gentle fingers of well-mannered and pious women.

When considered old enough to leave home the boy was sent to the private school of Dr. Dyne in Highgate, another suburb of London, hallowed by having been at one time associated with such illustrious names in literature as Coleridge, Charles Lamb, Keats, and De Quincey. Here he obtained whatever scholastic lore he possessed, and was, according to the opinion of a schoolfellow, known as a humorously eccentric boy, with a most tenacious memory and an insatiable desire to read everything he could lay hands on. Owing to his physical inability to indulge in the usual boyish sports, he was in the habit of wandering about in search of knowledge wherever it was to be gleaned, and not infrequently this restless curiosity, which remained with him to the last, led him into quarters which it had been better for his yet unformed mind he had never entered. Here especially was felt the absence of a mother's guidance, which was unfortunately replaced by the carelessness of an indulgent father. Of his schooldays little is known, save what can be gathered from a note-book kept by him at that period; and even in this the information is but fragmentary. According to this book he seems to have had only two friends with whom he was upon terms of great intimacy. They were brothers, Cyril and Gerald Hopkins, who appear, judging from jottings and sketches of theirs in his scrap album, to have been talented beyond the average schoolboy. Among the jottings to be found in this school record is one bearing the initials G. H., and referring to one " Marcus Scrivener " as a " Kaleidoscopic, Parti-colored, Harlequinesque Thaumatropic " being. Another item which may not be uninteresting to read, as indicating the turn for humorous satire, which, even at so early a period of his life the author had begun to develop, is an epitaph written on himself, and runs thus :—

Hic Jacet
MARCUS CLERICUS,
Qui non malus, 'Coonius
Consideretus fuit
Sed amor bibendi
Combinatus cum pecuniæ deficiens
Mentem ejus oppugnabat—
Mortuus est
Et nihil ad vitam restorare
Posset.

To his schoolmaster, the Reverend Doctor Dyne, the following dedication to a novel *(Chatteris)* commenced by his former pupil shortly after his arrival in Australia was written. From this it is apparent that the master had not failed to recognise the talents of his gifted pupil, nor yet be blind to his weaknesses. It reads—

To
T. B. DYNE, D.D.,
Head Master of Chomley School, Highgate.
This Work
Is respectfully dedicated in memory of the advice so tenderly
given, the good wishes so often expressed, and the
success so confidently predicted for the author.

But whatever good influences might have been at work during his residence at Dr. Dyne's school, they were, unfortunately for their subject, more than counterbalanced by others of a very dissimilar character met with by him at his father's house. It seems scarcely credible that so young a boy was allowed to grow up without any restraining influences except those of a foolishly-indulgent father, as we are led to believe was the case from the following extract, which the writer knows was intended by the subject of the biography as a reference to his boyish days when away from school. Doubtless the picture is somewhat over-coloured, but substantially it is true :—

My first intimation into the business of "living" took place under these auspices. The only son of a rich widower, who lived, under sorrow, but for the gratification of a literary and political ambition, I was thrown when still a boy into the society of men twice my age, and was tolerated as a clever impertinent in all those witty and wicked circles in which virtuous women are conspicuous by their absence. I was suffered at sixteen to ape the vices of sixty. You can guess the result of such a training. The admirer of men whose successes in love and play were the theme of common talk for six months ; the worshipper of artists, whose genius was to revolutionise Europe, only they died of late hours and tobacco ; the pet of women whose daring beauty made their names famous for three years. I discovered at twenty years of age that the pleasurable path I had trodden so gaily led to a hospital or a debtors' prison, that love meant money, friendship an endorsement on a bill, and that the rigid exercise of a profound and calculating selfishness alone rendered tolerable a life at once deceitful and barren. In this view of the world I was supported by those middle-aged Mephistopheles (survivors of the storms which had wrecked so many Argosies), those cynical, well-bred worshippers of self, who realise in the nineteenth century that notion of the Devil which was invented by early Christians. With these good gentlemen I lived, emulating their cynicism, rivalling their sarcasm, and neutralising the superiority which their existence gave them by the exercise of that potentiality for present enjoyment, which is the privilege of youth.

Again, in another sketch he wrote, referring to this period of his life :—

Let me take an instant to explain how it came about that a pupil of the Rev. Gammons, up in town for his holidays, should have owned such an acquaintance. My holidays, passed in my father's widowed house, were enlivened by the coming and going of my cousin Tom from Woolwich, of cousin Dick from Sandhurst, of cousin Harry from Aldershot. With Tom, Dick, and Harry came a host of friends—for as long as he was not disturbed, the head of the house rather liked to see his rooms occupied by the relatives of people with whom he was intimate, and a succession of young men of the Cingbars, Ringwood, and Algernon Deuceacre sort made my home a temporary roosting-place. I cannot explain how such a curious *ménage* came to be instituted, for, indeed, I do not know myself, but such was the fact, and "little Master," instead of being trained in the way he should morally go, became the impertinent companion of some very wild-bloods indeed. "I took Horace to the opera last night, sir," or " I am going to show Horatius Cocles the wonders of Cremorne this evening," would be all that Tom, or Dick, or Harry, would deign to observe, and my father would but lift his eyebrows in indifferent deprecation. So, a wild-eyed and eager school-boy, I strayed into Bohemia, and acquired in that strange land an assurance and experience ill suited to my age and temperament. Remembering the wicked, good-hearted inhabitants of that curious country, I have often wondered since "what they thought of it," and have interpreted, perhaps not unjustly, many of the homely tenderness which seemed to me then so strangely out of place and time.

In the midst of this peculiar and doubtful state of existence for a youth his father died suddenly, leaving his affairs in an unsatisfactory state. This unexpected change brought matters to a climax, and at seventeen years of age Marcus Clarke found that instead of inheriting, as expected, a considerable sum of money, he was successor to only a few hundred pounds, the net result of the realisation of his late father's estate. With this it was arranged by his guardian relatives that he should seek a fresh field for his future career, and accordingly in 1864 he was shipped off to Melbourne by Green's well-known old liner, " The Wellesley," consigned to his uncle, Judge Clarke, above mentioned. Referring to this episode of his life, he has written in the following sarcastic and injured strain :—

My father died suddenly in London, and to the astonishment of the world left me nothing His expenditure had been large, but as he left no debts, his income must have been proportionate to his expenditure. The source of this income, however, it was impossible to discover. An examination of his bankers' book showed only that large sums (always in notes or gold) had been lodged and drawn out, but no record of speculations or investments could be found among his papers. My relatives stared, shook their heads, and insulted me with their pity. The sale of furniture, books, plate, and horses, brought enough to pay the necessary funeral expenses and leave me heir to some £800. My friends of the smoking-room and of the supper-table philosophised on Monday, cashed my I O U's on Tuesday, were satirical on Wednesday, and cut me on Thursday. My relatives said "Something must be done," and invited me to stop at their houses until that vague substantiality should be realised, and offers of employment were generously made; but to all proposals I replied with sudden disdain, and, desirous only of avoiding those who had known me in my prosperity, I avowed my resolution of going to Australia.

After one of those lengthy voyages for which the good old ship " The Wellesley" was renowned, the youth of bright fancies and disappointed fortune set foot in Melbourne ; and, after the manner of most "new chums" with some cash at command and no direct restraining power at hand, he set himself readily to work, fathoming the social and other depths of his new home. The natural consequence of this was that one who had prematurely seen so much "life" in London, soon made his way into quarters not highly calculated to improve his morals or check his extravagantly-formed habits. In other words, he began his Bohemian career in Australia with a zest not altogether surprising in one who had been negligently allowed to drift into London Bohemianism. And naturally, a youth with such exceptional powers of quaint humour, playful satire, and *bonhomie* became a universal favourite wherever he went, much, unfortunately, to his own future detriment. But, in due course, a change came of necessity o'er this Bohemian dream, when the ready cash was no longer procurable without work. It was then, through the influence of his uncle the Judge, that the impecunious youth was relegated to a high stool in the Bank of Australasia. As might have been expected of one who spent most of his time in drawing caricatures and writing satirical verses and sketches he was a *lusus naturæ* to the authorities of the bank, and this is not to be wondered at when one learns that his mode of adding up long columns of figures was by guesswork, to wit, he would run his eye over the pence column, making a guess at the aggregate amount, and so on with the shillings and pounds columns.

After a patient trial of some months it was considered, in the interests of all concerned, that he should seek his livelihood at a more congenial avocation, and thereupon he left the bank. But here must be mentioned the manner in which the severance took place, as being characteristic of him. Clarke applied for a short leave of absence. The letter containing this request not having been immediately answered he sought the presence of the manager for an explanation, when the following scene took place :—Clarke : " I have come to ask, sir, whether you received my application for a few weeks' leave of absence." The Manager : " I have." Clarke : " Will you grant it to me, sir?" The Manager : "Certainly, and a longer leave, if you desire it." Clarke: "I feel very much obliged. How long may I extend it to, sir?" The Manager: "Indefinitely, if you do not object!" Clarke: "Oh! I perceive, sir; you consider it best for us to part; and perhaps it is best so, sir?" And Mr. Clarke ceased to be a banker. Here it will not be inopportune to quote from an article on "Business Men," written by him subsequently, referring to this banking experience:—

It has always been my misfortune through life not to be a Business Man. When I went into a bank—The Polynesian, Antarctic and Torrid Zone—I suffered. I was correspondence clerk, and got through my work with immense rapidity. The other clerks used to stare when they saw me strolling homewards punctually at four. I felt quite proud of my accomplishments. But in less than no time a change took place. Letters came down from up-country branches. "I have received cheques to the amount of £1 15s. 6d., of two of which *no* mention is made in your letter of advice." "Sir! how is it that my note of hand for £97 4s. 1¾d., to meet which I forwarded Messrs. Blowhard and Co.'s acceptance, has been dishonoured by your branch at Warrnambool?." "*Private.*—Dear Cashup: Is your correspondent a hopeless idiot? I can't make head or tail of his letter of advice. As far as I can make out, he seems to have sent out the remittances to the wrong places.—Yours, T. TOTTLE." I am afraid that it was all true. The manager sent for me, said that he loved me as his own brother, and that I wore the neatest waistcoats he had ever seen, but that my genius was evidently fettered in a bank. Here was a quarter's salary in advance, he had no fault, quite the reverse; but, but, well—in short—I was not a Business Man

In addition to this the following remark, bearing on the same subject, written in one of the "Noah's Ark" papers in the *Australasian*, may also here be quoted:

A Man of Business, said Marston, oracularly, is one who becomes possessed of other people's money without bringing himself under the power of the law.

Finding commercial pursuits were not his *forte*, the youthful ex-banker bethought him of turning his attention to the free and out-door existence of a bushman. Accordingly he, shortly after leaving the bank in 1865, obtained, through his uncle, Judge Clarke, a "billet" on Swinton Station, near Glenorchy, belonging to Mr. John Holt, and in which the Judge had a pecuniary interest. Here he remained for some two years mastering the mysteries of bushmanship in the manner described in the sketch in this volume, styled "Learning Colonial Experience." It was during his sojourn in this wild and mountainous region that our author imbibed that love for the weird, lonely Australian Bush, which he so graphically and pathetically describes in so many of his tales—notably in "Pretty Dick," a perfect bush idyll to those who know the full meaning of the words Australian Bush. Although sent up to learn the ways and means of working a station, it is to be feared that the results of the lessons were not over fruitful. Indeed, beyond roving about the unfrequented portions of the run in meditation wrapped, pipe in mouth and book in pocket, in case of thoughts becoming wearisome, the sucking squatter did little else till night set in, and then the change of programme simply meant his retiring after the evening meal to his own room and spending the time well into midnight writing or reading. From one who was a companion of his on the station at the time, viz., the popular sportsman—genial, generous—Donald Wallace, I have learned that though Clarke wrote almost every night he kept the product of his labour to himself. But we now know that the work of his pen appeared in several sketches in the *Australian Magazine*, then published by Mr. W. H. Williams. These were written under the *nom de plume* of Marcus Scrivener. It was while residing in this district that he took stock of the characters which he subsequently utilised in all his tales relating to bush life. For instance, "Bullocktown," is well known to Glenorchy, the post-town of the Swinton Station, and all the characters in it are recognisable as life portraits presented with that peculiar glamor which his genius cast over all his literary work. And to one of the characters in it—Rapersole—the then local postmaster, Mr. J. Wallace, I am under an obligation for supplying me with some incidents in our author's bush career. According to Mr. Wallace young Clarke was a great favourite with everybody, and was the life and soul of local entertainments such as concerts, balls, &c., in which he took part with great zest. He was also at that time a regular attendant at church, and a frequent visitor to the local State-school, in which he evinced a lively interest, giving prizes to the boys. He was, moreover, an omnivorous reader, getting all the best English magazines and endless French novels from Melbourne regularly. But whatever progress he may have been making in his literary pursuits, it was found by Mr. Holt that as a "hand" on the station he was not of countless price. Indeed, it was discovered after he had been there some months, that not only did the gifted youth pay little heed to his unintellectual work, but that he had to a great extent imbued others engaged on the station, with such a love for reading—more particularly the novels of Honoré Balzac—that the routine duty of their daily existence became so irksome that they sought consolation by taking shelter from the noonday sun under some umbrageous gum-tree, listening to their instructor as he translated some of the delicate passages from the works of the Prince of French novelists.

Accordingly it was mutually agreed by the employer and employé that the best course to pursue under the circumstances was to part company. But, fortunately for the literary bushman, it was just at this time, when he had tried two modes of making a living and had hopelessly failed in both, that a person appeared on the scene who was destined to direct his brilliant talents to their proper groove. There came as a visitor to Mr. Holt, in the beginning of 1867, Dr. Robert Lewins. As Dr. Lewins had no small share in shaping the after career of Marcus Clarke, it behoves me to briefly refer here to him and his theories. Dr. Lewins, who had been staff-surgeon-major to General Chute during the New Zealand war, had shortly before this arrived in Melbourne with the British troops, *en route* to England ; and, being a friend of Mr. Holt's, went on a visit to him to Ledcourt, on which station Clarke was then employed. Learning while there of the peculiar youth whom Mr. Holt had as assistant, Dr. Lewins, who was like most thinking men of his class, always on the look-out for discoveries, whether human or otherwise, sought an introduction to the boy, whom practical Mr. Holt considered a "ne'er do weel." And no sooner was the introduction brought about than the learned medico discovered that, buried within view of the Victorian Grampians, lay hidden an intellectual gem of great worth. Rapidly a mutual feeling of admiration and regard sprang up between the young literary enthusiast of twenty and the learned medico of sixty—an attachment which lasted through life. The *savant* admired the rare talents of his *protegé* with the love of a father ; while the fanciful boy looked up to the learned man who had discerned his abilities, and placed him on the road to that goal for which he was destined. But the influence of the elder on the younger man did not cease here, as without doubt the former converted the latter to his views regarding existence. What these views were the Doctor explained in more than one pamphlet addressed to eminent men in England and Europe. As regards his pet theory, which he affirmed he had proved beyond doubt by experiments, extending over forty years, in all parts of the world, it may be, for the curious, briefly explained in his own words, as follows :—

"1. That there is no distinct vital principle apart from ordinary inorganic matter or force,

"That oxygen is capable of assuming an imponderable form, and that it is identical with the Cosmic '*primum mobile*,' the basis of light, heat, chemical affinity, attraction, and electric force.

"3. That the theory of materialism is, in fact, the only tenable theory."

The result of this tuition as regards Clarke was a remarkably able article on "Positivism," which he wrote some months afterwards, and which, I believe, saw light in one of the Liberal English reviews. But I am forestalling the order of the biography. Having satisfied himself upon the merits of the newly-found intellect, the doctor, on his return to Melbourne, told the proprietor of the *Argus*, with whom he was acquainted, of his discovery, advising him to secure the unknown genius for his journal, and so, in the course of a few weeks after meeting Dr. Lewins, Marcus Clarke appeared in Melbourne, and in February, 1867, became a member of the literary staff of the *Argus*. After an initiation into the mysteries of a newspaper office the young journalist was allotted the task of theatrical reporter, which routine drudgery he performed satisfactorily till one night he took upon himself to criticise an entertainment, which, unfortunately, through the indisposition of the chief performer, did not come off. This carelessness on the part of the imaginative critic led to his withdrawal from the *Argus* reporting staff, but his relations with that paper and the *Australasian* were, however, continued as a contributor. It was during this period that Marcus Clarke contributed to the *Australasian* the two masterly reviews on Doré and Balzac, published in these pages, besides writing weekly for the same journal those sparkling and humorous papers, "The Peripatetic Philosopher," which brought his name prominently before the public and placed him at once in the front rank of Australian journalists—and here it may be mentioned that the letter "Q.," under which he wrote the weekly contributions, was the stock brand of the station on which he had attempted to learn "colonial experience." Apart, however, from his contributions to the *Australasian*, he supplied special articles to the *Argus*, and acted as the theatrical critic of that paper for some time, during which he wrote some admirable critiques on the late Walter Montgomery's performances—critiques which gained for him the admiration and regard of that talented actor, though unhappily they fell out afterwards for some foolish reason or another.

But the active brain of the sparkling *littérateur* was not satisfied with journalistic work merely. With the pecuniary assistance of a friend and admirer, the late Mr. Drummond, police-magistrate—whose death shortly afterwards by poison received from one of the snakes kept by the snake-exhibitor Shires, whom he held to be an impostor as regarded his antidote, caused so much excitement—he purchased from Mr. Williams the *Australian Magazine*, the journal in which had appeared his earliest literary attempts. The name of this he altered to the *Colonial Monthly*; and with praiseworthy enthusiasm set about encouraging Australian literary talent by gathering around him as contributors all the best local literary ability available. But, despite his laudable efforts to create an Australian literature, racy of the soil, he was doomed to disappointment and loss. The primary cause of this unfortunate result may be ascribed to the sneers which any attempt made by an Australian received at the hands of a few self-sufficient, narrow-minded individuals, who, sad to say, had the ear of the then reading public, because they unfortunately happened to be in a position to dictate on literary matters.

It was in the *Colonial Monthly* that Clarke's first novel, *Long Odds*, appeared in serial form. Of this, however, he only wrote a few of the first chapters, as shortly after its commencement he met with a serious accident through his horse throwing him and fracturing his skull—an accident from the effects of which he never totally recovered.

Some months prior to this mishap—about May, 1868—Clarke, in conjunction with some dozen literary friends, started a modest club for men known in the fields of Literature, Art, and Science—THE YORICK. This has developed in the course of the past fifteen years into one in which the three elements predominating originally are lost in the multifarious folds of "Professionalism."

The Yorick Club was the outcome of the literary and Bohemian—analogous terms in those days—spirits who used then to assemble nightly at the Café of the Theatre Royal to discuss coffee and intellectual subjects. These gatherings grew so large in the course of time that it was found necessary, in order to keep the communion up, to secure accommodation where the flow of genius, if nothing else, might have full play without interruption and intrusion from those deemed outside the particular and shining pale. Accordingly a room was rented and furnished in Bohemian fashion, with some cane chairs, a deal table, a cocoa-nut matting and spittoons. In this the first meeting was held in order to baptise the club. The meeting in question debated, with the assistance of sundry pewters and pipes—not empty, gentle reader—the subject warmly from the first proposition made by Clarke, that the club should be called "Golgotha," or the place of skulls, to the last, "alas, poor Yorick!" This brief name was accepted as appropriate, and the somewhat excited company adjourned to a Saturday night's supper at a jovial Eating-House, too well known to fame. The first office-bearers of the club were:—*Secretary*, Marcus Clarke; *Treasurer*, B. F. Kane; *Librarian*, J. E. Neild; *Committee*, J. Blackburn, G. C. Levey, A. Semple, A. Telo, J. Towers. The first published list of members gives a total of sixty-four, but Time has made many changes in that list, and Death has been busy too. Of the sixty-four original members there have passed away the following well-known intellectuals :—B. C. Aspinall, Marcus Clarke, Lindsay Gordon, Henry Kendall, T. Drummond, J. C. Patterson, Jardine Smith, A. Telo, Father Bleardale, etc.

It was at the "Yorick" that Marcus Clarke first met one of whose abilities he entertained a very high opinion, and towards whose eccentric and mournful genius he was drawn by a feeling of sympathetic affection, namely, Adam Lindsay Gordon, poet, and the once king of gentleman Jocks. Nothing could have shown more assuredly the deep feeling and regard felt by Marcus Clarke for Lindsay Gordon than the pathetic preface he wrote for the posthumous edition of the poet's works (an extract from which preface is given in this volume under the title of " The Australian Bush ") when the poet himself put an end to his life, to the horror of the community, which did not learn till after the heartbroken poet's death that it was only the want of the wherewith to live upon which drove one of the brightest geniuses Australia has seen into a suicide's grave. To those who knew Gordon and Clarke intimately, the keen sympathy of genius existing between them was easily understood, for there was, despite many outward differences of manner, a wonderful similarity in their natures. Both were morbidly sensitive; both broodingly pathetic; both sarcastically humorous; both socially reckless; both literary Bohemians of the purest water—sons of genius and children of impulse. That the deep feeling for the dead poet and friend lasted till death with Marcus Clarke was evidenced by his frequently repeating when in dejected spirits those pathetically regretful lines of the " Sick Stockrider "—

> I have had my share of pastime and I've done my share of toil,
>   And life is short—the longest life a span ;
> I care not now to tarry for the corn or for the oil,
>   Or for the wine that maketh glad the heart of man.
> For goods undone and gifts misspent and resolutions vain
>   'Tis somewhat late to trouble. This I know—
> I should live the same life over if I had to live again ;
>   And the chances are I go where most men go.

And to see him seated at the piano humming these lines to his own accompaniment, while the tears kept rolling down his cheeks, was proof enough that the tender chords of a beloved memory were being struck, and that the living son of genius mourned for his dead brother as only genius can mourn.

Turning to a more lively memento of Lindsay Gordon, characteristic of him when the spirit of fun possessed him, the following note, written to Clarke and kept by him sacredly, will interest his many admirers :—

Yorick Club.

Dear Clarke,—Scott's Hotel, not later than 9.30 sharp. Moore will be there. Riddock and Lyon, Baker and the Powers, beside us ; so if 'the Old One' were to cast a net—eh ?—Yours,

A. LINDSAY GORDON.

It was shortly after Gordon's untimely and sad death that Clarke became acquainted with another erratic though differently constituted son of genius— Henry Kendall, the foremost of Australian-born poets. Kendall met with warm sympathy from the friend of Gordon, and, moreover, with a helping hand in the hard life-struggle—which the poet feelingly referred to in the following memorial verses written on the death of his friend and benefactor :—

> The night wind sobs on cliffs austere,
>   Where gleams by fits the wintry star ;
> And in the wild dumb woods I hear
>   A moaning harbour bar.
>
> The branch and leaf are very still ;
>   But now the great grave dark has grown,
> The torrent in the harsh sea-hill
>   Sends forth a deeper tone.
>
> Here sitting by a dying flame
>   I cannot choose but think in grief
> Of Harpur, whose unhappy name
>   Is as an autumn leaf.
>
> And domed by purer breadths of blue,
>   Afar from folds of forest dark,
> I see the eyes that once I knew—
>   The eyes of Marcus Clarke.
>
> Their clear, bright beauty shines apace ;
>   But sunny dreams in shadow end.
> The sods have hid the faded face
>   Of my heroic friend.
>
> He sleeps where winds of evening pass—
>   Where water songs are soft and low.
> Upon his grave the tender grass
>   Has not had time to grow.

Few knew the cross he had to bear
  And moan beneath from day to day.
His were the bitter hours that wear
  The human heart away.

The laurels in the pit were won ;
  He had to take the lot austere
That ever seemed to wait upon
  The man of letters here.

He toiled for love, unwatched, unseen,
  And fought his troubles band by band ;
Till, like a friend of gentle mien,
  Death took him by the hand.

He rests in peace. No grasping thief
  Of hope and health can steal away
The beauty of the flower and leaf
  Upon his tomb to-day.

So let him sleep, whose life was hard !
  And may they place beyond the wave
This tender rose of my regard
  Upon his tranquil grave.

The idiosyncrasies of the two men were in many respects widely dissimilar—Clarke's belonging to the polished school of the Old World while Kendall's were akin to those of his own native land, in the New World, but the acquaintanceship ripened into mutual admiration and friendship ; and together they worked on *Humbug*, the brilliant weekly comic journal, started about this time by Clarson, Massina & Co., under the editorship of Clarke. Probably one factor which exercised an influence over Clarke in the interests of Kendall was the poem written to Lindsay Gordon's memory by Kendall, of which the following few lines may here be given :—

The bard, the scholar, and the man who lived
That frank, that open-hearted life which keeps
The splendid fire of English chivalry
From dying out ; the one who never wronged
Fellowman ; the faithful friend who judged
The many, anxious to be loved of him,
By what he saw, and not by what he heard,
As lesser spirits do; the brave, great soul
That never told a lie, or turned aside
To fly from danger ; he, I say, was one
Of that bright company this sin-stained world
Can ill afford to loose.

During this period, 1868-69, Clarke was a regular contributor to the *Argus* and *Australasian*, writing leaders for the former journal, and, besides the "Peripatetic Philosopher" papers for the latter, a series of remarkably able sketches on "Lower Bohemia." These articles, as their name implies, were descriptive of the life then existing in the lowest social grades of Melbourne, composed to a great extent of broken-down men of a once higher position in life, drawn hither by the gold discovery. They made a great impression upon the public, being full of brilliantly realistic writing, reminding one greatly of Balzac's ruthless style of exposing without squeamishness the social cancers to be found among the vagrant section of a community. Apart from his connection with the two journals named, the prolific and sparkling journalist contributed at this time to *Punch* some of the best trifles in verse and prose that ever adorned its pages. This connection, however, he severed about the middle of 1869, on undertaking the editorship of *Humbug*, a remarkably clever publication. In *Humbug* appeared, perhaps, the best fugitive work Marcus Clarke ever threw off. Besides his own racy pen, those of such well-known writers as Dr. Neild, Mr. Charles Bright, Mr. A. L. Windsor and Henry Kendall were busy on the pages of the new spirited, satirical organ, which was ably illustrated by Mr. Cousins. Notwithstanding, however, all this array of talent the venture was not financially a success, as at that time the taste for journalistic literature was very much more limited than now, and a writer, however gifted, had then a poor chance of earning a livelihood by the efforts of his pen.

While thus rapidly rising in the rank of Australia's *littérateurs*, Clarke was unfortunately induced, by the foolish advice of friends, who felt flattered by his company, to live at a rate far exceeding his income, naturally becoming involved in debt. From this there was no recourse but to borrow, and so the presence of the usurer was sought. Thus commenced that course of life which, after a few years of ceaseless worry, brought, long ere his time, the brilliant man of genius, with the brightest of prospects before him, to the grave broken-hearted. Surely those who led him into the extravagances, men his seniors in years and experience, must bear their share of responsibility for the dark end to so bright a beginning. And yet some of these were his bitterest enemies afterwards.

Undeterred, however, by the pecuniary difficulties in which he found himself, he, with characteristic thoughtlessness, plunged into matrimony by espousing Miss Marian Dunn, the actress-daughter of genial John Dunn, Prince of Comedians. This young lady was at the time of her engagement to Clarke playing with great success a series of characters with the late Walter Montgomery, who entertained so high an opinion of her histrionic abilities, as to urge her to visit England and America with him. But the little lady preferred to remain in Australia as the wife of the rising *littérateur*, and so they were married on the 22nd of July, 1869, the only witnesses of the marriage being the bride's parents and the best man, the late Mr. B. F. Kane, Secretary of the Education Department. And the strangest—but characteristic of him—part of the ceremony was that the bridegroom, after the connubial knot was tied, left his bride in charge of her parents, while he went in search of lodgings wherein to take his "better half."

Having settled down as a Benedict, so far as it was possible for him to do so, our author, doubtless inspired by the society he had married into, set himself to work for the first time as a playwright, the result being the production of a drama styled *Foul Play*, a dramatisation of Charles Reade's and Dion Boucicault's novel of that name. It met with but partial success. But not discouraged by this comparative failure, the newly-fledged dramatist wrote, or rather adapted from other sources, for the Christmas season of 1870 at the Theatre Royal, a clever burlesque on the old nursery story of *Goody Two Shoes*, which met with considerable success both from the Press and the public. But even in this, his almost initial piece, he betrayed that weakness, theatrically speaking, which, more or less, marred all his dramatic efforts, namely, writing above the intelligence of the average audience.

Soon after this overwork had told its tale upon the restless brain, and the doctors ordered change of air to the more salubrious climate of Tasmania. But as funds were, as usual with him, decidedly low, how was the change to be effected? Eureka! He would ask the publishers of the now defunct *Humbug* to bring out a tale of his in their *Australian Journal*. The tale should be full of thrilling incidents relating to the old convict days in Tasmania. Brimming over with the idea he sought the presence of the publishers in question—Clarson, Massina & Co.—and made his suggestions. The offer was at once accepted, and the needy writer received the necessary aid to take him over to Van Diemen's Land, in order to improve his health and enable him to pore over prison records. Thus was the now deservedly celebrated novel, *His Natural Life*, initiated. But as to how it was completed is another matter. Let the unfortunate publisher testify his experience. And in such manner was produced *His Natural Life*. But the reader must remember that the work, as now published by Messrs. Bentley in London, is very different, as regards the construction and ending, to that which appeared in serial form in the *Australian Journal*.

As without doubt this is the best and most sustained effort of Marcus Clarke's genius, and the one upon which will chiefly rest his fame in literature, it is only right to publish here some extracts from the various reviews written of the novel in English, American and German papers.

The Daily Telegraph, London :—"And who," some thousands of readers may ask, "is Mr. Marcus Clarke? Until a recent period we should have confessed the very haziest knowledge of Mr. Marcus Clarke's existence, save that in the columns of Melbourne newspapers his name has appeared. Mr. Marcus Clarke has hardly entered into the ken of perhaps more than a hundred persons in England; but, having read the forcible and impressive novel entitled *His Natural Life*, we have not only come to an acquaintance as admiring as it is sudden with the author's name, but esteem it by no means a venturesome or hazardous act to predict for it a fame as great as that achieved by any living novelist. Indeed this wonderful narrative, which, despite the thrilling incident, bears on every page the honest impress of unexaggerated truth, has the material of a whole circulating library of tragic romance within itself. The only fault is the over-abundance which necessitates hurry in its disposal. But if Mr. Clarke's future has been embarrassed in some measure by its own riches, the author may well be satisfied with the result, for he has furnished readers in the old and new countries with matter for grave and earnest reflection ; he has re-opened a discussion that has too soon been abandoned to torpor, and he has, in short, rendered better service than the State of Letters is wont to receive at the hands of a mere novel writer. . . . We have by no means over-praised this novel. The temptation to run into superlatives is great, and it has been resisted here for the one reason, if for no other, that, highly meritorious as Mr. Marcus Clarke's first English publication seems in our eyes, we are yet of belief, after its perusal, that he is destined to give the world yet greater and more effective because more concentrated work."

Boston Gazette, America :—"One of the most powerfully written and most absorbingly interesting novels that has lately attracted our notice is *His Natural Life*, by Marcus Clarke. It is a story dealing with convict life in Australia, and has been written ' for a purpose.' The plot is constructed with remarkable skill, and in the depicting of character the author manifests a talent we have rarely seen surpassed in any modern writer of fiction. A similar high degree of praise may be awarded him for his description of scenery. The book is intensely dramatic both in subject and treatment, but it is quite free from ' sensationalism ' in the objectionable sense of the word. The style is healthy, manly and vigorous, and shows a surprising facility in word-painting. Mr. Clarke professes to have drawn his characters, localities and incidents directly from nature, and his work bears internal evidence that he has. It is the most stirring story of its class that has appeared since Victor Hugo's *Les Misérables*, of which it has all the fire and artistic feeling, minus the affectation. This novel cannot fail to make its mark."

The Spectator, London :—" It is something to write a book so powerful, especially as all the power is directed to the noblest end."

Saturday Review, London :—" There is undeniable strength in what Mr. Clarke has written."

Morning Post, London : " This novel appals while it fascinates, by reason of the terrible reality which marks the individual characters living and breathing in it. The tragic power of its situations, the knowledge of the sombre life which the author shows so vividly in the able handling of its subject, the pathos which here and there crops up like an oasis in a sandy desert, lead the reader from the beaten track of fiction."

The Graphic, London :—" It is, of course, possible that Mr. Marcus Clarke may turn out to be a man of one book, and out of his element in any atmosphere but that of convict and penal settlements. He shows, however, too much knowledge of human nature generally to make us think this at all likely, and if so, he must be hailed as a valuable recruit to the ranks of novelists of the day."

Vanity Fair, London :—" There is an immensity of power in this most extraordinary book."

The World, London :—" Few persons will read his remarkable descriptions of convict life and antipodean scenery without recognising an author of commanding originality and strength."

The Reform, Hamburg (translated from the German.)—" This novel treats of a terrible subject. The life of the prisoners in Van Diemen's land is set before us in a panorama painted by a master hand. Ladies of a sentimental turn had better abstain from reading this story, unless they choose to risk a nervous fever. The romance is full of power. The writer illuminates the lowest depths of human nature in a manner which holds us spell-bound, despite ourselves. Marcus Clarke is a master of psychology, and his descriptions of nature are as effective as his style is pure."

And from no less a giant in literature than Oliver Wendell Holmes, of Boston, America, the following complimentary letter was received by Clarke in acknowledgment of a copy of the novel sent to the author of the *Autocrat of the Breakfast Table* :—" The pictures of life under the dreadful conditions to which the convicts were submitted are very painful, no doubt, but we cannot question the fact that they were only copied from realities as bad as their darkest shadows. The only experiences at all resembling these horrors which our people have had were the cruelties to which our prisoners were subjected in some of the southern pens for human creatures during the late war. I do not think they were driven to cannibalism, but the most shocking stories were told of the condition to which they were reduced by want of food and crowding together. There are some Robinson Crusoe touches in your story, which add greatly to its interest, and I should think that the colonists, and thousands at home in the mother country, would find it full of attraction in spite of its painful revelations. This work cannot fail to draw attention, and make your name widely known and appreciated as an author throughout the world."

Besides contributing this historical romance to the columns of the *Australian Journal* Clarke was busy writing in the *Australasian* those sketches of the early days of Australia, which were afterwards published in book form under the title of *Old Tales of a Young Country*. These sketches, like his great novel, though highly interesting as historical records of the colonies, were for the most part worked up from governmental pamphlets and old journals. But in the casting they were stamped by the genius of the master-hand, which could appropriate and improve upon the appropriation as only men of original *calibre* are able to do. In the meantime the " Peripatetic Philosopher " ceased to adorn the pages of the *Australasian* with his caustic and eccentric dissertations, because, through the influence of one of the noblest patrons of letters in Victoria—the late Sir Redmond Barry—the Philosopher had been found a congenial post as Secretary to the Trustees of the Public Library, of whom Sir Redmond himself was the respected President. This appointment was made in June, 1870, and from that time Clarke ceased to be connected with the staff of any journal, though remaining a brilliant and valued contributor all his life to newspapers, magazines, reviews, &c., instead of, unfortunately, concentrating his exceptional powers on the production of works of a class with *His Natural Life.* Among other articles contributed by him about this time were the "Buncle Letters," which appeared in the *Argus* and attracted much attention, being running comments of a satirically humorous character, on the social and political events of the day, supposed to be written by one brother resident in town to his less sophisticated brother in the country. In the same journal, Clarke wrote a descriptive sketch of the mining mania which had seized upon Sandhurst at the time; and for piquancy the sketch was among his best in descriptive journalism. At this period, also, he once more tried his hand at the drama, and adapted for John Dunn, his father-in-law, Moliére's celebrated comedy, *Le Bourgeois Gentilhomme,* into English, under the title of *Peacock's Feathers,* which was produced with great success at the Theatre Royal.

Mention has been made of the interest Sir Redmond Barry evinced in the rising *littérateur,* whom he took under his parental wing when obtaining for him the post in the Public Library. And this interest and regard the respected judge retained for his *protégé,* despite his oft-repeated thoughtless acts, to the end of his life, which end arrived, strange to say, only some few months before that of the much younger man, who, on hearing of Sir Redmond's death, expressed himself as having lost his best and truest friend. But with all the warm regard existing between the venerable judge and the youthful author, there was always a certain characteristic *hauteur* on the one hand, and a reverential respect on the other, in their official and social relationships. In proof of this a couple of examples may be related.

It was a hot summer's day, and, as was his style in such weather, the librarian was dressed dandily in unspotted white flannel, a cabbage-tree hat shadowing his face. So clothed he was leisurely wending his way up the steps of the library when he met the President, looking more starched, if possible, than ever, and wearing the well-known, flat-rimmed, tapering, belltopper, which shone sleekily in the glare of the noonday sun. The following brief dialogue then ensued:— President: "Good morning, Mr. Clarke." Librarian: "Good morning, sir." President: "I scarcely think your hat is exactly suited to the position you occupy in connection with this establishment, Mr. Clarke—Good morning," and with a stiff bend of the erect body the President took his departure with just a glimmer of a smile playing round the firmly-closed lips. Again, not long before Sir Redmond's death, and when the librarian had got himself into "hot water" among the "unco guid" section of the Trustees, through writing his clever though caustic reply to the Anglican Bishop, Dr. Moorhouse's criticism on Clarke's article, "Civilisation without Delusion," the President appeared one evening in the librarian's office with a clouded countenance, and said, "Good evening, Mr. Clarke." The librarian, with an intuitive feeling that something was wrong, returned the salutation, when the President remarked: "Mr. Clarke, you would oblige me greatly if you were to leave *some* things *undone.* For instance, that unfortunate article of yours—attacking so estimable a man as the bishop. Very indiscreet, Mr. Clarke. I—think—I—should require—to—have—some—thousands a year of a private income before *I* would—venture—upon writing such an—article on—such a subject, and among so punctillious a community as exists here. Good evening, Mr. Clarke:" and the librarian was left dazed and speechless at the solemnity of the rebuke, and the dignified departure of his President.

Recurring back to the literary work being done by our author, we find that it was during the next two years—namely, in 1872-73—that his prolific pen was in its busiest mood, for within the space of those twenty-four months he wrote the psychological dialogues styled "Noah's Ark," in the *Australasian ;* these were interspersed with those exquisitely told stories, subsequently published in book form, under the names of *Holiday Peak* and *Four Stories High.* The former was dedicated to Oliver Wendell Holmes upon whom he looked as one of the brightest gems in the literary firmament, and from whom he had received much literary encouragement; the latter was dedicated to an appreciative friend, the late kind-hearted though explosive William Saurin Lyster, the man to whom Australian lovers of music owe a deep debt of gratitude as the first introducer of high-class opera and oratorio to these shores. Of these stories, *Pretty Dick* is perhaps the finest piece of work as regards execution done by Australia's greatest literary artist. And in this opinion I am not alone, as the following letter, from one who stands very high in the world's estimate as a master of true pathos and humour will show :—

BOSTON, 23rd December. 1872.

DEAR MR. CLARKE,—

I received your letter and MS., with the newspaper extract, some two or three days ago, and sat down almost at once and read the story. It interested me deeply, and I felt as much like crying over the fate of " Pretty Dick " as I did when I was a child and read the *Babes in the Wood*. I *did* cry then—I will *not* say whether I cried over " Pretty Dick " or not. But *I* will say it is a *very* touching story, *very* well told.

I am, Dear Mr. Clarke,
Most sincerely yours,
O. W. HOLMES.

Apart from these tales, there appeared among the " Noah's Ark " papers some excellent original verse, at times approximating to poetry and several metrical translations from Greek, Latin, German and French poets. He also composed in this year—1872—his most effectively written drama, *Plot*, which was produced at the Princess' Theatre with success. Following on *Plot*, he wrote, or rather adapted, the pantomime of *Twinkle Little Star*, which was played at the Theatre Royal during the Christmas season making quite " a hit."

It was about this time that the relations between Marcus Clarke and the journals with which he had from the commencement of his journalistic career been connected became strained, as is said in diplomatic jargon, and shortly afterwards all connection between them ceased for ever.

As a good deal of misconception exists about the breach that took place between the subject of this biography and the representatives out here of the proprietors of the *Argus* and *Australasian*, it is advisable in the interest of the author to explain the cause of the breach. It was in this year that Mr. Bagot, the " indefatigable " Secretary of the Victoria Racing Club, declined while under some peculiar influence to issue free tickets to the press, as had been the universal custom from time immemorial. The very natural reply of the press to this uncalled-for and blundering affront was simply not to report the races. This was agreed to by the morning journals then published in Melbourne. But in the *Evening Herald*, which was not, through questionable motives, consulted in the matter, there appeared the night the Cup was run, a remarkably clever report of the event—perhaps the cleverest description of the Cup meeting which has been seen in the pages of any Melbourne journal. Naturally the sparkling report caused no small consternation in the ranks of journalism in the city ; more especially among the authorities of the *Argus*, who did not fail to recognise it to be the ingenious brainwork of their own contributor—Marcus Clarke. When questioned on the subject the erratic journalist denied having been at the races, but admitted writing the sketch, claiming his right to do so on the ground that, as the *Argus* did not choose to employ him because of a disagreement with Mr. Bagot he had every moral right to earn an honest penny from the proprietors of another journal who afforded him the opportunity of so doing. This, however, did not satisfy the ruling power of the *Argus* (Mr. Gowen Evans), who was probably chagrined to read in another journal the work of one whom he looked upon as that paper's property. The result of this attempt at autocratic interference and dictation was the loss to the journals in question of the writer whose work above that of all others had adorned their columns, and increased their popularity.

Having parted from the journals which he had so greatly aided by his rare abilities, Clarke became attached as a contributor to the *Herald* and *Daily Telegraph* and subsequently to the *Age* and *Leader*.

The next, most important and unfortunate, event which overtook him about this period was his insolvency. Though long expected, and known to be inevitable, the victim of untoward circumstances put off the evil day by every means in his power, thereby sinking deeper and deeper in the mire, till at last his doom had to be met, and his name appeared in the bankruptcy list. What those who had helped to lead him into this position felt when the disagreeable fact became known can only be conjectured, but, at any rate, their foolish dupe felt the position more acutely than any acquaintance of his could possibly imagine, judging by the light-hearted manner in which he discussed the subject with one and all. Only those who knew Marcus Clarke intimately—and they were few—realised how keenly he suffered from the thought that one, like himself, with a name and a fame, who had had every chance of being independent, should become what he, poor, generous, thoughtless fellow, had become. Still, it was unavoidable, and his fate was sealed. Would that the first mistake had acted as a warning, but it was not to be, for no sooner was one difficulty overcome than another commenced, ending only when life was no more—that life which was driven to its death by the merciless snares of the crafty usurer, against whom, at the last, he fought as desperately as man does against the remorseless python, who knows his prey is safe in the fatal embrace.

Yet despite all these monetary troubles, the inherently strong sense of humour in him would trifle with the seriousness of the position, for it was about this time that he penned the following remarks as the real excuse for his chronically impecunious condition :—

I have made a scientific discovery. I have found out the reason why I have so long been afflicted with a pecuniary flux. For many years past I have tried to find out why I am always in debt, and have consulted all sorts of financial physicians, but grew no better, but rather the worse. The temporary relief afforded by a mild loan or an overdraft at the bank soon vanished. I once thought that by the judicious application of a series of bills at three months I could check the ravages of disease ; but, alas ! my complaint was aggravated, while I had not courage for the certain but painful remedy of the actual cautery, as recommended by Dr. Insolvent Commissioner Noel. My friends said I had "got into bad hands," that I had been deceived by advertising quacks, whose only object was to depress the financial system, and keep me an invalid as long as possible. I applied for admission into the Great Polynesian Loan Company's Hospital, and pawned myself there. in fact, at the ridiculously low rate of 350 per cent. I was insured in the Shylock Alliance Company (which afterwards. to my great disgust, amalgamated with the Polynesian), and there I sold the reversionary interest in my immortal soul, I believe, to a bland gentleman who calculated the amount of blood in my body and flesh on my bones by the aid of a printed money-table. Yet my financial health did not seem to improve. I grew anxious, and began to reason. I resolved to write a book. I wrote one, and called it *A Theory for the Causation, and Suggestions for the Prevention of Impecuniosity; together with Hypotheses on the Causation, and Views as to the Prevention of Composition-with-creditors, Bankruptcy, Fraudulent Insolvency, and other Pecuniary Diseases.* In the course of examination of Bills of Sale, Acceptances, Liens on Wool, and other matters, I discovered by accident the cause of my disease. It was the simplest thing in the world. The idiots of doctors had been treating me for extravagance, whereas the fact was that *I was cursed with so powerful and innate a passion for economy that I never could bring myself to the expenditure of ready money.*

But turning to a pleasanter and more interesting subject, the Cave of Adullam has to be mentioned. The Cave of Adullam ! "What is that?" may ask the uninitiated reader. Well, the particular cave alluded to was a club house, once situated in Flinders Lane, behind the *Argus* office, where stands now some softgoods palatial structure. To this only a very select body of members was admitted, the selectness in this case necessitating that a member should be happily impecunious, and, if possible, be hunted by the myrmidons of the law. From this brief description it will be seen that the Adullamites were a family *sui generis.* The entrance to the modest building was not easy of access, being only reached by a tortuous lane of ominous appearance, guarded by an animal who boasted the bluest of blue bulldog blood. The pass-words were—"Honor! No Frills!" The members were mostly composed of literary Bohemians, whose wordly paths were not strewn with roses, and between whom and the trader there existed a mutual disrespect. Chief among the members of this exclusive brotherhood was the subject of this biography, who, having discarded the more conventional surroundings of the Yorick Club, became a shining light within the shades of the Cave of Adullam. And to commemorate the genius of the members of the Cave was written a Christmas tale, yclept *'Twixt Shadow and Shine,* which contains fanciful portraitures of the leading Adullamites. But, alas ! the destroyer of all things, Time, has one by one scattered its members, till now the place that knew the members of that eccentric Bohemian band knows them no more. *Sic transit gloria,* &c. And with Hamlet we may say, addressing that once coruscating group—"Where be your gibes now ? Your gambols? Your songs? Your flashes of merriment that were wont to set the table in a roar? Not one now to mock your own jeering ? Quite chap-fallen ! "

Notwithstanding, however, all the merry goings on at the Cave, Clarke was, perhaps, harder at work in those years than at any other time, although certainly the work was thrown off without much effort, and with as little care for a future reputation. It was at this time he first became a contributor to the *Age* and *Leader,* with which his connection lasted up to his death, having gone through the trying ordeal incident upon the *Age cum* Berry Reform Agitation of 1877, '78, '79, into which he threw himself with all the zest of a thorough hater of Shoddocracy, writing some of the most telling articles which illumined the pages of these journals at that time. And he fought the more zealously in the fray, because he wrote under the editorial guidance of one upon whom he looked as, at once, the best read and the ablest journalist on the Australian press—Mr. A. L. Windsor. It was during this period he enjoyed the friendship and confidence of the then Governor of Victoria, Sir George Bowen, and was offered by Mr. Graham Berry (now Sir) the Librarianship of the Parliament Library, which he declined, relying upon securing that of the Public Library, in which, however, he was doomed to disappointment a year or two later.

Clarke, apart from Melbourne journals, contributed largely to the *Queenslander* as also to the *Sydney Mail*, through the introduction of the late Mr. Hugh George, the gentleman who as general manager of the *Argus* raised that paper to a high position, and who subsequently was the valued general manager of the Messrs. Fairfax's newspapers in Sydney. Of all those connected prominently with the *Argus* when Marcus Clarke was its brightest ornament, Mr. Hugh George alone remained to the end the generous advocate of his exceptional abilities, of which he never lost an opportunity to avail himself in the Sydney journals, over which he exercised a control. And about the last negotiations Clarke entered into, only a few weeks before his unexpected death, were with that gentleman, in connection with a proposal that he should start on a tour through the colonies and South Sea Islands as the accredited " Special " of the Messrs. Fairfax's newspapers, and of the London *Daily Telegraph*, for which brilliantly written journal he had been acting for some years as " Australian Correspondent ; " and that he was held in high estimation by the authorities of that remarkable paper the following letter, written by its proprietor and editor, speaks for itself. Wrote Mr. Lawson Levy :—

"Without having the pleasure of your personal acquaintance, I am sure you will pardon me if I venture to address you on a subject which may not be without interest. I have read your books with very great pleasure, and it has occurred to me that you possess most of the qualifications for journalism of the highest order. Has the idea ever occurred to you of adopting this branch of literature, and would it suit your views to come to England? I am, of course, ignorant of what your position may be, and ignorant of any feeling that you may have upon the subject. It is quite possible that ties may bind you to Australia—ties that you cannot break. If, however, the idea should have entered into your mind, tell me in a letter what your position is, what income you would require to entice you to come to London, whether you feel yourself competent for journalistic work, whether you have ever done any, and if you have, you would perhaps think it advisable to send me by the next mail, samples of such work. If, moreover, for the moment, the notion should seem acceptable to you, sit down and write me three or four leading articles on any subjects that may seem best to you—articles that will make about a column of our newspaper matter ; and put into them as much of your force and vigor as you can command. Under any circumstances, whether my ideas waken any sympathy in your mind or not, I am sure you will permit me to congratulate you on the success your works have met with here."

Why Marcus Clarke did not avail himself of the chance of going to London under such auspices it is difficult to imagine, the more particularly that he was well aware that such talent as his had no possible scope in this, a new country, whereas in London literary circles it would have been appreciated at its proper value.

Surely, in the face of such encouragement, a genius, well nigh suffocated by the denseness of the *quasi*-intellectual atmosphere surrounding it, should have seized the opportunity to move from scenes clouded over with trouble, and from a community which gave but a feeble response to its bright efforts ? But, somehow, it did not, or could not.

Returning to the year 1876, an event happened which deeply affected Marcus Clarke. In August of that year his father-in-law, genial, witty John Dunn, for whom he had a sincere affection, fell down dead in the street. The bitterness of this loss was greatly aggravated by his inability to publish the autobiography of the deceased actor, which he had together with Dr. Neild revised at the author's request, with a view to its publication after his death. But the wish of the deceased was not carried out, owing, it is said, to an objection taken by a daughter of the actor, who had married into so-called Society circles, to have the ups and downs of a poor player's family career submitted to public view.

Accordingly, the autobiography of Australia's clever comedian was not brought out, and the early history of the Australian stage has been lost to the public. For the next three years, besides the journalistic work alluded to, Clarke was busy at dramatic composition, producing, in conjunction with Mr. Keely, *Alfred the Great*, a burlesque, which achieved a success at the Bijou Theatre, during the Christmas season of 1877. This was followed by the adaptation for the Theatre Royal of Wilkie Collins' sensational novel *Moonstone*. This play was not the success anticipated, but it must be said in justice to the author that it was considerably spoiled by the pruning-knife of the management, which did its slashing with little judgment. Another piece, a comedietta, styled, *Baby's Luck*, was subsequently written for Mr. J. L. Hall, in which that popular actor appeared to great advantage. *Fernande*, a clever adaptation of Sardou's emotional drama of that name, was also written about this time, but never produced owing to a disagreement over the matter. Of this adaptation Miss Genevieve Ward expressed to the writer a high opinion of its merits, which, coming from so great an artist and one who had read the play in the original, is no small compliment to the author. It may also be surmised that it was during this period that the fanciful extravaganza of *The King of the Genii* was composed. This piece is written in a Gilbertean manner, and is not unlike that author's *Palace of Truth*. Yet Clarke's ability as a playwright was thrown away, as theatrical managers in the colonies had not, unfortunately, either the capacity to know a good thing, or the enterprise to encourage local talent. But not only was Clarke's pen busy at dramas—it was tempted into an entirely new field—that of history. At the suggestion of the then Minister of Education, the late Mr. Justice Wilberforce Stephen, he was engaged to write a history of Australia for the State-schools, which had just come under the new secular, compulsory, and free Education Act. This work entailed upon the writer more routine labour than was to his taste, and consequently, instead of devoting himself to the somewhat tedious task, he, after commencing the book, handed it over, in his usual good-hearted way to some impecunious friends, who did not possess any literary qualification for such work, the consequence being that the book turned out to be a miserable *fiasco*, and was never used in the schools for which it was intended. Some notion of its value may be gleaned from the following critical notice of it in a leading journal :—"In short, the book before us is calculated to impress the reader with the idea that it has been compiled by some literary charlatan, rather than by an author of Mr. Marcus Clarke's ability and reputation." But because little or no attention was given by the supposed author of the history to the work, it must not be imagined that the fertile mind was inactive. That clever, though eccentric, *brochure, The Future Australian Race*, was written at this period. Of it an English paper wrote :— "It deals with a subject of considerable ethnological and social interest in language more forcible than philosophical. Mr. Clarke considers that vegetarians are Conservatives, and ' Red Radicals,' for the most part meat-eaters, while ' fish-eaters are invariably moderate Whigs.' He thinks that ' the Australasians will be content with nothing short of a *turbulent democracy*,' and that in five hundred years the Australasian race will have ' changed the face of nature, and swallowed up all our contemporary civilisation,' but it is fortunately ' impossible that we should live to see this stupendous climax. *Après nous, le déluge.*'" Besides this his restless mind was weekly giving out articles, reviews, and sketches, bearing his own mint mark, in the *Age*, the *Leader*, the *Sydney Mail* and *Morning Herald*, and *London Daily Telegraph*. It was also at work on the *Melbourne* and *Victorian Reviews*, in a somewhat significant, albeit imprudent manner, for it was in the *Victorian* that his " disturbing" article on " Civilisation Without Delusion" appeared, and in the *Melbourne* his clever rejoinder, to Dr. Moorhouse's reply to the original article, saw light.

The last efforts of Clarke in the direction of dramatic work, were the two comedies written for his wife on her re-appearance, after an absence of some years, at the Bijou in the winter of 1880. Of the two, the one, *A Daughter of Eve*, was original ; the other, *Forbidden Fruit*, being an adaptation from the French. The former is undoubtedly clever, being on the lines of Sheridan's comedies ; and in the leading character of " Dorothy Dove," Mrs. Clarke did every justice to her histrionic abilities.

Besides these comedies, the author left unfinished the libretto of *Queen Venus* an *Opera Bouffe* on which he was engaged with M. Kowalski, the eminent pianist, at the time of his death ; also the plots and a portion of the matter of the following ;—*Reverses*, an Australian Comedy ; *Paul and Virginia*, a burlesque ; *Fridoline*, an opera comique, and *Salome*, a comedy.

And now reference has to be made to that which more than any other single cause led to the unfortunate pecuniary and other complications in which the subject of this memoir became involved during the last year or two of his short life —namely his appointment as agent with power-of-attorney to act as he deemed desirable for his cousin, Sir Andrew Clarke, in connection with some landed property owned by that gentleman in this colony.　Paradoxical as this statement may appear it is nevertheless too true that the confidence placed by Sir Andrew Clarke in his cousin's ability to act as his sole and unchecked agent in business matters was one of the most fatal errors ever committed both for the principal and the agent.　For the former it meant pecuniary loss, for the latter neglect of all literary work.　That Marcus Clarke was altogether to blame for the "mixed" condition into which the business affairs of his cousin got is simply absurd.　All that can be urged against him in the matter is that he was negligent and thoughtless in connection with them as he had always been with his own.　However, the less said the better in connection with this episode of the brilliant *littérateur's* life for after all it was not his fault but misfortune, as he has said himself, that he was not a Business Man.　Indeed, no reference would have been made to this matter were it not that it was the greatest misfortune that ever happened to Clarke that he had anything to do with this business, as it not only led him to abandon his proper duties, but led him, also, deeper into the clutches of usurers, who eventually wrought him to death before his time.　And it is probably owing to this "bungle" that Sir Andrew Clarke has not seen his way to help (although receiving a handsome pension from this colony) the widow and children of him of whose abilities he could think so highly as to induce the Prince of Wales, when on his visit to India where Sir Andrew was Minister of Public Works, to read *His Natural Life*.　The Prince did read the book, and was so struck by its powers that he expressed a desire to meet the author, who, he suggested, ought to go to that intellectual centre of the world—London.

It may be assumed that it was owing to this unfortunate business craze which had seized hold of our author, that there had been left behind in an unfinished state a novel which began so brilliantly as *Felix and Felicitas*.　Commenced years before, it was allowed to lie by during his "landlord" days, and until a few months previous to his demise, when it was re-commenced; but too late, for the hand of Death was already upon him, as he himself too well knew and frequently remarked during the last few weeks of his life—notably on the Queen's Birthday, preceding his decease—when, walking with a friend in the vicinity of the Yarra Bend Asylum he mournfully remarked, "Which shall it be—the Mad Asylum or the Pauper Grave?　Let a toss of the coin decide—head, grave; tail, asylum."　And forthwith a florin was tossed, and fell tail uppermost.　"Not if I know it, my festive coin.　No gibbering idiot shall I e'er be; rather the gleeful, gallows-tree."

That English literature has lost through the incompletion of *Felix and Felicitas*, no judge who has perused the opening chapters can deny; and that the promise of artistic merit held out by these chapters was fully realised by authorities on the subject is proved by the anxiety of Messrs. Bentley and Sons to urge on the writer to complete the work for publication in London; and so capable a critic as Mrs: Cashel Hoey, writing from London to the *Australasian* of the story, remarked :—

The literary world here has received with great regret the intelligence of Mr. Marcus Clarke's death.　His tales of the early days of the colonies, and his very striking novel, *His Natural Life*, made a deep impression here.　We were always expecting another powerful fiction from his pen. I fear he has not left any finished work, and I regret the fact all the more deeply that I have been allowed the privilege of reading a few chapters of a novel begun by Mr. Marcus Clarke, under the title of *Felix and Felicitas*.　The promise of those chapters is quite exceptional; they equal in brilliancy and vivacity the best writing of Edward Whitty, and they surpass that vivid writer in construction.　It is difficult to believe, while reading the opening chapters of this, I fear, unfinished work, that the author lived at the other side of the world from the scenes and the society which he depicts with such accuracy, lightness, grace, and humour.

In order to enable the reader to have some idea of the interesting nature of the plot of the story ideally drawn, it is said, from the author's own experiences, the following sketch of it written by him for the publishers will doubtless be welcome :—

The following is a synopsis of my novel now in MS.　The title is FELIX AND FELICITAS. Those who were in the Academy Exhibition of 18— remember the picture " Martha and Mary."

The artist was a Mr. Felix Germaine, the son of a country parson having a rectory near Deal. I'
know the place well. The brother of this clergyman is travelling tutor and friend to Lord Godwin
(one like Lord Pembroke), who has just returned from a cruise in the South Seas in his yacht.
Ampersand, the idler (everybody knows him), meets Godwin on his return, and tells him of the
success of his old schoolfellow—Felix. He brings both to a concert at Raphael Delevyra's, the
famous pianoforte maker; and there they hear some good musical and witty talk, Stivelyn,
Carbeth, Storton,—not unlike Swinburne, Buchanan, and Albert Grant—are there amongst others.
Felix, who is married to a charmingly domesticated wife, falls in love with Mrs. Delevyra, who, as
all the world knows, was Felicitas Carmel—the niece of Carmel, the violinist, who retired from.
public life, having paralysis of the left hand. (N.B.—The great Beethoven was deaf; but his
torments were nothing to Carmel's.) Mr. Delevyra is a rich, thriving man—some say that his name ·
is really Levi—but Felicitas doesn't care for him. She and Felix you see—want to live that Higher
Life of which we have heard so much lately; and consequently they resolve to break the Seventh
Commandment. They get away in Godwin's yacht; and now begins my effort at mental
analysis. In a little time they grow weary; then blame each other; then they are poor; and
finally they hate each other—each blaming each for causing the terrible fall from the high standard'
of Ideality settled by them in their early interviews. In the midst of this Delevyra arrives. The
Jew has made up his mind. He loves his wife; but she has betrayed him. He will not forgive
her; or rather he cannot forgive himself. He explains the common-sense view of the matter. He
shows her that she has spent two-thirds of his income—that her desertion was not only treacherous,
but foolish, inasmuch as she loses respect, position, and *money*. In fine, with some sarcasm and
power, he strips adultery of its poetic veil, and shows it to be worse than a crime—a blunder.
Felix expects a duel—not at all. Delevyra discourses him sweetly upon the "Higher Life," and
says to his wife—"If this is the congenial soul you pine for I will allow him £300 a year to live
with you and make you happy." Felicitas travels—divorced and allowanced (Teresa Perugino did
the same). She writes books, poems, and travels—very recondite stuff they say. Felix, utterly
shamed, goes home in Godwin's yacht. He is wrecked at Deal, near his own house, and his body
is brought to his wife. He, however, recovers and lives happily. Ampersand says in the last
chapter—"You ask what the Modern Devil is." It is an Anti-Climax. We haven't the strength to
carry anything to the end. These people ought to have taken poison or murdered somebody. I
saw Felix the other day. He is quite fat and rubicund. His wife henpecks him. He makes lots
of money by pictures—but they are not as good as "Martha and Mary."

The romance is musical, æsthetic, and sensational. It is not written *virginibus puerisque*, but
the effect is a moral one. Some of the characters may be recognised, but I have avoided direct
personality.

And now comes the last scene of all, and it is with a sorrowful heart I pen
these lines, for Memory flies back to the bright days of our early friendship, when,
boys together, we never found "the longest day too long," and whispers, in
mournful tones, "Ah! what might have been." But it was not to be, and I
bow in silent submission to the Omnipotent Will.

Some months before the end came the never strong constitution of my friend
began to give forth ominous signs of an early break-up. The once-active brain
became by degrees more lethargic, and the work which at one time could be
executed with rapidity and force became a task not to be undertaken without
effort. The vivid, humorous imagination of the Peripatetic Philosopher assumed
a more sombre hue, yielding itself up to the unravelling of psychological puzzles.
The keen vein of playful satire which was so marked a feature of his mental calibre
turned into a bitterness that but reflected the disappointed mind of this son of
genius; and hence, for upwards of six months, from the opening of the year 1881
to the day of his death in the August of that year no literary work of consequence
was done with the exception of the *Mystery of Major Molineux*, which opened in
his usual finished style, but which through force of untoward pecuniary circumstances was wound up suddenly, leaving the mystery as mysterious as ever. But
above all other matters that occupied his thoughts during the few weeks preceding
his death and the one which may be set down as the chief cause of that death, was
the compulsory sequestration of his estate by Aaron Waxman, usurer (since
gone to render his account before the Almighty Tribunal), which meant the
loss of his position in the Public Library. All these mental troubles came upon
the broken-down body in a cluster, and the burden was too heavy to bear.
Struggling against his bitter fate—the more bitter that he knew he was himself
greatly to blame—he fell by the way, crushed in mind and body, and the bright
spirit passed away from the weakly tenement of clay which held it, to, let us hope,
more congenial realms, leaving behind it a blank in the social and literary circles
it was wont to frequent, which cannot be filled up, for that spirit was *sui generis*.

The illness which immediately caused his decease commenced with an attack
of pleurisy, and this developing into congestion of the liver, and finally into
erysipelas, carried him off in the space of one short week. Indeed he had, during
the last year of his life, suffered so frequently from attacks brought on by a
disordered liver, that little heed was given to the final attack till a day or two

previous to his death, when the wife, who had so unwearyingly attended him night and day, found that matters were more serious than anticipated and sent for an old companion and friend of her husband's, Dr. Patrick Moloney. From the beginning he held out little hopes, as the constitution was sadly worn out, and the mental worry of the latter weeks had completed the task of dissolution. But the dying man himself did not evidently realise his position even up to the time of the insensibility which preceded death setting in, for only a few hours before his decease he remarked jocularly to his watchful wife, "When I get up I will be a different man with a new liver," and then asked for and put on his coat. But the end came upon him rapidly. Losing his speech he beckoned for pencil and paper, and seizing hold of the sheets moved his hand over them as if writing. Shortly afterwards the mind began to wander, but still the hand continued moving with increasing velocity, and every now and then a futile attempt to speak was made. But the tongue could not utter what the fevered brain wished apparently to explain; and then, by degrees, the arms grew weary, the body fell back on the pillows, the large, beautiful eyes, with a far off gaze in them, opened widely for a second—then closed—and all was over on this earth with—Marcus Clarke.

At 4 o'clock on the afternoon of Tuesday, 2nd August, 1881, he died, aged 35.

Reader, let us draw the veil over this sad scene. The sorrow caused by the passing away of so bright a spirit is too mournful to dwell upon.

AUSTRALIAN TALES AND SKETCHES.

AUSTRALIAN SCENERY.

WHAT is the dominant note of Australian Scenery? That which is the dominant note of Edgar Allan Poe's poetry—Weird Melancholy. A poem like " L'Allegro " could never be written by an Australian. It is too airy, too sweet, too freshly happy. The Australian mountain forests are funereal, secret, stern   Their solitude is desolation. They seem to stifle in their black gorges a story of sullen despair. No tender sentiment is nourished in their shade. In other lands the dying year is mourned, the falling leaves drop lightly on his bier. In the Australian forests no leaves fall. The savage winds shout among the rock clefts. From the melancholy gums strips of white bark hang and rustle. The very animal life of these frowning hills is either grotesque or ghostly. Great gray kangaroos hop noiselessly over the coarse grass. Flights of white cockatoos stream out shrieking like evil souls. The sun suddenly sinks, and the mopokes burst out into horrible peals of semi-human laughter. The natives aver that when night comes, from out the bottomless depths of some lagoon the Bunyip rises, and in form like a monstrous sea-calf, drags his loathsome length from out the ooze. From a corner of the silent forest rises a dismal chant, and around a fire, dance natives painted like skeletons.   All is fear-inspiring and gloomy. No bright fancies are linked with the memories of the mountains.   Hopeless explorers have named them out of their sufferings—Mount Misery, Mount Dreadful, Mount Despair. As when among sylvan scenes in places

> " Made green with the running of rivers,
> And gracious with temperate air,"

the soul is soothed and satisfied, so, placed before the frightful grandeur of these barren hills, it drinks in their sentiment of defiant ferocity, and is steeped in bitterness.

Australia has rightly been named the Land of the Dawning. Wrapped in the midst of early morning her history looms vague and gigantic. The lonely horseman, riding between the moonlight and the day, sees vast shadows creeping across the shelterless and silent plains, hears strange noises in the primeval forests, where flourishes a vegetation long dead in other lands, and feels, despite his fortune, that the trim utilitarian civilisation which bred him shrinks into insignificance beside the contemptuous grandeur of forest and ranges coeval with an age in which European scientists have cradled his own race.

There is a poem in every form of tree or flower, but the poetry which lives in the trees and flowers of Australia, differs from those of other countries. Europe is the home of knightly song, of bright deeds and clear morning thought. Asia sinks beneath the weighty recollections of her past magnificence, as the Suttee sinks jewel-burdened upon the corpse of dread grandeur, destructive even in its death. America swiftly hurries on her way, rapid, glittering, insatiable even as one of her own giant waterfalls. From the jungles of Africa, and the creeper-tangled groves of the Islands of the South, arise, from the glowing hearts of a thousand flowers, heavy and intoxicating odours—the Upas-poison, which dwells in barbaric sensuality. In Australia alone is to be found the Grotesque, the Weird, the strange scribblings of Nature learning how to write. Some see no beauty in our trees without shade, our flowers without perfume, our birds who cannot fly, and our beasts who have not yet learned to walk on all fours. But the dweller in the wilderness acknowledges the subtle charm of this fantastic land of monstrosities. He becomes familiar with the beauty of loneliness. Whispered to by the myriad tongues of the wilderness, he learns the language of the barren and the uncouth, and can read the hieroglyphs of haggard gum-trees, blown into odd shapes distorted with fierce hot winds, or cramped with cold nights, when the Southern Cross freezes in a cloudless sky of icy blue. The phantasmagoria of that wild dreamland termed the Bush interprets itself, and the Poet of our desolation begins to comprehend why free Esau loved his heritage of desert sand, better than all the bountiful richness of Egypt.

LEARNING "COLONIAL EXPERIENCE."

THERE were three of us, Dougald M'Alister, Jack Thwaites, and myself. The place was called in the grandiloquent language of the bush, "The Dinkledoodledum Station"(I like these old native names), because it was situated in the Dinkledoodledum Creek. Dinkledoodledum—as any philologist can guess by the sound of it—means the Valley of the Rippling Streamlets; but alas! never a rippling streamlet did our eyes behold during our stay in the inhospitable valley.

The station had just been purchased by Thwaites' brothers—is not his name now synonymous with gold, from the Great Glimmera to the Adelaide Desert?—and had been overstocked by its former proprietor. Along the Glimmera banks, where jovial but family-burdened Boschman kept his boundary-riding habitation, the ground was as bare as a billiard-table, and the travelling sheep that called the Great Glimmera their "feeding track," were only too glad to escape beyond the Dinkledoodledum boundary into the pleasant paths of Whistlebinkie. Let it not, however, be imagined that our station was always in this condition. On the contrary, it had been renowned as a place flowing with milk and honey. It was reported that Clibborn had made his fortune out of it; that Wallum had retired to independence and hot grog after twelve months of it; and that Thwaites was in a fair way to do exceedingly well if he could but "hold on" to it.

Unluckily, what with the former proprietor's mania for feeding two sheep to every three acres (one sheep to every five acres was about the Dinkledoodledum standard) and a succession of bad seasons, the "holding on" was hard work. Economy was absolutely needful, and M'Alister, Jack and I practised it healthily. Mutton and damper all the week, and damper and mutton on Sundays, was the order of the day, and we carried it out to the letter. No epicurean feasts of beef or of pork disgraced the frugality of our board. Never to our table came the feeble fowl or the enervating kitchen-garden vegetable. We had no milk, for our dairy cattle were starving; no eggs, for our poultry refused to lay; no pumpkin pie, for our soil was too poor to grow even that harmless esculent. Yet on Spartan fare we led Spartan lives, and were happy.

Oh, that bark hut! Never shall I forget the first day when I, a slim and somewhat effeminate youth, with London smoke not yet cleared from my throat, beheld its dilapidated walls. "You will sleep here," said Jack, pointing to a skillion which seemed to have been used as a sheep-pen, so marked was the "spoor" of those beasts. "With all my heart," said I, as that organ sank within me—down,

down, down, until I could feel it palpitating in the very tips of my riding-boots. But I did not regret my acquiescence. How many nights in that humble shelter have I listened to the skirr of the wild cats, and watched the one bright star that pertinaciously peeped through the chinks of the bark sheets. How many nights have I lighted my lonely pipe, and wrestled alone with my own particular angel, even as Jacob wrestled at Pennel. Happy Jacob! would I owned thy cunning of wrist and elbow. How many nights have I trimmed the reed in the pannikin of tallow, and read the half-dozen books I possessed until I could read no more. How many nights have I slept the unutterably sweet slumber of virtuous weariness, until my Jack, bursting in with clanking spurs, would rouse me with his "All aboard!" Aye, old skillion, I have had some happy hours. in thee; so peace to thy ashes, for, sooth to say, thou art now but fit for burning.

It is proper to boast of the Australian summer. Those who have lived in tents, camped by rocky water-holes, kept dew-sprinkled watch beneath the yellow moon, and ridden through fiery noons hard upon the tails of the head-long herd, can with justice boast of the wild intoxication of that burning ether. I have known it, I! Not the draught which the great spirit gave to eager Faust maddens so gloriously. Australian summer, dost thou say? I am with thee. With open shirt ballooned behind thee, with streaming hair and. bloody spurs, urge, urge the straining steed across the level plain! No tree mars the prospect of immensity. In front, the flying emu, and behind—naught but the whistling air! The grey grass spins, the grey plain reels, the cloudless sky glows molten brass above. It comes—the hot wind of the desert! Bitter-fierce from the sand-hills of the scorching north, it sweeps upon thee! Ride! Ride! There are fifty miles of grass before thee, and the blood of an Emperor's battle steed beats beneath thy saddle-flaps. What are fears, griefs, loves? Throned upon the rocking saddles of our stretching barbs, we laugh at fate. Stand in thy stirrups now, and shout! Ha! ha! Tell me what draught of love or wine compares with *this*—the champagne nectar of a hot-wind gallop!

But the time to enjoy our hut was in the winter—the wild, wet winter that lashed the groaning gums, and scourged to white rage the risen river. All the hot summer wooed us to the air. Through parching noons and dewy nights we rode and revelled. Then camped the cattle by the shrinking swamp, and the wild horses came down to drink at the famished springs. Then we went expeditions in the balmy moonlight, and roused the drowsy township with the clattering echoes of our hurrying hoofs. Then came Harry of the Gap, Tom of the Scano, and Dare-devil Dick, of Mostyn's Folly, to "foregather" with us. Then were Homeric days, musical with chanted melody, and fierce with the recklessness of horse-taming youth. Then were our hearts great within us, and in that glowing atmosphere, beneath that burning sun, our bright blood bounded, and we lived!

But in gray, chill winter the bark hut, so long deserted, repaid our ingratitude by generous kindness. Creeping, all wet, and weary

with travel, splashed with mire, and torn by prickly scrub, to its
friendly shelter, it glowed warm welcome, its rough but honest sides
laughing in the beams of the roaring logs till they were nigh to crack
again. How cheery were those evenings. How we ate the ewe
mutton, and laughed at the mishaps of the day; how we smoked,
and toasted our toes and "yarned;" three sworn comrades, singing
the songs of our native Britain to the accompaniment of the whistling
Austral wind.

The hut was not commodious. When duly camped within it,
indeed, we had but scant room. When M'Alister had flung his lazy
length upon the lounging chair (a wool bale stretched upon the rack-
toothed iron skeleton of some long-forgotten patent) and I had
usurped the cane-bottomed American importation, there was but one
place for Thwaites, and that the table top. Thwaites would roost
there, like some intelligent bird, and chant the lays of his native
country. We called him the "Little Warbler." Thwaites was a
young man of military tendencies. He had belonged in the old country
to the Diggleshire Yeomanry Cavalry (who received the thanks of
their Lord-Lieutenant and county, you may remember, for their
conduct in the great insurrection of the cider-sellers against the
patent bottling process), and in our excursions into the bush he was
perpetually waving a brass-headed whip which he affected, and with
wild cries of "St. George and Diggleshire!" charging the brush
fences. Paddy, his big-boned horse, put him down badly one afternoon, and he gave up this method of exhilaration. M'Alister, who
owned that sense of dry humour which is a fungoid growth peculiar
to Scotland, would artfully excite Thwaites to wrath by the assumption
of anti-Hanoverian tendencies, and induce in him a violent outburst
of loyalty, and frequent reference to a lady of whom he habitually
spoke as "My gracious sovereign, whom God preserve." McAlister
himself was not without his prejudices, for on one occasion I
distinctly remember that we removed the table, and fought over the
merits of poor Mary Queen of Scots. I had ventured to hint that her
conduct in the matter of Bothwell was not quite incapable of
impeachment, and M'Alister challenged me to trial by battle. In
justice to the soundness of a reasoning which has sent so many
honest men to Hades, I will presume that my cause was a bad one,
for I received a very sound and complete drubbing.

One of poor Thwaites's duties was to "keep the books," and
once a week he would labour painfully but religiously at his task.
The "books" could not have been very difficult to "keep," I think,
but somehow or other we never could keep them. I am now inclined
to think that our system was too comprehensive, for, as we put
everything down in a volume called a day-book, (*lucus a non lucendo*,
I suppose, for we never wrote anything in it until night), and
transferred it bodily to a ledger, our accounts were pretty mixed.
After I had been there a month, Thwaites mounted his horse solemnly
and mysteriously one morning, and rode off one hundred and
twenty miles to his brother. Two days afterwards he returned, dusty
but calm, and big with intelligence of importance. After supper, he

said to me gravely, "you have been in a bank, haven't you?" I replied that I had for a month or so, until my ravages among the well kept books were presumed to have permanently affected the brain of Napoleon Smith, the manager. "Then," said Jack, "since you've been used to banking, my boy, my brother thinks that *you* can keep the books." I was ready for any hazardous experiment in those days, and I consented. I think on the whole I did pretty well, though three rams (half-bred Leicesters, and as strong as bullocks), got into Derwent Joe's account, and could not be got out again by any financial operation I could devise, while I was always dropping boots and things in "carrying over." Jack would endeavour sometimes to see how I was getting on, but he told me one day that he couldn't understand why I should keep four plugs of Barrett's twist in the Long Swamp Paddock, and put our married couple's wages to the debit of Weathers and Weaners. I really don't think he understood much about it.

In the Long Swamp Paddock, by the way, lived one Long Tom, who was an oddity. He was nearly seven feet high and thin as a harpoon. He had been a sailor, digger, explorer, stockman, everything but a quiet stop-at-home. For the last ten years, however, he had rested in the hut by the Long Swamp, and the place was known as Long Tom's Waterhole; indeed, Long Tom and his dog were better known at the stations round about, than the name of the Chief Secretary of the Colony. His dog was one of the biggest impostors—for a dog—that I have ever met. He was called Old Moke, and was supposed to be of marvellous sagacity; he was a stumpy-tailed, long-bodied, shambling beast, who worked just when he chose, and as he chose. Long Tom, when riding to muster, would remark that if we didn't get the sheep soon, he would have to put "Old Moke on 'em," as though the act was equivalent to working a miracle, or dissolving Parliament. By-and-by Old Moke was "put on." "Moke!" Tom would remark in tones of conscious superiority, "get away forward!" We would hear a howl, and see a streak of white lightning slip out from under the belly of Tom's horse. Moke had obeyed the summons. By-and-by, in the depths of the forest, faint barks would be heard, and Tom would grow uneasy. He would whistle. Still the barking would continue, and presently, with a rushing sound, a flock of ewes would fly past us bewilderedly. Tom would shift in his saddle, and we would grin.

Presently M'Alister gallops up, raging. "Call off your cursed dog, Tom!" he shouts. "Hi, Moke!" roars Tom. "Moke! Moke! Sink, and burn, and—and—and——the dog. Moke! Hi! Moke!" Then would Long Tom, vomiting fury, gallop madly into the bush, some agonised howls would be heard, and old Moke would be seen no more until supper, when he would meet us at the hut wagging his delusive stump defiantly. Yet everybody around believed in the beast. Old Moke was a sort of religion at the Dinkledoodledum, and to express doubt of his immense value would be heresy of the deepest dye. One would meet stockmen going home with puppies squeaking at their heels. "Any good?" one

6

would ask, nodding at the black and white mass. "Good! I believe you. That's one of old Moke's," would be the proud reply. Alas! old Moke—honest impostor, thou and thy crack-brained master are both gone! Gone, let us hope, old dog, to a place where the faults of both of ye will be as lightly dealt with as in the pleasant days of old.

When Thwaites had gone to bed in the corner—he was a most determined sleeper—M'Alister and I would pitch another log on the fire and prepare for enjoyment. Carefully filling our pipes, we placed the grease-pannikin on a mark made exactly in the centre of the table, and "yarned." By "yarning," dear reader, I don't mean mere trivial conversation, but hard, solid talk. M'Alister was a man of more than ordinary natural talents, and had he been placed in other circumstances, would have cut a figure. It was not easy to argue with him, and some of our discussions lasted until cock-crow. The arguments not unfrequently merged into story-telling, and in that department my memory served me in good stead. I had been a sickly brat in my infancy, and having unfettered access to the library of a man who owned few prejudices for moral fig-leaves, had, with the avidity for recondite knowledge which sickly brats always evince, read many strange books. I boiled down my recollections for M'Alister, and constituted myself a sort of Scherezade for his peculiar benefit. He would smoke and I would fix my eyes on a long strip of bark which hung serpentwise from the ridge pole, and relate. I think if that strip of bark had been removed, my power of narration would have been removed with it. In this fashion we got through a good deal of Brantome, several of the plays—or rather plots of the plays—of Wycherley, Massinger, and Farquahar, and most of Byron. We rambled over the Continent with Gil Blas, discussed the Alchemists, strolled up and down Rome with Horace, and investigated the miracles of the early Saxon churchmen in company of a lot of queer fellows who lived somewhere about the time of the Venerable Bede. We talked *Candide* and Dr. Lardner's *Encyclopædia;* we saw Hogarth with Ireland's descriptions; we quarrelled bitterly over Tom Paine's *Age of Reason*, and made friends again over the pathetic adventures of one Moll Flanders, a friend of Daniel Defoe.

Oh, cheery bark hut, despite all miseries of rough ways and rougher weather, despite all hideousness of lamb-cutting and sheep-slaughtering, despite the figs of tobacco that *would* get mixed up with my record of maiden-ewes and two-toothed wethers, despite rain, storm, and tough mutton, I recall thy memory with unfeigned regret. Thither "never came the trader, never waved a European flag;" no smiling bill-discounters ever invaded thy sacred precincts; no severe duns, rightly claiming that which is, alas! their own, and that which I am unable to pay them, ever darkened thy hospitable doorway; no folio documents, demanding instant official attention, were ever brought by the merry black-boy to thy rude letter-box; no monstrous civilisation with its luxurious necessities overshadowed, Upas-like, thy imperfect roof. A glorious barbarism was thine, a jovial freedom from the cares of the morrow was the charter of thy liberties. I disliked thee once, and grumblingly did abuse thy hospitable shelter, but I have since found other roofs less pleasant than thine, have since—pent within stucco and inurned in marble mockery of grandeur —yearned for the careless fortune of thy uncultured surroundings, cried often in vain amid the uncomfortable comfort of the city.

> " Give me again my hollow tree,
> My crust of bread and liberty."

PRETTY DICK.

HOT day. A very hot day on the plains. A very hot day up in the ranges, too. The Australian sun had got up suddenly with a savage swoop, as though he was angry at the still coolness of early morning, and was determined to drive the cattle, who were munching complacently in the long rich grass of the swamp, back up under the hill among the thick she-oaks. It seemed to be a settled thing on the part of the sun to get up hotter and hotter every morning. He even went down at night with a red face, as much as to say, "Take care, I shall be hotter than ever to-morrow!"

The men on the station did not get into smoking humour until he had been gone down at least an hour, and as they sat on a bench and a barrel or two, outside the "men's hut" on the hill, they looked away across the swamp to that jagged gap in the ranges where he had sunk, and seeing the red flush in the sky, nodded at one another, and said, "We shall have a hot day to-morrow." And they were right. For, when they had forgotten the mosquitoes and the heat, and the many pleasant things that live in the crevices between the slabs of the hut, and gone to sleep, up he came again, hotter than ever, without the least warning, and sent them away to work again.

On this particular morning he was very hot. Even King Peter, who was slowly driving up the working bullocks from the swamp, felt his old enemy so fierce on his back, that he got up in his stirrups and cracked his whip, until the hills rang again, and Strawberry, and Punch, and Doughboy, and Damper, and all (except that cynical, wicked Spot, who hated the world, and always lived away by himself in a private clump of she-oak) straightened their tails and shook their heads, and galloped away up to the stockyard in mortal terror. The horses felt the heat, and King Peter's brother, who was looking for them on the side of the Stony Mount, had a long ride up and down all sorts of gullies before he found them out, and then they were unusually difficult to get together. The cockatoos knew it was hot, and screamed themselves away into the bush. The kangaroos, who had come down like gigantic shadows out of the still night, had all hopped away back into the scrub under the mountains, while the mist yet hung about the trees around the creek-bed. The parrots were uneasy, and the very station dogs got under the shadow-lee of the huts, in case of a hot wind coming up. As for the sheep—when Pretty Dick's father let them out in the dawn, he said to his dog, "We shan't have much to do to-day, old woman, shall we?" At which Lassie wagged her tail and grinned, as intelligent dogs do.

But who was Pretty Dick?

Pretty Dick was the seven-years-old son of Richard Fielding, the shepherd. Pretty Dick was a slender little man, with eyes like pools of still water when the sky is violet at sunset, and a skin as white as milk—that is, under his little blue and white shirt, for where the sun had touched it, it was a golden brown, and his hands were the colour of the ripe chestnuts his father used to gather in England years ago. Pretty Dick had hair like a patch of sunlight, and a laugh like rippling water. He was the merriest little fellow possible, and manly, too! He understood all about milking, did Pretty Dick; and could drive up a refractory cow with anybody. He could chop wood, too—that is, a little, you know, because he was not very strong, and the axe was heavy. He could ride, not a buck-jumper—that was his ambition—but he would take Molly (the wall-eyed mare) into the home station for his father's rations, and come out again quite safely.

He liked going into the station, because he saw Ah Yung, the Chinaman cook, who was kind to him, and gave him sugar. He had all the news to hear too. How another mob of travelling sheep were coming through the run; how the grey mare had slipped her foal; how the bay filly had bucked off Black Harry and hurt his wrist; how Old Tom had "got the sack" for being impudent to the overseer, and had vowed to fire the run. Besides, there was the paper to borrow for his father, Mr. Trelawney's horses to look at, the chat with the carpenter, and perhaps a peep at the new buggy with its silver-mounted harness (worth, "oh, thousands of pounds!" Pretty Dick thought;) perhaps, too, he might go down to the house, with its garden and cool verandah, and bunches of grapes; might get a little cake from Mary, the cook; or even might be smiled upon by Mrs. Trelawney, the owner's young wife, who seemed to Dick to be something more a lady—to be a sweet voice that spoke kindly to him, and made him feel as he would feel sometimes when his mother would get the Big Bible, that came all the way from England, and tell him the story about the Good Man who so loved little children.

He liked to go into the station, because everyone was so kind to him. Everyone loved Pretty Dick; even old Tom, who had been a "lag," and was a very wicked man, hushed the foul jest and savage oath when the curly head of Pretty Dick came within hearing; and the men always felt as if they had their Sunday clothes on in his presence. But he was not to go into the station to-day. It was not ration-day; so he sat on the step of his father's hut door, looking out through a break in the timber-belt at the white dots on the plain, that he knew to be his father's sheep.

Pretty Dick's father lived in the Log Hut, on the edge of the plains, and had five thousand sheep to look after. He was away all day. Sometimes, when the sheep would camp near home, Pretty Dick would go down with some fresh tea in a "billy" for his father, and would have a very merry afternoon watching his father cut curious notches a his stick, and would play with Lassie, and look about for 'possums in the trees, or, with craning neck, cautiously inspect an ant-hill. And then when evening came, and Lassie had got the sheep together—quietly, without any barking, you know—when father and son jogged homewards through the warm, still air, and the trampling hoofs of the sheep sent up a fragrance from the crushed herbage round the folding ground, Pretty Dick would repeat long stories that his mother had told him, about "Valentine and Orsen," and "Beauty and the Beast," and "Jack the Giant Killer;" for Pretty Dick's mother had been maid in the rector's family in the Kentish village at home, and was a little above Pretty Dick's father, who was only a better sort of farm-labourer. But they were all three very happy now in their adopted country. They were all alone there, these three—Pretty Dick, and mother and father—and no other children came to divide the love that both father and mother had for Pretty Dick. So that when Pretty Dick knelt down by his little bed at night, and put his little brown hands together, and said, "God bless my dear father and mother, and God bless me and make me a good boy," he prayed for the whole family, you see. So they all three loved each other very much—though they were poor people—and Pretty Dick's mother often said that she would not have any harm happen to Pretty Dick for Queen Victoria's golden crown. They had called him Pretty Dick when he was yet a baby on board the "Star of Peace" emigrant ship, and the name had remained with him ever since. His father called him Pretty Dick, and his mother called him Pretty Dick, and the people at the home station called him Pretty Dick; and even the cockatoo who lived on the perch over Lassie's bark-kennel, would call out "Pretty Dick! Pretty Dick! Pretty Dick!" over and over again.

Now, on this particular morning, Pretty Dick sat gazing between the trunks of the gum-trees into the blue distance. It was very hot. The blue sky was cloudless, and the sun seemed to be everywhere at once. There was a little shade, to be sure, among the gum-tree trunks, but that would soon pass, and there would be no shade anywhere. The little fenced-in waterhole in the front of the hut glittered in the sunlight like a piece of burnished metal, and the tin milk-pail that was turned topsy-turvy on the pole-paling, was quite dazzling to look at. Daisy, the cow, stood stupidly under the shade of a round, punchy little she-oak close by, and seemed too lazy even to lie down, it was so hot. Of course the blow-flies had begun, and their ceaseless buzz resounded above and around, making it seem hotter than ever, Pretty Dick thought.

How hot father must be! Pretty Dick knew those terrible plains well. He had been across them two or three times. Once in the early spring, when it was pleasant enough with a cool breeze blowing, and white clouds resting on the tops of the distant mountains, and the broad rolling levels of short, crisp, grass-land sweeping up from their feet to the horizon unceasingly. But he had been across there once in the summer, when the ground was dry and cracked, when the mountains seemed so close that he almost thought that he could touch them with his hand, when the heavens were like burning brass, and the air (crepitant with the ceaseless chirping of the grasshopper) like the flame of a heated furnace. Pretty Dick felt quite a fresh accession of heat as he thought of it, and turned his face

11

away to the right to cool himself by thinking of the ranges. They were deep in the bush, past the creek that ran away the other side of the Sandy Rises; deep in the bush on the right hand, and many a weary stretch of sandy slope, and rough-grassed swamp, and solemn wood, and dismal, deserted scrub, was between him and them. He could see the lofty purple peak of Mount Clear, the highest in the range, grandly rising above the dense level tops of the gum-tree forests, and he thought how cool it must be in its mighty shadow. He had never been under the mountain. That there were some strange reaches of scrub, and sand, and dense thickets, and tumbled creeper-entwined rock in that swamp-guarded land, that lay all unseen under the shadow of the hills, he knew, for he had heard the men say so. Had he not heard how men had been lost in that awesome scrub, silent and impenetrable, which swallowed up its victims noiselessly? Had he not heard how shepherds had strayed or slept, and how, at night, the sheep had returned alone, and that search had been in vain, until perhaps some wandering horseman, all by chance, had lighted upon a rusty rag or two, a white skull, and perhaps a tin pannikin, with hopeless scratchings of name and date? Had he not been told fearful things about those ranges? How the bushrangers had made their lair in the Gap, and how the cave was yet visible where their leader had been shot dead by the troopers; how large sums of stolen money were buried there, hidden away behind slags and slabs of rock, flung into fathomless gullies, or crammed into fissures in the mountain side, hidden so well that all the searching hands and prying eyes of the district had not yet discovered them? Did not Wallaby Dick tell him one night about the Murder that had been done down in the flat under the large Australian moon—when the two swagmen, after eating and drinking, had got up in the bright, still night, and beaten out the brains of the travelling hawker, who gave them hospitality, and how, the old man being found beside his rifled cart, with his gray hairs matted with blood, search was made for the murderers, and they were taken in a tap-room in distant Hamilton, bargaining with the landlord for the purchase of their plunder?

What stories had he not heard of wild cattle, of savage bulls, red-eyed, pawing, and unapproachable? What hideous tales of snakes, black, cold, and deadly, had not been associated in his mind with that Mountain Land? What a strange, dangerous, fascinating, horrible, wonderful place that Mountain Land must be, and how much he would like to explore it! But he had been forbidden to go, and he dismissed, with a childish sigh, all idea of going.

He looked up at his clock—the sun. He was just over the top of the big gum-tree—that meant ten o'clock. How late! The morning was slipping away. He heard his mother inside singing. She was making the bread. It would be very hot in the hut when the loaf was put in the camp-oven to bake. He had nothing to do either. He would go down to the creek; it was cool there. So he went into the hut and got a big piece of sweet cake, and put it in the pocket of his little jumper.

"Mother," said Pretty Dick, "I am going down to the creek."

"Take care you don't get lost!" said she, half in jest, half in earnest.

"Lost! No fear!" said Pretty Dick.

—And when he went out, his mother began to sing again.

It was beautifully cool down by the creek. Pretty Dick knew that it would be. The creek had come a long way, and was tired, and ran very slowly between its deep banks, luscious with foliage, and rich with grass. It had a long way to go, too, Pretty Dick knew where it went. It ran right away down to the river. It ran on into the open, desolate, barren piece of ground where the road to the station crossed it, and where its bright waters were all red and discoloured with the trampling of horses and cattle. It ran by the old stockyard, and then turned away with a sudden jerk, and lost itself in the Five Mile Swamp, from whence it re-appeared again, broader and bigger, and wound along until it met the river.

But it did not run beyond the swamp now, Dick knew, because the weather had been so hot, and the creeks were all dried up for miles around—his father said—all but this one. It took its rise in the mountains, and when the rainfall was less than usual, grew thinner and thinner, until it became, what it was now, a slender stream of water, trickling heavily between high banks—quite unlike the dashing, brawling, black, bubbling torrent that had rushed down the gully in flood-time.

Pretty Dick took off his little boots, and paddled about in the water, and found out all kinds of curious, gnarled roots of old trees, and funny holes under the banks. It was so cool and delicious under the stems and thick leaves of the water frondage that Pretty Dick felt quite restored again, and sang remembered scraps of his mother's songs, as he dodged round intervening trees, and slipped merrily between friendly trunks and branches. At last he came out into the open. Here his friend, the creek, divided itself into all sorts of queer shapes, and ran here, and doubled back again there, and twisted and tortured itself in an extraordinary manner, just out of pure fun and frolic.

There was a herd of cattle camped at this place, for the trees were tall, and big, and spreading. The cattle did not mind Pretty Dick at all, strange to say. Perhaps that was because he was on foot. If he had been on horseback now, you would have seen how they would have stared and wheeled about, and splashed off into the scrub. But when Pretty Dick, swinging a stick that he had cut, and singing one of his mother's songs, came by, they merely moved a little farther away, and looked at his little figure with long, sleepy eyes, slowly grinding their teeth from side to side the while. Now the way began to go up-hill, and there were big dead trees to get over, and fallen spreading branches to go round; for the men had been felling timber here, and the wasted wood lay thick upon the ground. At last Pretty Dick came to the Crossing Place. The Crossing Place was by the edge of the big swamp, and was a notable place for miles round. There was no need for a crossing place now though, for the limpid water was not a foot deep.

Pretty Dick had come out just on the top of a little sandy rise, and he saw the big swamp right before him, speckled with feeding cattle, whose backs were just level with the tall rushes. And beyond the big swamp the ranges rose up, with the sunlight gleaming here and there upon jutting crags of granite, and with deep cool shadows in other places, where the noble waving line of hills sank in, and made dark recesses full of shade and coolness. The sky was bluer than ever, and the air was heavy with heat; and Pretty Dick wondered how the eagle-hawk that was poised—a floating speck above the mountain top—could bear to swoop and swing all day long in that fierce glare.

He turned down again, and crossing the creek, plunged into the bush. There was a subtle perfume about him now; not a sweet, rich perfume like the flowers in the home station garden, but a strange intoxicating smell, evolved from the heat and the water, and the many coloured heath blossoms. The way was more difficult now, and Pretty Dick left the bank of the creek, and made for the open space—sandy, and bunched with coarse clumps of grass. He went on for a long time, still upwards, and at last his little feet began to tire; and, after chasing a dragon-fly or two, and running a long way after a kangaroo rat, that started out from a patch of broom and ran in sharp diagonal lines away to hide itself in among the roots of a she-oak, he began to think of the piece of sweet cake in his pocket. So when, after some little time, emerging from out a dense mass of scrub, that scratched and tore at him as though it would hold him back, he found himself far up the hills, with a great gully between him and the towering ranges, he sat down and came to the conclusion that he was hungry. But when he had eaten his sweet cake, he found that he was thirsty too, and that there was no water near him. But Pretty Dick knew that there was water in the ranges; so he got up again, a little wearily, and went down the gully to look for it. But it was not so easy to find, and he wandered about for a long time, among big granite boulders, and all kinds of blind creeks, choked up with thick grass and creeping plants, and began to feel very tired indeed, and a little inclined to wish that he had not left the water-course so early. But he found it at last—a little pool, half concealed by stiff, spiky, rush grass, and lay down, and drank eagerly. How nice the first draught was! But at the second, the water felt warm, and at the third, tasted quite thick and slimy. There had been some ducks paddling about when he came up, and they flew away with a great quacking and splashing, that almost startled him. As soon as they had disappeared though, the place was quite still again, and the air grew heavier than ever. He felt quite drowsy and tired, and laid himself down on a soft patch of mossy grass, under a tree; and so, after listening a little while to the humming of the insects, and the distant crackling of mysterious branches in the forest, he put his little head on his little arm, and went fast to sleep.

How long he slept Pretty Dick did not know, but he woke up suddenly with a start, and a dim consciousness that the sun had shifted, and had been pouring its heat upon him for some time. The moment he woke he heard a great crashing and plunging, and started up just in time to see a herd of wild cattle scouring off down the side of the range. They had come up to drink while he was asleep, and his sudden waking had frightened them. How late it must be! The place seemed quite changed. There was sunlight where no sunlight had been before, and shadow where had been sunlight. Pretty Dick was quite startled at finding how late it was. He must go home, or mother would be frightened. So he began to go back again. He knew his way quite well. No fear of his losing himself. He felt a little tired though, but that would soon wear off. So he left the little pool and turned homewards. He got back again into the gully, and clambered up to the top, and went on sturdily. But the trees did not seem familiar to him, and the succession of dips in the hills seemed interminable. He would soon reach the Big Swamp again, and then he could follow up the creek. But he could not find the Swamp. He toiled along very slowly now, and at last found the open plot of ground where he had stopped in the morning. But when he looked at it a little, it was not the same plot at all, but another something like it, and the grim ranges, heavy with shadow, rose all around him.

A terrible fear came into poor little Pretty Dick's heart, and he seemed to hear his mother say, quite plainly, "Take care you don't get lost, Pretty Dick!" Lost! But he put the feeling away bravely, and swallowed down a lump in his throat, and went on again. The cattle-track widened out, and in a little while he found himself upon a jutting peak, with the whole panorama of the Bush at his feet. A grand sight! On the right hand towered the Ranges, their roots sunk deep in scrub and dense morass, and their heads lifted into the sky, that was beginning to be streaked with purple flushes now. On the left, the bush rolled away beneath him—one level mass of tree-tops, broken here and there by an open space of yellow swamp, or a thin line of darker foliage, that marked the meanderings of some dried-up creek. The sun was nearly level with his face, and cast a long shadow behind him. Pretty Dick felt his heart give a great jump, and then go on beating quicker and quicker. But he would not give in. Lost!—Oh no, he should soon be home, and telling his mother all the wonders of the walk. But it *was* too late! He must make haste. What was that!—somebody on horseback. Pretty Dick shaded his eyes with his little hand, and peered down into the valley. A man with a white puggarree on his hat, was moving along a sort of cattle-track. Joy!—It was Mr. Gaunt, the overseer. Pretty Dick cooeed. No answer. He cooeed again,—and again, but still the figure went on. Presently it emerged from the scrub, and the poor little fellow could see the rays of the setting sun gleam redly for an instant on a bright spur, like a dying spark. He gave a despairing shout. The horseman stopped, looked about him, and then glancing up at the fast clouding heavens, shook his horse's bridle, and rode off in a hand-gallop.

Poor Pretty Dick! He knew that his cry had been unheard—mistaken, perhaps, for the scream of a parrot, the cry of some native bear, or strange bird, but in his present strait, the departure of the presence of something human, felt like a desertion. He fairly gave way, and sat down and cried. By-and-by he got up again, with quite a strange feeling of horror, and terror, and despair; he ran down the steep side of the range in the direction in which Mr. Gaunt had gone, and followed his fast fading figure, calling and crying with choked voice. Presently he lost him altogether, and then he felt his courage utterly fail. He had no idea of where he was. He had lost all power of thought and reason, and was possessed but by one overpowering terror, and a consciousness that whatever he did, he must keep on running, and not stop a moment. But he soon could run no longer. He could only stagger along from tree to tree in the gloomy woods, and cry, "Mother! Mother!" But there was no mother to help him. There was no human being near him, no sound but the hideous croaking of the frogs in the marshes, and the crackling of the branches under his footsteps. The sun went down suddenly behind the hills, and the air grew cool at once. Pretty Dick felt as if he had lost a friend, and his tears burst forth afresh. Utterly tired and worn out, he sat down at the foot of a tree, and sobbed with sheer fatigue. Then he got up and ran round and round, like some hunted animal, calling, "Mother! Mother!"

But there was no reply. Nothing living was near him, save a hideous black crow who perched himself upon the branch of a withered tree, and mocked him, seeming to the poor boy's distorted fancy to say, "Pretty Dick! Pretty Dick! Walk! walk! walk!"

In a burst of passionate, childish despair, he flung a piece of stick at the bird, but his strength failed him, and the missile fell short. This fresh failure made him cry again, and then he got up and ran—stumbling, and falling, and crying—away from the loathsome thing. But it followed him, flapping heavily from tree to tree, and perched quite close to him at last, croaking like an evil presence—"Pretty Dick! Pretty Dick! Walk! walk! walk!"

The sweet night fell, and the stars looked down into the gullies and ravines, where poor Pretty Dick, all bruised, bleeding, and despairing, was staggering, from rock to rock, sick at heart, drenched with dew, hatless, shoeless, tear-stained, crying, "Mother! mother! I am lost! Oh, mother! mother!"

The calm, pitiless stars looked down upon him, and the broad sky spread coldly over him, and the birds flew away terrified at him; and the deadly chill of loneliness fell upon him, and the cold, cruel, silent night seemed to swallow him up, and hide him from human sympathy.

Poor Pretty Dick! No more mother's kisses, no more father's caresses, no more songs, no more pleasures, no more flowers, no more sunshine, no more love—nothing but grim Death, waiting remorselessly in the iron solitude of the hills; in the sad-eyed presence of the

16

speechless stars. There, among the awful mystery and majesty of nature, alone, a terrified little human soul, with the eternal grandeur of the forests, the mountains, and the myriad voices of the night, Pretty Dick knelt trembling down, and, lifting his little, tear-stained face to the great, grave, impassable sky—sobbed.

"Oh! take me home! Take me home! Oh! please, God, take me home!"

The night wore on—with strange sounds far away in the cruel bush, with screamings of strange birds, with gloomy noises, as of the tramplings of many cattle, with movements of leaves and snapping of branches, with unknown whirrings as of wings, with ripplings and patterings as of waterfalls, with a strange heavy pulsation in the air, as though the multitudinous life of the forest was breathing around him. He was dimly conscious that any moment some strange beast —some impossible monster, enormous and irresistible, might rise up out of the gloom of the gullies and fall upon him;—that the whole horror of the bush was about to take some tangible shape and appear silently from behind the awful rocks which shut out all safety and succour. His little soul was weighed down by the nameless terror of a solitude which was no solitude,—but a silence teeming with monsters. He pictured the shapeless Bunyip lifting its shining sides heavily from the bottomless blackness of some lagoon in the shadow of the hills, and dragging all its loathsome length to where he lay. He felt suffocated; the silence that held all these indistinct noises in its bosom, muffled him about like a murderous cloak; the palpable shadow of the immeasurable mountains fell upon him like a grave-stone, and the gorge where he lay was like the Valley of the Shadow of Death. He screamed to break the silence, and the scream rang around him in the woods, and up above him in the mountain clefts, and beneath him in the mute mystery of the glens and swamps,—his cry seemed to be re-echoed again and again by strange voices never heard before, and repeated with indistinct mutterings and moanings in the caverns of the ranges. He dared not scream a second time lest he should wake some awful sound whose thunder should deafen him.

All this time he was staggering on,—not daring to look to right or left, or anywhere but straight on—straight on always. He fell, and tore his hands, and bruised his limbs, but the bruises did not hurt him. His little forehead was cut by a sharp stone, and his bright hair was all dusty and matted with blood. His knees shook and trembled, and his tongue clove to his mouth. He fell at every yard, and his heart seemed to beat so loud, that the sound filled the air around him.

His strength was leaving him; he tottered from weakness; and, at last, emerging upon a little open platform of rock, white under the moon, he felt his head swim, and the black trunks, and the masses of fern-tree leaves, and the open ground, and the silent expanse of bush below him, all turned round in one crimson flash; and then the crimson grew purple-streaked, and spotted with sparks, and radiations, and bursting globes of light and colour, and then the ranges closed in and fell upon him, and he was at once in his little bed at home—oh, so-fast-asleep !

But he woke at last, very cold and numbed, and with some feeling that he was not himself, but that he had been dreaming of a happy boy named Pretty Dick, who went away for a walk one afternoon many years ago. And then he felt for the blankets to pull them up about his shoulders, and his little fingers grasped a prickly handful of heather, and he woke with a terrible start.

Moonlight still, but a peaceful, solemn, sinking moon. She was low down in the sky, hanging like a great yellow globe over the swamp that rose from far beneath him, straight up, it seemed to a level with his face. Her clear cut rim rested on the edge of the morass now. He could almost touch her, she looked so close to him; but he could not lift his little arm so high, and besides, he had turned everything upside down before he went to sleep, and the moon was down below him and the earth up above him! To be sure ! and then he shut his eyes and went to sleep again.

By-and-by it dawned. The birds twittered, and the dew sparkled, and the mists came up and wreathed themselves all about the trees, and Pretty Dick was up in the pure cool sky, looking down upon a little figure that lay on an open space among the heather. Presently, slowly at first, and then more quickly, he found out that this little figure was himself, and that he was in pain, and then it all came back with one terrible shock, and he was Lost again.

He could bear to think of it now, though. His terror, born of darkness, had fled with the uprising of the glorious golden sun. There was, after all, no reason to be afraid. Boys had been lost before, and found again. His father would have missed him last night, and the station would be speedily roused. Oh, he would soon be found ! He got up very painfully and stiffly, and went to look for water. No difficulty in that ; and when he had drunken, and washed his face and hands, he felt much better. Then he began to get hungry, and to comfort himself with the thought that he would soon be found. He could almost hear the joyful shout, and the welcome, and the questioning. How slowly the time went on! He tried to keep still in one place, for he knew now that his terror-driven feet had brought him to this pass, and that he should have kept still in the place where he saw Mr. Gaunt the night before.

At the recollection of that bitter disappointment, and the thought of how near he had been to succour, his tears began afresh. He tried hard to keep his terrors back—poor little fellow,—and thought of all kinds of things—of the stories his mother told him—of the calf-pen that father was putting up. And then he would think of the men at the station, and the remembrance of their faces cheered him ; and he thought of Mrs. Trewlawney, and his mother. O—suppose he should never see his mother again! And then he cried, and slept, and woke, and forgot his fears for awhile, and would listen intently for a sound, and spring up and answer a fancied shout, and then lie in a dull, stupid despair, with burning eyes, and aching head, and a gnawing pain that he knew was

Hunger. So the hot day wore out. The same heat as yesterday, the same day as yesterday, the same sights and sounds as yesterday—but oh! how different was yesterday to to-day,—and how far off yesterday seemed. No one came. The shadows shifted, and the heat burnt him up, and the shade fell on him, and the sun sank again, and the stars began to shine,—and no one came near Pretty Dick. He had almost forgotten, indeed, that there was such a boy as Pretty Dick. He seemed to have lived years in the bush alone. He did not know where he was, or who he was. It seemed quite natural to him that he should be there alone, and he had no wish to get away. He had lost all his terror of the Night. He scarcely knew it was night, and after sitting on the grass a little longer, smiling at the fantastic shadows that the moonlight threw upon the ground, he discovered that he was hungry, and must go into the hut for supper. The hut was down in the gully yonder; he could hear his mother singing;—so Pretty Dick got up, and crooning a little song, went down into the Shadow.

*   *   *   *   *

They looked for him for five days. On the sixth, his father and another came upon something, lying, half-hidden, in the long grass at the bottom of a gully in the ranges. A little army of crows flew heavily away. The father sprang to earth with a white face. Pretty Dick was lying on his face, with his head on his arm.

God had taken him home.

19

POOR JOE.

HE was the ostler at Coppinger's, and they called him Poor Joe.
Nobody knew whence he came ; nobody knew what misery
of early mutilation had been his. He had appeared one
evening, a wandering swagman, unable to speak, and so explain his
journey's aim or end—able only to mutter and gesticulate, making
signs that he was cold and hungry, and needed fire and food. The
rough crowd in Coppinger's bar looked on him kindly, having for
him that sympathy which marked physical affliction commands in the
rudest natures. Poor Joe needed all their sympathies : he was a
dwarf, and dumb.

Coppinger — bluff, blasphemous, and good-hearted soul —
dispatched him, with many oaths, to the kitchen, and when the next
morning the deformed creature volunteered in his strange sign-speech
to do some work that might "pay for his lodging," sent him to
help the ostler that ministered to King Cobb's coach-horses. The
ostler, for lack of a better name, perhaps, called him " Joe," and
Coppinger, finding that the limping mute, though he could speak no
word of human language, yet had a marvellous power of communication with horseflesh, installed him as under-ostler and stable-helper,
with a seat at the social board, and a wisp of clean straw in King
Cobb's stable.

"I have taken him on," said Coppinger, when the township
cronies met the next night in the bar.

"Who," asked the croniest, bibulously disregarding grammar.
"Poor Joe," said Coppinger.

The sympathetic world of Bullocktown approved the epithet,
and the deformed vagabond, thus baptized, was known as Poor Joe
ever after.

He was a quiet fellow enough. His utmost wrath never sufficed
to ruffle a hair on the sleek backs of King Cobb's horses. His
utmost mirth never went beyond an ape-like chuckle, that irradiated
his pain-stricken face, as a stray gleam of sunshine lights up the
hideousness of the gargoyle on some old cathedral tower.

It was only when " in drink " that Poor Joe became a spectacle for
strangers to wonder at. Brandy maddened him, and when thus excited
his misshapen soul would peep out of his sunken fiery eyes, force his
grotesque legs to dance unseemly sarabands, and compel his pigeon-
breast to give forth monstrous and ghastly utterances, that might
have been laughs, were they not so much like groans of a brutish
despair that had in it a strange chord of human suffering. Coppinger
was angry when the poor dwarf was thus tortured for the sport of the

whisky-drinkers, and once threw Frolicksome Fitz into the muck midden for inciting the cripple to sputter forth his grotesque croonings and snatches of gruesome merriment. "He won't be fit for nothin' to-morrer," was the excuse Coppinger made for his display of feeling. Indeed, on the days that followed these debauches, Poor Joe was sadly downcast. Even his beloved horses failed to cheer him, and he would sit, red-eyed and woe-begone, on the post-and-rail-fence, like some dissipated bird of evil omen.

The only thing he seemed to love, save his horses, was Coppinger, and Coppinger was proud of this simple affection. So proud was he, that when he discovered that whenever Miss Jane, the sister of Young Bartram, from Seven Creeks, put her pony into the stable, the said pony was fondled and slobbered over and caressed by Poor Joe, he felt something like a pang of jealousy.

Miss Jane was a fair maiden, with pale gold hair, and lips like the two streaks of crimson in the leaf of the white poppy. Young Bartram, owner of Seven Creeks Station—you could see the lights in the house windows from Coppinger's—had brought her from town to "keep house for him," and she was the beauty of the country side. Frolicksome Fitz, the pound-keeper, was at first inclined to toast an opposition belle (Miss Kate Ryder, of Ryder's Mount), but when returning home one evening by the New Dam, he saw Miss Jane jump Black Jack over the post-and-wire into the home station paddock, he forswore his allegiance.

"She rides like an angel," said pious Fitz, and the next time he met her he told her so.

Now this young maiden, so fair, so daring, and so silent, came upon the Bullocktown folk like a new revelation. The old Frenchman at the Melon Patch vowed tearfully that she had talked French to him like one of his countrywomen, and the schoolmaster—Mr. Frank Smith—duly certificated under the Board of Education—reported that she played the piano divinely, singing like a seraph the while. As nobody played (except at euchre) in Bullocktown, this judgment was undisputed. Coppinger swore, slapping with emphasis his mighty thigh, that Miss Jane was a lady, and when he said that he said everything. So, whenever Miss Jane visited the township, she was received with admiration. Coppinger took off his hat to her, Mr. Frank Smith walked to the station every Sunday afternoon to see her, and Poor Joe stood afar off and worshipped her, happy if she bestowed a smile upon him once out of every five times that he held her tiny stirrups.

This taming of Poor Joe was not unnoticed by the whisky-drinkers, and they came in the course of a month or so to regard the cripple as part of the property of Miss Jane—as they regarded her dog, for instance. The schoolmaster, moreover, did not escape tap-room comment. He was frequently at Seven Creeks. He brought flowers from the garden there. He sent for some new clothes from Melbourne. He even borrowed Coppinger's bay mare "Flirt," to ride over to the Sheep-wash, and Dick the mail-boy, who knew that Coppinger's mare was pigeon-toed, vowed that he had seen another horse's tracks besides her's in the sand of the Rose Gap Road.

"You're a deep 'un, Mr. Smith " said Coppinger. "I found yer out sparking Miss Jane along the Mountain Track. Deny it if yer can ?"

But Frank Smith's pale cheek only flushed, and he turned off the question with a laugh. It was Poor Joe's eyes that snapped fire in the corner.

So matters held themselves until the winter, when the unusually wet season forbade riding parties of pleasure. It rained savagely that year, as we all remember, and Bullocktown in rainy weather is not a cheerful place. Miss Jane kept at home, and Poor Joe's little eyes, wistfully turned to the Station on the hill, saw never her black pony cantering round the corner of Archie Cameron's hayrick.

A deeper melancholy seemed to fall on the always melancholy township. Coppinger's cronies took their "tots" in silence, steaming the while, and Coppinger himself would come gloomily to the door, speculating upon evil unless the leaden curtain lifted.

But it did not lift, and rumour of evil came. Up the country, by Parsham and Merrydale, and Black Adder's Gully, there were whole tracts of grass-land under water. The neighbouring station of Hall's, in the mountains, was a swamp. The roads were bogged for miles. Tim Doolan was compelled to leave his dray and bullocks at Tom and Jerry's, and ride for his life before the advancing waters. The dams were brimming at Quartzborough, St. Rey reservoir was running over. It was reported by little M'Cleod, the sheep-dealer, that the old bridge at the Little Glimmera had been carried away. It was reported that Old Man Horn, whose residence overlooked the river, had fastened a bigger hook to a larger pole (there was a legend to the effect that Old Man Horn had once hooked a body from the greedy river, and after emptying its pockets, had softly started it down stream again), and was waiting behind his rickety door, rubbing his withered hands gleefully. Young Bartram rode over to Quartzborough to get M'Compass, the shire engineer, too look at his new dam. Then the coach stopped running, and then Flash Harry, galloping through the township at night, like the ghost-rider in Bürger's ghastly ballad, brought the terrible news :—THE FLOODS WERE UP, AND THE GLIMMERA BANK AND BANK AT THE OLD CROSSING-PLACE.

"It will be here in less than an hour," he shouted, under Coppinger's red lamps; "make for the high ground if you love your lives ;" and so wet, wild-eyed, and white, splashed off into the darkness, if haply he might warn the poor folk down the river of the rushing death that was coming upon them.

Those who were there have told of the horrors of that night. How the muddy street, scarce reclaimed from the river-bed, was suddenly full of startled half-dressed folk. How Coppinger's was crowded to the garret. How the schoolmaster dashed off, stumbling through the rain, to warn them at Seven Creeks. How bullies grew pale with fear, and men hitherto mild of speech and modest of mien, waxed fiery-hot with wrath at incapacity, and fiercely self-assertive in relegating fools to their place in the bewildered social economy of that general overturn. How the roaring flood came down, bearing huge trees, fragments of houses, grotesquely terrible waifs and strays of house-hold furniture upon its yellow and turbid bosom, timid women grew brave, and brave men hid their faces for a while. How Old Man Horn saved two lives that night. How Widow Rae's cottage, with her light still burning in the windowsill, was swept off, and carried miles down stream. How Archy Cameron's hayrick stranded in the middle of the township. How forty drowned sheep were floated into the upper windows of the "Royal Mail." How Patey Barnes's cradle, with its new-born occupant sucking an unconscious thumb, was found jammed in the bight of the windlass in Magby's killing-yard. How all this took place has been told, I say, by those who were present, and needs no repeating. But one thing which took place shall be chronicled here. When the terror and confusion were somewhat stilled, and Coppinger, by dint of brandy and blankets, had got some strength and courage into the half-naked, shivering creatures clustered in his ark, a sudden terrible tremor went through the crowd, like an electric current. In some mysterious way, no one knew how originating, or by what fed and fostered, men came to hear that Bartram's dam was breaking. That is to say, that in ten minutes or less, all the land that lay between Coppinger's and the river, would be a roaring waste of water—that in less than ten minutes the Seven Creeks Station, with all its inmates, would be swept off the face of the earth, and that if Coppinger's escaped, it would be a thing to thank God for.

After the first sharp agony of self-apprehension, one thought came to each—Miss Jane.

"Good God," cries Coppinger, "can nobody go to her?"

Ten men volunteered to go.

"It's no good," said faint-hearted Riley, the bully of the bar.

"The dam 'll burst twice over 'fore you can reach the Station."

It was likely.

"I'll go myself," cries brave old Coppinger; but his wife clung to his arm, and held him back with all the weight of her maternity.

"I have it," says Coppinger; "Poor Joe 'll go. Where is he?"

No one had seen him. Coppinger dashed down the stairs, splashed through the yard into the stable. The door was open, and Blackboy, the strongest of King Cobb's horses, was missing. Coppinger flashed round the lantern he held. The mail-boy's saddle had disappeared, and faintly mingling with the raging wind and roaring water, died the rapid strokes of a horse pat.

Poor Joe had gone.

*　　　*　　　*　　　*　　　*

The house was already flooded out, and they were sitting (so I was told) with their arms round each other, not far from where poor Bartram's body was found, when the strange misshapen figure, bestriding the huge horse, splashed desperately through the water, that was once the garden.

"Rescue," cried Frank, but she only clung to him the closer.

Poor Joe bit his lips at the sight of the pair, and then, so Frank Smith averred, flung him one bitter glance of agony, and dropping his deformed body from the back of the reeking horse, held out the bridle with a groan.

In moments of supreme danger one divines quickly. Frank placed his betrothed upon the saddle, and sprang up behind her. If ever Blackboy was to prove his metal, he must prove it then, for already the lightning revealed a thin stream of water trickling over the surface of the dam.

"But what is to become of *you*?" cried Miss Jane.

Poor Joe, rejecting Frank's offered hand, took that of Miss Jane, patted it softly, and let it fall. He pointed to Coppinger's red light, and then to the black wall of the dam. No man could mistake the meaning of that trembling finger, and those widely-opened eyes. They said "Ride for your lives! ride!" plainer than the most eloquent tongue owned by schoolmaster could speak.

It was no time for sentiment, and for the schoolmaster there was but one life to be saved or lost that night. He drove his heels into the good horse's sides, and galloped down the hill. "God bless you Joe!" cried Miss Jane. Poor Joe smiled, and then, falling down on his knees, waited, straining his ears to listen. It was not ten minutes, but it seemed ten hours, when, through the roar, he heard a distant shout go up. They were saved. Thank God! And then the dam burst with a roar like thunder, and he was whirled away amid a chaos of tree trunks.

*   *   *   *   *

They found his little weak body four days afterwards, battered and bruised almost out of recognition; but his great brave soul had gone on to judgm nt.

GENTLEMAN GEORGE'S BRIDE.

CHAPTER I.

WHEN it was known at Bullocktown that old Keturah Gow was going to be married to Gentleman George, there was some laughter and much shaking of heads.

"Keturah was a woman of hard middle age. Scotch by birth, and Presbyterian by religion, she had come to Australia as the nurse of Flora M'Leod, now Mrs. Marrable, of Seven Creeks, and had lived twenty years in the bush. The man whom she was about to marry was named George Harris. No one knew whence he came, or how long he had lived in the colonies. He had no religion worth mentioning, and no accomplishment save that of horsemanship. His age was three-and-twenty, or thereabouts, and being impatient of temper, handy with his fists, prodigal of his money, and possessed of a certain gipsy beauty of face and figure, the intelligent stockmen called him 'Gentleman George.'

"In vain did the gossips of Bullocktown animadvert upon the match. In vain did Longbow borrow Mumford's spring-cart and Coppinger's grey mare for the express purpose of making a pilgrimage to the Gap, and warning Neil Gow, the shepherd, of the misery which awaited his sister. 'She must just gang her ain gate,' said crippled Neil, wagging the stump of his arm in a feeble circle as though he would fain have waved the hand that was wanting. 'I've said a' I can, I'll say nae mair.' 'Shall *I* speak to her?' asked Longbow. 'As ye please,' quoth Neil; 'but Kitty's the deevil's temper, and maybe she'll claw oot ye're e'en, man!' So Longbow sighed and shot ducks. In vain did Mrs. Marrable implore the headstrong old woman to reconsider her determination. 'The fellow's a ne'er-do-well, Keturah—John says he is: he only wants your money (for Keturah had saved some £200 during her servitude). He's a bad man.' Keturah only sighed and vowed that all the world was prejudiced against puir Geordie. In vain did John Marrable—not without a hearty English curse or two—command Gentleman George not to make a fool of himself and to let the old woman alone. 'If she's minded to marry me,' said the young man, with a droop of his thickly-lashed lids, 'it isn't for you to interfere, sir—excuse *me*. I suppose a man can marry anyone he likes.' 'I suppose he can, confound him,' replied honest John Marrable. In vain did Coppinger, the publican, suggest—over a nobbler of P.B.—that George was throwing himself away. 'You'll have the whole township laughing at you, George.' 'Shall I?'

25

returns George, fiercely, and catching Alick, the blacksmith, in the very dead waste and middle of a grin, forthwith pitched him into the sandy street. 'Folks won't laugh at me *twice*, I'll pound it,' said he, and Alick—his mouth full of sand—re-echoed the sentiment with spluttering humility. So the pair were married in due form, and the wedding feast was held at the 'Saw-pits.'

"The 'Saw-pits' was a public-house situated half-way between the Gap (where, under the shadow of the hills, nestled Neil Gow's hut), and the distant Glimmera, on whose farther bank smoked the chimneys of Coppinger's and drowsed the world of Bullocktown. The High Road was wont to run through Bullocktown and bend abruptly westward to avoid crossing the chain of water-holes called the Great Glimmera River; but three floods and a new Postmaster-General, with a turn for economy, had altered all that. The mail-carrying coaches had been directed to take the shortest cut, and a bridge had been built, in order that they might do so with convenience. The building of this bridge had established a colony of sawyers, and the bridge completed, the mill was converted into a tavern. Where the carcass is, there will the eagles be gathered together. Where is liquor, there flock the bushmen. It is thus that townships are formed.

"The keeper of the 'Saw-pits' was one Trowbridge, who with his two daughters had migrated from Bullocktown. Neil Gow was a great crony of his, and despite the orders of Marrable (who, when a public-house was established on his run, thought the end of the world was come) frequently rode the bob-tailed pony through the sweet summer night, and 'hung him up' to Trowbridge's verandah-post. Trowbridge and the one-armed boundary rider had often seriously conversed on the subject of Keturah's approaching marriage, and it had been agreed that the wedding feast should be held at the 'Saw-pits.'

"'She may do what she likes, lad,' said Trowbridge; 'and if the match turns out ill, neither thou nor I will be to blame. But if we don't make every mother's son of 'em as drunk as a fiddler's bitch, my name ain't Tom Trowbridge!'

"The laudible purpose of the publican seemed likely to be fulfilled. Before the wedding party arrived, the 'Saw-pits Hotel' was crowded. Trowbridge's Sunday shirt had come to torment him before the time, and Alick anticipated the daily period of his intoxication by full three hours. In the hollows round about the creek were camped tilt-waggons galore, and in the half-acre of mud that did duty for the stable-yard of the 'Saw-pits,' the brand new buggy of Jim Porter, the lucky reefer, lay stranded like a skeleton-wreck upon a bleak, inhospitable shore. Festoons of such wild-flowers as were procurable, decorated the front of the hostelry, and wreathed themselves lovingly about the transparent beauties of Hennessy and Otard, while in the long room, where dancing was to be undergone, the air was pungent with the exhilarating odour of smashed gum-leaves. To these preparations arrived presently, in a cloud of dust, the bridal party.

"Let the classical reader recall the triumphs of old Rome, the glittering spears, the hollow-clanging shield, the sound of the trumpets, the thunder of the captains, and the shouting. First, galloping furiously, a crowd of horsemen, bearded and long-haired, cracking their whips like pistol-shots, and filling the air with Homeric laughter. Then a mass of vehicles, bumping, jolting, leaping, filled with men in white shirts, and women with yellow shawls. Then were stockriders, some with led horses, in order that the swift pace of the morning might be preserved on the homeward journey. Now behind, now before, in the midst of this fury and clamour, borne along and . overwhelmed by dust and friendship, clattered the triumphal car—a hooded buggy lent by Coppinger, to which were attached four grass-fed nags, postillioned by the two sons of Archy Fletcher, youths to whom, in the matter of rapidity of locomotion, Jehu, the son of Nimshi, would have appeared but as a farmer's wife, jogging with egg-laden panniers to market. From the buggy— jerked to a swaying standstill in the most approved bush method when the fore legs of the leaders threatened the skillion window of the inn—descended, to shouts that rent the hot heaven, the happy pair.

"Gentleman George was dressed in the height of bush fashion. A cabbage-tree hat, so browned and battered that it boasted the colour of a well-smoked meerschaum, adorned his handsome bullet-head. A short linen coat served but to enhance the purity of a white shirt, from the falling collar of which fluttered the ends of one of those gaily-coloured kerchiefs known to London costermongers as ' Kingsmen.' Round his supple waist was girded a red silk sash, and tightly-fitted breeches of creamy whiteness met, and defied boots, so marvellously black, so astonishingly wrinkled, that Mr. Rapersole, bootmaker and parish clerk, had forgotten an Amen in gazing at them. As this hero walked, the rowels of huge German-silver spurs, loosely fastened by one broad semicircular strap, click-clacked upon the boards in the musical manner so dear to the stockman's soul. Keturah, now Mrs. Harris, was none the less imposing in her attire. She wore a purple shot-silk dress, on the shifting surface of which played rays of crimson and gold, as shoot the colours of the prism across a mass of molten metal. From beneath this marvel two white boots played in and out—not so much like Sir John Suckling's mice as like plump mill-rats newly escaped from a flour-bag. Keturah wore a red velvet bonnet adorned with blue and white flowers; her shawl, fastened by a plaid brooch, was a glowing yellow with a green border, and her hands swelled in all the magnificent mockery of mauve kid gloves. Yet, with all this, her honest brown face shone with an honesty of purpose and a hopefulness of future happiness that rendered it almost beautiful.

"She hung lovingly on her husband's arm, smiling up at him, nor removing her eyes from his face but to gaze proudly at the cheering crowd. *He* walked rather quickly, and his lips tightly compressed, and his black eyes set forward steadily, seemingly wrought up to endure the scene, but anxious to be quit of it. *She* seemed to say, 'See what a noble husband I have won!' He seemed to say, 'I guess your thoughts, but my marriage is none of your business.'

"'He's a temper, Jenny,' said Susie Barnes.

"'My word!' assented Jenny.

"'She ain't such a bad-looking bit of stuff after all,' said Jim Porter. 'I'd rather marry *her* than break my leg, blowed if I wouldn't.'

"So the wedding feast began.

"It is not for my feeble pen to detail the glories of that day. The little township—buried as it was beneath the shadow of the purple hills, and yet preserving in itself all the petty malice, the local jealousy, the blatant conceit of larger towns—gave loose on this one occasion to the wildest merriment. Local feuds were forgotten, personal hatreds forgiven or suspended. Even Mr. M'Taggart, a rabid Orangeman from Derry, forbore to attack Mr. Michael Murphy, a rabid Ribbandman from Clare, and going out into the solitude of the bridge, drank in silence his favourite toast of 'Here's the Pope in the devil's belly, and Martin Luther pitching red hot priests at him!' a toast which was wont to cause Mr. Murphy's 'bhlood to bhoil, bhoys,' and to bring about wrathful combats. Fighting Fitz, the poundkeeper, who was at daggers drawn with Dick Mossop, Scabby Barton's overseer, on account of a brindled poley bullock branded P.W. over T.S. on the off rump, with a notch in both ears, and a star on the forehead, consented to be friends again, and even offered to sell Dick a certain bay mare in defiance of the Impounding Act. Rapersole, of course, could not be kept from politics, and insisted on putting what he was pleased to call 'supposititious' cases in such numbers that Neil Gow, vowing him a bletherin' bumbee's byke, took him by the collar, and flourishing the stump of his arm menacingly, deposited him in an empty buggy. The breakfast was an immense success. Tom Trowbridge presided, having formally asked permission to lay aside his unaccustomed coat, and carved a noble round of beef with the air of a gold stick in waiting. But a round of beef was not the only viand. There was mutton broth and cow-heel, and an ox's head decorated with flowers, and rump steaks, and sweetbreads, and a haggis, and lamb's head, and sheep's trotters, and cold saddle of mutton, and preserved peaches, and tins of jam, and sago pudding, and plum duff, and bottled ale, and tea, and sweet cake, and brandy, and rum, and one bottle of champagne for the ladies.

"'My eyes that's a merry tightener!' said Chirrup, the mail-boy. 'Could *you* eat any more, Archy?' 'No fear!' said Archy, ruefully, 'them blessed puff-tillooners did my business.' After the breakfast and the speeches—you should have heard Rapersole's!—and the digestive smoke, drinking and dancing commenced, Trowbridge doing his best to carry out his promise to Neil Gow and vindicate his self-impugned title to his name. Some notion of the result may be gleaned from a glance at his bill, duly paid by Mrs. Keturah Harris two days afterwards.

"To Mr. George Harris' weding brakefast :—

					Pounds	shilg.	d.
The brakefast	...	...	...	...	10	0	0
Noblers	...	...	...	...	0	2	0
8 spiders	...	...	...	...	0	8	0
Dit o	...	...	...	...	0	8	0
Refreshments for lades		...	...	...	2	0	0
Peppermint drops	...	...	...	...	0	1	0
ginger Bear and bitters		...	...	...	0	0	6
Drinks, phromiskus	...	...	...	...	1	10	0
Squar gin for six		...	...	...	0	3	6
Kake speshul	...	...	...	...	1	10	0
Shout round	...	...	...	...	5	0	0
Dit o	...	...	...	...	5	0	0
Music	...	...	...	...	2	0	0
Drinks for same	...	...	...	...	0	10	0
Rossin	...	...	...	...	0	2	6
10 noblers	...	...	...	...	0	5	0
24 spiders	...	...	...	...	1	4	0
Tobaco	...	...	...	...	0	2	0
24 noblers	...	...	...	...	1	4	0
2 broken chares	...	...	...	...	1	0	0
1 winder	...	...	...	...	2	10	0
Hoarse feed	...	...	...	...	9	0	0
Shout all round	...	...	...	...	5	10	0
Dit o parting	...	...	...	...	5	10	0
Beds for 12	...	...	...	...	2	0	0
Shampane for lades	...	...	...	...	1	0	0
Tottal	...	...	...	...	58	0	6
Recieved by cash	...	...	...	...	58	0	6

T. TROWBRIDGE.

"In the consumption of such items as those mentioned above -did the day wear out; and Trowbridge nobly fulfilled his promise. Of the sixty or seventy persons present, but a very insignificant number went home sober. Indeed, had it not been for the coquetry of Jenny Joyce, who, riding her father's bay horse, Walkover, dared any of the young men to give her five minutes' start and catch her before she reached the Bluff, there is no saying what might have happened. Eight or nine of the best-mounted followed laughing Jenny, but no one got within arm's length of her supple waist save Harry Scallan, and they *do* say that she checked her nag to let him snatch the kiss he had begged for in vain. However, Harry never confessed the fact; but as Dick Mossop, his rival, broke his horse's knees at Mount Hopeless, but half-way to the Bluff, and Jenny became Mrs. Scallan a month afterwards, Harry could afford to be generous. Two or three horse-accidents happened that day. Jim Porter saddled his new buggy-horse, and attempting to ride him, despite the advice of Gentleman George himself, was bucked ignominiously, and his collar-bone ingloriously fractured. Lucy Sperrin's grey pony kicked Chirrup in the stomach and hurt him badly. 'Serves him right for fossicking round me,' Miss Lucy had said. 'I told him the mare was handy with her heels.' Poor Cooke —Mad Cooke, who wore a silver plate on his head, to the wonder of Bullocktown—must needs bring out his old stock-horse and witch the world with noble horsemanship. 'Heigh, boys! Heigh, boys!' he would cry while at full gallop. 'There's none of ye can go up the hills like Ballie!' And indeed no one attempted to do so, all standing aghast at the feats Ballie performed upon the side of the steep hill that shadowed the inn, until poor Ballie put his foot into a hole, or slipped on a rolling stone, and his master came to earth with a fresh brain concussion—the third in his short mad life-time.

"Amid such sports the hot, sweet day wore out to cool evening. The pure perfume of grass and earth scented the air. The red sun sunk in glory behind the ragged shoulder of the B'uff. A purple mist slowly enveloped the hills; the laughing jackasses, merry fellows, set up a tremendous chattering; the frogs began to babble in the marshes, the sheep to move off their camps, the cattle to make for water. The wedding-day was over, and as, amidst a hurricane of cheers, Gentleman George handed his wife to the spring-cart that was to bear them to their home in the Swamp Hut, the great stars came slowly out and looked with tender eyes upon this hopeful, ill-dressed bride.

"A week afterwards frolicsome Fitz, wandering in search of prey wherewith to feed his ravenous Pound, met jolly Polwheal, the butcher, coming from the Swamp Hut.

"'Have you seen the bride?' asked Fitz.

"'Ay, and a comely wench she's grown. She looks a young 'oman, Fitz.'

"'Does she?' says Fitz. 'That's rum, too.'

"Polwheal laughed. 'You're not a felosopher, Fitz! Don't you know,' he added, borrowing a metaphor from his own profession, 'that a working bullock, if you get him fat after a spell, makes the best beef.'

"In regard to the appearance of Keturah Harris, Mr. Polwheal was right. She had become a very comely woman. The lines in her face had faded, her spare figure had rounded, her withered arms had fattened, her grey eyes had a youthful sparkle, and her step a youthful lightness; she seemed a younger woman by twenty years. If you passed by the Swamp Hut, at any hour of the day, you could hear her singing, and the good-tempered woman who brought you out a pannikin of tea, or asked you to have a slice of sweet cake, was a very different being from 'old Ketty,' of the home station, the shrewish-tongued and withered maiden who was the terror of wandering swagmen. Bullocktown wondered at the change, and were not disinclined to roughly jest upon the subject with Gentleman George. That worthy, however, went about his business of stock-riding in silence, and seemed determined by honest attention to his business to merit the kindness shown him by Mrs. Marrable, and deserve the 'married couple' billet which John Marrable had bestowed upon him.

"The astute reader will no doubt have come to the conclusion that this conduct of Gentleman George was but assumed for his own ends; and the astute reader will be right. Gentleman George had not the least intention of passing his life as a stockrider to Mr. Marrable and as the young husband of an old woman. He had married Keturah for her money, and intended, as soon as he could obtain that money, to take himself off. Until he was in a position to do this securely, it was his interest to be kind and gentle, and the scoundrel was kind and gentle accordingly. I trust, however, that the astute reader who has discovered this will not consider Mr. Harris a very great villain. For a young man to marry an old woman for her money is not such a very rare thing, nor have there been wanting cases in the best society where the lady has been deserted afterwards. I admit, however, that to perpetrate such an offence for two hundred pounds does show a coarseness of intellect. If Keturah had been possessed of two hundred thousand pounds now, the case would have been different, and good society might have admitted Mr. Harris to its bosom without a pang. Yet men can but act according to their opportunity, and I am sure that had Gentleman George seen his way to marry a lady with two hundred thousand, or even one hundred thousand pounds, he would have left poor Keturah alone.

"There is no necessity to protract the story at this period. In six months George had got possession of the endorsed deposit receipt of the Bank of Australia, Quartzborough, for £201 8s. 6d., had kissed his wife, told her he was going to look after the mare and foal last seen in Ponsonby's paddock. Once clear of the hut he saddled his own nag Peppercorn, secured his swag already 'planted' on the river bank, set out a smart canter for Quartzborough; drew the money, and slept that night at Hamilton, doing ninety-five miles in eleven and-a-half hours.

"Poor Keturah was like a mad woman. At first she thought that some accident had befallen him, then that he was detained at a neighbouring station. She would fain have roused all the station to look for him. She ran to her mistress raging, and upbraided her for not suffering the dam to be dragged. Then she began to suspect, then to weep, then to vow revenge. 'He's left ye missis,' said the wife of the other boundary-rider. 'He's a bad lot. Ye'd better forget him.'

"'I'll no forget him, the black villain,' said the deserted woman. 'I'll pray to God on my bended knees that I may meet him, and if he's a heart o' flesh I'll wring it.'

"'Come, Ketty,' said her mistress, some days after, 'It's no use greeting, woman. The fellow's gone.'

"'Let him go,' said Ketty. 'I'll find him oot. Ef he's on his dying bed, I'll find him oot, and dinna let him ask me to raise a finger to save him.'

"'I must take her away,' said Mrs. Marrable to her husband. 'She can't bear the sneers and looks of the folk about.'

"'All right; take her with you to town when you go,' said John Marrable.

"Thus it came to pass that having been twenty years in the bush, Keturah Harris became upper nurse in the family of Mr. Thomas Marrable, of the firm of Marrable and Davis, softgoods-men."

CHAPTER II.

"The soft-goods firm of Marrable and Davis was a wealthy one. The Marrable interest consisted of Thomas Marrable (the brother of the station-owner) with his son Harry, and Mr. Israel Davis, once chief clerk, now partner. The office was in Flinders Lane—a big stuccoed building of four storeys, having swing-doors embellished with double plates of brass. Mr. Marrable was a politician and an importer. His son dressed in the latest London fashions, played loo and billiards equally badly, and cherished a secret ambition to belong to the Melbourne Club. He was a thin young man, with a blotched face; rode fairly to hounds, had large private expenses of a disreputable sort, and avowed a profound contempt for cads—which was unselfish. Mrs. Thomas was the daughter of a buttonmaker of Birmingham; she brought 'money' into the business, painted her face daily, had four unhealthy children, and compelled Marrable to reside at Toorak, in case she should ever 'go into society.'

"Mr. Davis lived in a cottage at St. Kilda, and was remarkable for his bachelor parties. He was a tall, slim man of irreproachable manners, and the slightest suspicion of an accent. He drank the best wine procurable, smoked the best cigars, was a patron (and a judicious one) of the fine-arts, owned a cultivated musical taste, and flattered himself that he was utterly without principle. 'My dear fellows,' he would say to the guests (gentlemen who ate his admirable dinner and d——d him going home 'for an infernal Jew, sir'), 'I have no principle, and no religion. My father was a slopseller in Monmouth Street. What's that to me? I am myself—with a good dinner, and a good digestion. You call yourself Christians—bah— you're asses. Every man his own creed, that's my motto. I am Israel Davis—that's my religion. Harry, here, who has been drinking too much claret, thinks himself superior to me. Let him—that's *his* religion, and quite sufficient for him.'

"Flinders Street respected Mr. Davis. 'He's a crafty beast, that beast Davis,' said Mr. Podosokus, the bill-broker. 'He did me out of £50 as easy as kiss my hand. Dam him. I like that fellow. He's such a beast.'

"'A thorough business man,' said Cammolard, of the Border Bank. A hard head. A hard heart. A *thorough* business man.'

"'I don't like that Mr. Davis,' said Milly Smith, who met him at the Marrables' once. 'He's so polite.'

"'What do you mean, dear?' asked Mrs. Smith, but Milly couldn't explain.'

"'I wonder if he has as large an interest in the firm as young Mr. Marrable,' said the mother.

"'I don't like young Mr. Marrable, either,' said poor Milly. '*He's* so rude.'

" 'That wasn't what I asked you, Miss,' said the old lady sharply, and fell into a financial reverie.

"Now, despite his hard-headed and hard-heartedness, Mr Davis had done one kind thing. He had 'taken up' a bill signed 'Marrable and Davis,' which was written by Mr. Harry. This bill was for £250, and had been discounted by Mr. Davis's unacknowledged brother, Zebulon Davis, the proprietor of the Victorian Loan and Discount Company, capital £300,000,000, offices 29 Elizabeth Street East. Mr. Zebulon Davis was the 'Company,' and the capital was supplied by Mr. Israel. When some poor devil of a borrower took his miserable acceptance to the offices at 29 Elizabeth Street, he would be received by Zebulon, who would scan the oblong slip doubtfully, saying, 'It ish an unushual transhaction, Mr. Blank, but I'll lay it before the Board,' and so send a messenger round to Israel, with particulars. If Israel said 'Yes,' the cash, less 90 per cent., was handed to applicant. If Israel said 'No,' Zebulon would put off the transaction for a day or two, on pretence of making inquiries, and then suggest that, perhaps, 'with another namesh '—&c.

"When a bill for £120, with the signature of the firm, was presented to Israel, he saw the state of the case at once, and being a business man he directed it to be discounted on easy terms. 'It is a forgery,' said he to his brother when they met that evening. 'It is sure to be taken up. Sure enough it was taken up by Mr. Harry in person, who had borrowed £120 from Davis 'just for twenty-four hours.' The next day Harry brought the company another bill for £250—'I don't like to put it through the bank,' he said, 'but it's all right.' By his brother's directions, the 'Company' cashed this second forgery, and on the day it fell due, Mr. Davis called Harry into his private room and showed him the document.

" 'Do you see this?'

"Harry turned very pale.

" 'The money-lender to whom you took it had his suspicions, and brought it here. Fortunately *I* saw him, and not your father. I have paid it.'

"Harry, stammering thanks and excuses, stretched out his hand for the document, but Mr. Davis twitched it away.

" 'Oh, no,' he said. 'Excuse me, dear boy, I shall keep this until you repay me the £250.'

"It was after this transaction that Harry Marrable's face became blotchy, and that he had that awkward fit. Dr. Dignato knew it was brandy, so he said it was blood, and ordered the boy to go into the country. Thomas Marrable sent him to his brother's station.

"At last Harry Marrable saw a way of paying his debt to the hated Davis—the very way by which he had incurred it. Honest Jack Griswold's 'Trumpeter' was certain to win the steeplechase, and as the 'talent' didn't think so, Harry could get 20 to 1 about him. A simple outlay of £12 10s. would free him from Mr. Israel Davis at once and for ever. Honest Jack Griswold was a man of honour (so the sporting world thought), and his horses ran straight, which was more than did those of some other men. The 'talent,' —consisting of Mr. Blackadder, Mr. Samuelson, Mr. Barnabas, Mr. Mephisto, and little Tobyman—had been assured that the horse for 'this event' was 'Bandoline' (by 'Cosmetic,' out of that famous mare 'Bearsgrease'), and laid their 20 to 1 accordingly. Harry got on his money, and being informed by some broken-down hanger-on of the 'Ring,' that 'Trumpeter' was 'meant,' felt happy. Mr. Israel Davis (who betted a little also) had invested against Honest John Griswold's stable, simply because he believed that a man who was called Honest must necessarily be a rogue.

Such were the conflicting interests that revolved round the house at Toorak in which old Keturah was upper nurse.

"Now there is—or was—a place called the Casino de Carambole. It stands midway in the street of Bourke, and is frequented by wicked people. Its pillars are mock-malachite, its glass is mock-crystal, is gooseberry-juice is mock-champagne, and its love-making is mock-turtle. The ostensible landlord of this saloon was one Oily O'Connor, a fighting man; the real owner was Zebulon Davis, and behind him was the gentlemanly partner of Marrable and Co. Not that Israel ever went there. Not he. His taste was too refined for such vulgar debaucheries, he simply drew a share of the profits. The sort of people who went were overseers of stations, juvenile owners of the same, young men of fashion (Heaven help them!) who came out from England superfluously oxygenated, betting-men, card-sharpers, day-waiters at hotels, and now and then some stray newspaper-man, or officer of the Frolicking Five Thousandth.

"'It isn't that I am a moral man,' said Davis, when urged to visit this scene of revelry, 'but the place is so deuced unwholesome.' He was right, it was very unwholesome. Perhaps one of the most unwholesome elements in it was the perpetual presence of the 'Talent.' Mr. Blackadder, shiny of eye, and flat of head; Mr. Samuelson, small of stature, and red crimpy of hair, freckled and moist of countenance; Mr. Barnabas, cold and reserved; Mr. Mephisto, perpetually grinning at the world through the horse-collar of his own whiskers; and little Tobyman, that loathsome pretender to childish gaiety and innocence. These worthies would knot in corners like vipers, would lean over bars until the crowns of their bran-new hats were the only objects visible to the spectator, would hoarsely 'shout' champagne, or dance on the waxed floor with exuberance of gesture. A variety of dimly-lighted bar-rooms surrounded this delightful spot, and to these such pigeons as Harry Marrable were admitted—as into traps. The 'talent'—presumedly under the influence of gooseberry-juice—were wont to drop awful hints of 'stable secrets,' upon the knowledge of which 'pots' of money could be put with absolute safety. When Mr. Davis spoke of the Casino to his brother, he always wiped his hands with his handkerchief.

"'I wish that confounded den of yours was burnt down,' he said one day. 'It is positively a disgrace to the city.'

" ' Oh, no, yer don't, Israel,' said Zebulon, grinning with all his yellow fangs (the teeth of this honest fellow were ringed near the gums, as though they were posts stuck into a spongy soil, which had sunk since their first embedding). 'Oh, no, yer don t. It's worth five thousand pounds any day.'

" ' I do with all my heart,' repeated Israel, earnestly. 'It's a disreputable hole, that's what it is, and—and I've just insured it for ten.'

" ' I can't understand how that ruffian O'Connor keeps that sink of iniquity going,' remarked Tom Provis the same evening at the dinner-table of Mr. Davis, 'I suppose the Jews—' and then he felt his host's keen eye upon him, and paused.

" ' Go on, dear sir,' said Davis ; 'you would say the Jews help him. So they do. O'Connor isn't his name. His name is Levison. I am connected with his family. We are all connected ; we all help each other. Do you ever see a Jew dig, or beg, or do menial service? Did you ever have a Jew servant? Did you ever know a Jew, however poor, who hadn't a sovereign to lend at interest ? My dear sir, we Jews rule the world. Freemasonry—stuff ! Priestcraft—bosh ! When we were turned out of that ill-built and inconvenient town, Jerusalem, we made a vow to take possession of the Universe—and we've done it, too.'

" ' But how ? ' asked Provis, ' how ? '

" ' By sticking together,' said Mr. Davis. ' All Jewry, my dear Provis, is one great firm—a huge bank which keeps the table against all Christendom. By the way, talking of banks, shall we cut the light pack or call the rattling main ? '

" ' All right,' said Provis, and presently proved his birthright as a Christian by losing £50.

" Now into this Casino there strolled one evening Mr. Finch, the gentleman who was to ride 'Bandoline.'

" ' Can you tell me where I can find Mr. Blackadder,' said he ; '. I want to see him immediately.'

" Harry Marrable, who, in company with a cigar and a friend (of equally bad odour in different ways), was gleaning 'information,' heard the question, saw that the long coat and neat boots belonged to a horsey-man, and guessed that something was wrong with Mr. Blackadder's property.

'Blackadder came out of an adjoining pigeon-hole, and bent to hear the news. ' I'll be out in the morning, Finch,' he said, and as Finch turned to go, Harry jumped up with an exclamation of surprise.

" ' George Harris, by Jove ! ' said he, and clapped him on the back.

" Gentleman George turned very red and then very pale when he saw who it was—the pair had often ridden together at Seven Creeks—and made as though he would fain get away. Harry held him fast, ' Look here, George,' he said, ' your old woman's living nurse at my mother's, do you know that ? '

" ' Don't say you saw me,' said the other. ' Well,' returned Harry, ' I don't see why I shouldn't. Come in here, and let us have a talk.'

"*Here* was the Yorick's Head, a theatrical tavern kept by one Porboy, and a place not likely to be visited by members of the Ring.

"'Sit down and have a drink,' said the young man, pointing to a chair situated beneath a portrait of G. V. Brooke. 'So you are going to ride 'Bandoline.' Two whiskies, Mrs. Porboy, please. Hot? No; cold. Cold, my girl. Now,' George, look here. Where have you been hiding? There's been a jolly row over this bolting.'

"'I don't see what business that is of *yours*, Mr. Harry,' said the stockman, his false eyes drooping. • 'It won't do *you* any good to set my wife on to me.'

"'Well, no; it wouldn't do *me* any good,' returned the boy, sipping the whisky: 'but it ain't right, you know, George. 'Pon my soul it ain't. The old soul's awfully cut up about it.'

"'What does she say?' asked Gentleman George, looking very hard at James Anderson as 'Ingomar.'

"'She don't say much,' replied the other, 'but she thinks a lot. She'll make *it* hot for you when she meets you, you be bound. It'll put you on the roads, my boy, or something like it,' he added with a shiver.

"Gentleman George seemed to read all the petty soul of the wretched young profligate in the evil glance he cast at him.

"'Would you like to make some money, Mr. Harry?' he asked.

"'Should I? By Jove, I should!' said Harry, thinking of the accursed bill, and the thrice-accursed Davis. 'Do you know a way?'

"'I ride "Bandoline" next week. Lay against him.'

"'I have.'

"'Then you'll lose.'

"'Well, you're a queer fellow. If I shall lose, why tell me to risk my money?'

"'If you won't say anything about me to the old woman, you *shan't* lose your money, for "Bandoline" shan't win!'

"'You are a pretty scoundrel!' said the young forger, feeling quite indignant at the mention of a sin to which he was unaccustomed.

"'Think of the money you can make,' said Gentleman George. 'If I pull "Bandoline," you can put the pot on "Trumpeter," and make money both ways. It's only holding your tongue for a week after all.'

"Harry Marrable took a turn up and down the room.

"'I won't tell your wife until after the race, at all events,' he said; 'and if "Bandoline" wins——'

"'He won't win, Mr. Harry,' returned the man. 'I've no wish to meet that old skeleton any more, I can tell you.'

"With this tacit agreement, they then parted."

CHAPTER III.

"THE appearance of a racecourse is much the same all the world over, and the Melbourne Racecourse differs only from that of Epsom in the regard of an octave. The melody of the turf is set a little lower to suit the less refined ears of our musicians. The grand opera of a steeplechase varies only in the class of singers; our tenor is not so good as he of London, our prima donna would not be thought much of at Liverpool, and our *corps de ballet* is neither so well dressed nor so well drilled as that which dances on the springy sward of the Downs, or joins in the tremendous chorus which salutes the winner of the Grand National. But we do our best to put the production of Signor Sathanas on the stage, and our libretto is translated into Australian by the best man we can discover. Our resources may be insufficient, but no one can doubt our willingness to please. The *dramatis personæ*—jockeys, fine ladies, *lorettes*, Jews, three-card-men, loafers, swindlers, gamblers, pickpockets, and police—are represented to the best of our ability, and if we do not raise the curtain upon so splendid an array of beauty and fashion as that which yearly beams from the dress-circle of the Epsom Grand Stand, we have at least equalled the legitimate theatre in our transpontine luxury of villains. The 'Ring' is over-poweringly admirable. No racecourse in the world can boast greasier, flashier, hoarser-voiced, or dirtier-handed bookmakers than Mephisto, Blackadder, Samuelson, Barnabas & Co.

"Young Harry Marrable, walking up and down the lawn—elbowed by bawling bookmakers shouting the odds beneath the charming noses of the soft-goods aristocracy—was ill at ease. He had not seen Gentleman George, otherwise Mr. Finch, since the evening he had met him so opportunely at the 'Casino,' and though he had followed the advice given him in the matter of backing 'Trumpeter,' he was by no means certain that the ingenious husband of poor Keturah would perform his promise. Mr. Davis—who, resplendent in white coat and lavender gloves, smoked a priceless cigar on the cynical retirement of a camp-stool—had taken occasion a few minutes before to remind him that he 'wanted that £250 to-morrow, dear boy.' The course buzzed with the name of 'Bandoline,' upon the result of whose performance the greatly little Tobyman was understood to have risked £2,000. In addition to these anxieties was the awkward feeling that he had no business there at all, for his father, Thomas Marrable, had been taken seriously ill two days before, and was even then in a 'critical' condition. So, with fevered hands, dry lips, and an unpleasant feeling as of mental indigestion, Harry watched the preparations for the event of the day.

"'—refused the jump,' and amid a furious medley of cheers, groans, and yells, 'Trumpeter' and 'Bandoline,' alone in the race, had but one fence between them and victory. 'Bandoline' led by half a length, Gentleman George sitting well back, composed, and easy.

"'That fellow can ride,' said Horsefall. 'Who is he?'

"'A man called Finch, a horse-breaker, I think,' returned Captain Pips. 'I don't know anything—ah! My God, he's killed.'

"It was 'Trumpeter's' race, for 'Bandoline,' swerving at the final fence, breasted it, toppled, and fell, crushing his rider beneath him.

"Harry turned sick. Was this an accident, or had the daring scoundrel, recklessly faithful to Luck and his promise, 'pulled' the beast as he had agreed, and so brought about this catastrophe ? Blackadder, muttering oaths, shouldered his way through the crowd.

" ' He has broken his neck,' said he to Tobyman.

" ' Has he ? ' said Tobyman, ruefully adjusting the hat upon which he had jumped three minutes before. ' I knowd he was ridin' too 'ard at it.'

" ' He be damned,' says Blackadder, roughly contemptuous, ' I mean the *horse*.'

"Harry felt a hand on his shoulder. It was that of Mr. Israel Davis, and its touch was not quite so firm as usual.

" ' How did you come off ? ' he asked.

" ' I've won,' said Harry. ' I can pay you that money the day after to-morrow.'

" ' I'm glad of that,' said Davis. ' I shall want all the money I can get. I have lost a small fortune—for me. Curse the brute !'

" ' I don't think it—it was the horse's fault,' said Harry. ' It— it seemed—'

" ' Of course it wasn't the horse's fault,' snapped Davis, no longer a Russian but a Tartar ; ' I meant the *man*.'

"While they were cheering Trumpeter and Griswold, somebody brought a hurdle, upon which the unhappy rider of the dead horse was lifted and borne off the course. When Harry, trembling to know the worst, reached the spot, he saw only turf, trampled with boot-heels, and ploughed with an insignificant furrow at the place where ill-fated ' Bandoline' had literally bitten the dust. He made for the gates and home.

"His father was no better, and Mrs. Harris, who had been invested with the responsibility of nursing the invalid, shook her head when questioned. By-and-by Dr. Dignato came, in a carriage accompanied by a kennel of dogs, and remarked that ' our patient must have quiet—perfect quiet. So I heard they killed a man to-day.' Mrs. Marrable had retired to her own room, and sent down her ' maid ' every hour to ' make inquiries.' The children had been ordered to refrain from noise, and were ' playing at visiting.' Miss Mabel was the lady of the house, and said, ' How do you *do ?*' to Miss Fanny. ' Did you go to the concert ? How are the *dear* children ?' After this they had a ' dinner party' at which little Toodles and Master Alfred personated the two ' poor relations,' and were instructed by Miss Mabel (a clever girl for her age) to refuse a second helping of pudding, while Fanny (as footman) took care to only give them ' *once* champagne.' Harry went into the garden and smoked bitterly.

" He had won his money, and released himself from Davis. So help him Heaven, he would never run risks of this nature again. He hoped that George hadn't done that purposely. It didn't look as if he had, although it was rumoured that people near the chair had *seen* him pull the horse off the jump. He hoped he wasn't dead. Should he tell old Keturah ? What would be the use ? He would ' sound' her, and see in what mood she would be likely to take the news that her husband had been found.

"He went to town next day as usual, and 'stuck to business.'

"On the evening he said to Keturah, 'Have you ever heard of your husband, Mrs. Harris?'

"'No sir,' said she, with a blush and a frown, 'and dinna want to.'

"'Ah! Somebody told me that they had seen him at—at Ballarat.'

"'It's like enough.' But, if you please, Mr. Harry, say nae mair; he's dead to me, let him be where he may, the black villain.'

"'But, Ketty, suppose now that you heard he were ill, would you go to him?'

"'No.'

"'—If you heard he was dead.'

"She turned pale. 'What do you mean, sir—it's ill jesting wi' me. I tell ye, I'd not go if he were dying in yon room, unless he sent for me; and then I'd tell the villain what I thought o' him,' and leaving her questioner with an iron face, she went straight to her own room and inconsequentially wept.

"The next day Mr. Marrable felt better.

"'Bring Davis home with you to-night, Harry,' he said 'I want to talk to him.'

"Mr. Davis started when Harry gave him the message, and asked if Mr. Marrable had quite recovered. 'No, but he's much better, thank God,' said Harry. 'I say Davis, I'll get that money for you this afternoon.' 'All right,' said Davis, frowning. 'I am glad to hear it.' But when Harry Marrable had shut the door of Mr. Israel Davis's room, that gentleman took the trouble to lock it after him, and then sat down to ruminate on his own position.

"The fact was—Mr. Israel confessed it to himself with many self-reproaches—that his vaunted sagacity had been at fault of late. His dubious speculations in 'bills' had not turned out so well as he thought he had a right to expect. Much 'paper,' of a kind which the 'Company' had imagined to be of the 'safest,' had been returned upon him. Some obnoxious journalist, in want of a 'subject,' had chosen to attack the Casino de Carambole, and a series of 'leaders' upon that institution—'leaders' which bristled with moral sentiments and blazed with Latin quotations, more or less incorrectly printed—had appeared in the daily press. The unlucky accident to 'Bandoline' had placed Mr. Davis in sore straights for money, and he confessed dismally that the £250 which that accident would enable young Marrable to pay him would be but a small instalment of the sum the bookmakers would demand that evening. He had counted upon this 'bill' being a tower of financial strength to him in days to come. When Mr. Harry Marrable was admitted to a larger participation in the profits of the firm, the astute Davis had promised himself that he would not part with the forgery for less than three times the amount which he had paid for it. Mr. Marrable was ill. It was possible that he might die. It was probable that he would take a less active part in business, and that the time for the 'sweating' of the foolish Harry was nigh at hand. It was provoking that by a turn of fortune Mr. Israel was to be a loser in a double sense. He went to the safe and took out the bill. There it lay—worth £1,000, at least, if he could only keep it a few months longer. The signature was well forged. The words 'Marrable and Davis' were capitally imitated; Mr. Israel smiled as he recognised the final flourish of his own ' s.' How provoking to be compelled to give up so splendid a prize! He began to wonder at the mood in which Master Harry must have found himself when he began forgery as a profession. He could imagine Harry Marrable—with the door locked, as it was locked now—playing with a pen, as he himself now played—scribbling the signature of the firm, as he himself now—! A bright notion occurred to Mr. Davis. He thought he saw a way to receive the £250, and keep the bill into the bargain. He would try.

"He was engaged in 'trying' for some time, and having at last succeeded to his satisfaction, he put on his hat and went out. 'If Mr. Henry should ask for me,' said he to the chief clerk, 'be good enough to tell him that I have gone home, and that I will see him at his father's this evening.' The clerk delivered the message, and Harry felt a little alarmed. Surely Davis did not intend to reveal the ugly secret! No, he could not imagine that.

"He sat with the sick man, on thorns, until the grinding of Mr. Davis's cab-wheels upon the gravel proclaimed his fate at hand.

"'Here he is,' he cried. 'I'll fetch him up,' and meeting Israel on the stairs, he dragged him from the stairs into the dressing-room adjoining the bed-chamber.

"'Where's the bill?'

"Mr. Israel was very calm.

"'I am sorry I was obliged to leave, Harry. How is your father?'

"'Better,' said Harry. Have you got it with you?'

"'I have,' said Mr. Davis, producing the bill from his pocket, and waving it gently in the air.

"'Then here's the money,' cried the poor boy, 'see, twelve £20 notes and a £10; count them.'

"'I do not know, sir,' returned Mr. Davis, 'if I am altogether justified in giving up this document. I really think, dear boy, that your father ought to be informed of the business.'

"'Oh, for God's sake!' cried Harry in great alarm.

"'I am sorry, dear boy, but really——'

"'Is that *you*, Davis?' said the voice of the sick man querulously; 'why don't you come in?'

"'Oh Davis! give it to me!' urged Harry, with dry lips. 'Here take the money. I'll give you £50 more, I will, upon my honour—Davis, I say.'

"Mr. Israel Davis seemed to relent. He set his back against the dressing-room door, and extending one hand for the money, held out the bill with the other.

"'Here then,' he said, nodding at the lowered gas-lamp, 'take it, and let me see it burned before I leave the room.'

"Harry clutched the bill, and had already held it towards the flame, when the dressing-room door was flung open with that violence which is natural in a person who wishes to hastily enter a room, and who is ignorant that any impediment is likely to prevent him so doing with ease. The effect of this accident was to propel the elegant Israel forcibly forward.

"'I beg your pardon,' cried Keturah, the intruder, aghast, 'but, the master's calling for ye.'

"Mr. Davis muttered something inelegantly like an oath, and Harry, seeing through the open·door his father's face, was seized with a sudden impulse.

"He ran into the room, flung himself by the bedside, and holding out the forged acceptance, sobbed out his story in a few hurried words.

"'I was in debt, father. They pressed me. I did this. Mr. Davis had it. I have paid him. See, here it is. Forgive me!'

"Mr. Israel Davis stood astounded. Of all things in heaven and earth, he had not calculated upon *this*!

"Thomas Marrable raised himself in his bed and called his partner.

"'What is this, Mr. Davis? My boy forged upon the firm— you should have told me. I would have paid it sooner than that this should happen.'

"'I thought, sir,' returned Mr. Davis, whose agitation had subsided into a wolfish calmness, 'that you would be glad to be spared the pang of knowing such an—an indiscretion. The note was presented to *me*, and *I* paid it. Do you blame me?'

"'No, no,' said poor Thomas Marrable. 'You did it for the best, I have no doubt; yet——'

"'Say no more, dear sir,' said Mr. Israel. 'Your son, I am sure, is truly penitent. Let us burn the bill, and forget that——'

"'Why!—Why!—Why, you infernal scoundrel!' burst out young Mr. Harry, who had been staring at the fatal paper. 'This— *this is not the bill I gave you!*'

"'Nonsense!' said Mr. Davis, showing his teeth in a vicious grin. 'What else should it be, give it to me, and let me burn it.'

"In his haste he made as though he would absolutely tear it out of the young man's hands, but Harry held it fast.

"'See, father, This is *not* the bill. I am sure it is not. That is *not* my signature.'

"'Mr. Davis,' says Thomas Marrable, 'what the devil is the meaning of this? Where is the bill that you say my son has forged?'

"'You have it in your hand, sir.'

"The old man looked from one to the other in bewilderment. He was an honest tradesman, and he did not comprehend such complications of finance. Harry—who was in advance of his father in knowledge of roguery, by virtue of the very forgery he had committed—came to the right conclusion.

"'I see what it is, father,' he said, 'he has forged this, so that I might burn it. He has got the original bill himself.'

"Mr. Israel Davis was no common rogue, and he saw that there was but one way to redeem his blunder.

"'My dear Mr. Marrable, your son is right. How much will you give me to return you the bill, and retire from the firm.'

"'I'll—I'll send you to gaol!' cries Marrable.

"'—And have the transaction explained in court? No, that would be a blunder worse than mine. Give me £500 and we will exchange documents.'

"'I'll see you —— first,' says Thomas Marrable.

"'Not first, dear sir, not first, returned Israel Davis, regaining all his composure. '*Afterwards* you may have that pleasure. Come, £500. I will forego 20 per cent. on my share in the business and leave on the day your cheque for the balance is honoured.'

"'I will see my solicitors,' groaned Thomas Marrable.

"'*I* will see them if you like, dear sir; I can explain matters more fully.'

"Thomas Marrable stared.

"'Are you not ashamed to talk like this,' he said at last.

"'Ashamed! why should I be ashamed?' said Davis, with coolness. 'I was ashamed when you found me out—ashamed that I had allowed so trivial an accident as the sudden opening of a door to disarrange my plans. But that is all, dear sir. You are a Christian, so is your dear boy there. *You* would be ashamed, perhaps. You have a "moral sense," a "society," a "parson." Bah. I am Israel Davis.'

"'You are a monstrous scoundrel! Go. I will write to my solicitors.'

"'Good evening, my dear sir,' said Mr. Israel Davis.

"They heard his cab-wheels scrunch the gravel, and then old Marrable looked at his son.

"'It was my fault, Harry. I should never have allowed you to come in contact with that scoundrel. He is enough to corrupt any one.'

"Harry Marrable suffered the excuse to be made, and left the sick-room with stern promise of repentance and amendment. On his way he met Keturah, cloaked and hooded.

"'Oh, Mr. Harry, tell me,' cried she, 'did you know anything?'

"'What do you mean?'

"'When you spoke to me last night about my husband. He's sent for me.'

"'The deuce he has!'

"'A cab's come to fetch me. I have seen the mistress. I am going at once. Tell me, Mr. Harry, is he sick or well?'

"'How should I know, Ketty,' said the young man, fearful of betraying himself. 'He can't be ill if he has sent for you. Go and make it up with him.'

"'No, I'll never do that,' said Keturah, her anger rising. 'I'll see him, and tell him my opinion o' him, as I vowed I would do.'

"The cab which had been sent for Mrs. Harris was not a handsome vehicle. The wheels were disagreeably loose, the iron step was bent and twisted, the cushions were mouldy, the tarpaulin-hood ragged and insufficient. The conduct of the driver, moreover,

was not calculated to inspire confidence. He was a large, loose man, with a white nose and a mottled face. His enemies said that he drank so much brandy that his nose had passed through the red stage and achieved a white heat. He wore a flapping Yankee hat, and drove at a great pace, shouting.

"So rapid was the manner in which the ricketty vehicle was whirled through space, that it was not until the panting horse dropped into a grateful walk at Prince's Bridge that the poor old woman felt herself enabled to ask questions.

"'Who sent ye? and how far's Flemington?'

"'Barney Welsher sent me,' returned white-nose, 'and it's about two mile.'

"'Who's Barney Welsher?' asks Keturah alarmed.

"'He keeps the "Horse and Jockey" on the Flemington course there. I'm a Flemington car, I am. I driven Joe Blueitt and another bloke, ye see, over there, ye see, when—cck!—out comes Barney, and ses "Go to Toorak and find Mr. Marrable's 'ouse, ask for a Mrs. Harris, and tell 'er 'er 'usban' wants 'er. Bring 'er out 'ere," he says, "and drive like 'ell" he ses. Ha'ay! Gu-u-u-ur!'

"—And the banging and slamming of the jolting car rendered further explanation impossible.

"Keturah was considerably relieved when the man, who had never ceased to howl at his horse, or to thwack him violently with a lashless whip, pulled up in safety beneath the solitary lamp of a lonely public-house, and sat gloomily waiting for Mr. Welsher to emerge. At sight of this worthy hirer of cabs poor Keturah felt a strange terror seize her. Mr. Welsher was in his shirt-sleeves, a pipe decorated his mouth, and in his left paw he held a very greasy 'hand' of cards. Nevertheless, when he espied the old woman, he handed her out with a solemnity that—contrasted with his appearance and evident pursuit—had something bodeful in it.

"'I heard that—that my husband was here,' said Keturah.

"'So he is, marm,' replied Mr. Welsher, scanning her curiously. 'Walk in. There's some coves in the parlour, but don't mind them. 'Ave a drop o' gin after your drive? No; well, then, this way.'

"The 'coves in the parlour' were not prepossessing. They were the sort of 'coves' engendered in the foul air of a stable ; the sort of 'coves' to whom the inside of a prison would not be unfamiliar, it might be wagered. In the 'parlour' was that atmosphere of oaths and brandy, onions, cheese, and humanity, which may be found in apartments where seven foul-fed, foul-clothed, foul-mouthed ruffians have been playing 'euchre' for nine consecutive hours. The cleanly Scotchwoman drew her honest petticoats about her and walked daintily. This was a strange place to where she had been brought, yet she felt that no harm was meant. Mr. Welsher politely aided her entrance, by saying, 'Now, then, make room there. Blarst yer, make room.' The terms in which the request was couched were not elegant, but they were intelligible, and Keturah felt that the sentence was dictated by a spirit of the truest politeness.

"She passed through the unsavoury crowd and entered a room beyond the adjoining passage. Something was lying on a bed there. Something bound up. Something which had candles burning at its bedside, and a cup of water within reach of the hand it could not move. Something which Keturah Harris would have taken for a corpse, but for the great black eloquent eyes of it, which gazed at her with all the dumb agony of a dying dog.

"Revenge melted into air.

"'Geordie! my bairn! Geordie, my jo!'

"Mr. Welsher reverently damned his soul, and shut the door, for the old faithful wife was on her knees at her husband's bedside.

*   *   *   *   *   *

"But what became of Israel Davis?"

"Who knows. He made good terms with the Marrables and left the colony—it is rumoured for America. But a man of his ability could get on anywhere."

"And now tell us the end of Mrs. Harris."

"I can only tell you this, that her story is true from beginning to end. Mrs. Harris is a 'charwoman.' She comes and washes stairs and so on at my house. When she gets her miserable wage, she goes home—to a wretched little house in a poor Melbourne suburb. In that house, there is a paralyzed and helpless man who has not yet reached middle-age. He is her husband. She expends her earnings in buying him nourishing food, and paying a child to 'mind him' when she is away. *She* lives on scraps and pieces, and broken victual. *He* has brandy and tobacco. Aye, I've seen the woman *hold the pipe* to the speechless lips of the poor blackguard while he pulled at it!"

"Ah! there is a great deal of poetry in the lives of some very unpoetical-looking people, isn't there?"

BULLOCKTOWN.

(GLENORCHY.)

BULLOCKTOWN is situated, like all up-country townships, on the banks of something that is a flood in winter and a mud-hole in summer. For general purposes the inhabitants of the city called the something a river, and those intelligent land surveyors that mark "agricultural areas" on the tops of lofty mountains, had given the river a very grand name indeed.

The Pollywog Creek, or as it was marked on the maps, the Great Glimmera, took its rise somewhere about Bowlby's Gap, and after constructing a natural sheepwash for Bowlby, terminated in a swamp, which was courteously termed Lake Landowne. No man had ever seen Lake Landowne but once, and that was during a flood, but Lake Landowne the place was called, and Lake Landowne it remained; reeds, tussocks, and brindled bullocks' backs to the contrary notwithstanding. There was a legend afloat in Bullocktown, that an unhappy new-comer from Little Britain had once purchased Lake Landowne from the Government, with the intention of building a summer residence on its banks, and becoming a landed proprietor. The first view of his estate, however, as seen from the hood of a partially submerged buggy, diverted his ambition to brandy and water, and having drunk hard for a week at the "Three Posts," he returned into his original obscurity by the first Cobb's coach driver that could be prevailed upon to receive him.

I do not vouch for the truth of the story, I only know that a peculiarly soapy part on the edge of the "lake" was known as "Smuggins' Hole," by reason of Smuggins, the landed proprietor, having been fished therefrom at an early period of his aforesaid landed proprietorship.

However, any impartial observer in the summer months could see Spot and Toby and Punch, and the rest of the station bullocks, feeding hard in the middle of the lake, and if, after that, he chose to make observations, nobody minded him. Mr. Rapersole, the bootmaker, and correspondent of the *Quartzborough Chronicle*, had a map in his back parlour, with Lake Landowne in the biggest of possible print on it, and that was quite enough for Bullocktown. Impertinent strangers are—locally speaking—the ruin of a township.

There was a church in Bullocktown, and there were also three public-houses. It is not for me to make unpleasant comments, but I know for a fact that the minister vowed that the place wasn't worth buggy-hire, and that the publicans were making fortunes. Perhaps

45

this was owing to the unsettled state of the district—in up-country townships most evils (including floods) are said to arise from this cause—and could in time have been remedied. I am afraid that religion, as an art, was not cultivated much in Bullocktown. The seed sown there was a little mixed in character. One week you had a Primitive Methodist, and the next a Hardshell Baptist, and the next an Irvingite or a Southcottian. To do the inhabitants justice, they endeavoured very hard to learn the ins and outs of the business, but I do not believe that they ever succeeded. As Wallaby Dick observed one day, " When you run a lot of paddocked sheep into a race, what's the good o' sticking half-a-dozen fellers at the gate ? The poor beggars don't know which way to run ! " The township being on a main road, and not owning a resident parson, all sorts of strange preachers set up their tents there. It was considered a point of honour for all travelling clergymen (" bush parsons," the Bullocktownians called them) to give an evening at the " brick edifice." Indeed, Tom Trowbridge, the publican (who owned the land on which the " edifice " was built), said that it was " only fair to take turn about, one down t'other come on, a clear stage and no favour," but, then, Tom was a heathen, and had been a prize-fighter. I think that of all the many " preachments " the inhabitants suffered, the teetotal abstinence was received with the greatest favour. The " edifice " was crowded, and Trowbridge, vowing that the teetotaler was a trump, and had during the two hours he had been in his house drunk gingerbeer enough to burst a gasometer, occupied the front pew in all the heroic agony of a clean shirt and collar. The lecture was most impressive. Tom wept with mingled remorse and whisky, and they say that the carouse which took place in his back-bar after the pledge was signed was the biggest that had been known in Bullocktown since the diggings. The lecturer invited everybody to sign, and I believe that everybody did. " Roll up, you poor lost lambs," he cried, " and seal your blessed souls to abstinence ! " He did not explain what " abstinence " meant, and I have reason to believe that the majority of his hearers thought it a peculiar sort of peppermint-bitters, invigorating and stimulating beyond the average of such concoctions.

The effect, however, was immense. The lambs signed to a wether, and where they could not sign, made their marks. The display of ignorance of the miserable art of writing nearly rivalled that shown at a general election. As the lecturer said afterwards, over a pint of warm orange-water in the bar-parlour, " It was a blessed time," and Mrs. Mumford, of the Pound, volunteered to take her " dying oath " (whatever that might be) that Jerry had never been so " loving drunk " in all his life before. Billy, the blackfellow, came up to the homestead two days afterwards, gaping like a black earthquake, and informed us that he had taken " big fellow pledge, big one square-bottle that feller," and felt " berry bad." M'Killop, the overseer, gave him three packets of Epsom salts, and sent him down to the creek with a pannikin. Strange to say, he recovered.

It was not often that we had amusement of this sort in Bullocktown. Except at shearing time, when the "hands" knocked down their cheques (and never picked them up again), gaiety was scarce. Steady drinking at the "Royal Cobb," and a dance at "Trowbridge's" were the two excitements. The latter soon palled upon the palate, for, at the time of which I write, there were but five women in the township, three of whom were aged, or as Wallaby said, "broken-mouthed crawlers, not worth the trouble of culling" The other two were daughters of old Trowbridge, and could cut out a refractory bullock with the best stockman on the plains. But what were two among so many? I have seen fifteen couples stand up in "Trowbridge's" to the "Cruiskeen Lawn," and dance a mild polka, gyrating round each other like intelligent weathercocks.

The stationary dance of the bush-hand is a fearful and wonderful thing. Two sheepish, grinning, blushing stockmen grip each other's elbows, and solemnly twirl to the music of their loose spurs. They don't "dance," they simply twirl, with a rocking motion like that of an intoxicated teetotum, and occasionally shout to relieve their feelings. If the "Cruiskeen Lawn" had been the "Old Hundredth," they could not have looked more melancholy. Moreover, I think that to treat a hornpipe as a religious ceremony is a mistake. The entertainment was varied with a free fight for the hands of the Misses Trowbridge. One of these liberal measures was passed every ten minutes or so, Trowbridge standing in the background, waiting to pick up the man with the most money. As a study of human nature the scene was interesting, as a provocative to reckless hilarity it was not eminently successful.

The other public-houses were much of the same stamp. The township was a sort of rule of three sum in alcohol. As the "Royal Cobb" was to "Trowbridge's," so was "Trowbridge's" to the "Three Posts," or you might work it the other way. As the "Three Posts" was to "Trowbridge's," so was "Trowbridge's" to the "Royal Cobb." The result was always the same—a shilling a nobbler. True, that "Trowbridge's" did not "lamb down" so well as the "Three Posts," but then the "Three Posts" put fig tobacco in its brandy casks, and "Trowbridge's" did not do that. True, that the coach stopped at the "Royal Cobb," but then the "Royal Cobb" had no daughters, and some passengers preferred to take their cut off the joint at "Trowbridge's." Providence—mindful of Mr. Emerson's doctrine of compensation—equalised conditions even in Bullocktown.

The "Royal Cobb" was perhaps the best house. Before Coppinger bought the place, it was kept by Mr. Longbow, a tall, thin, one-eyed, and eminently genteel man, who was always smoking. He was a capital host, a shrewd man of the world, and a handy shot with a duck gun. No one knew what he had been, and no one could with any certainty predict what he might be. He shot birds, stuffed beasts, discovered mines, set legs, played the violin, and was "up" in the Land Act. He was a universal genius, in fact, and had but one fault. His veracity was too small for his imagination.

It was useless to argue with Longbow. *He* was " all there," **no** matter where you might be, The Derby! He had lost fifty thou. in Musjid's year. The interior of Africa! He had lived there for months, and spoke gorillese like a native. Dr. Livingstone! They had slept all night with but an ant-hill between them. The Duke of Wellington! He had been his most intimate friend, and called him " Arthur " for years. I shall never forget one pathetic evening, when, after much unlimited loo, and some considerably hot whisky, Longbow told me of his troubles. "Beastly colony!" he said, "beastly! Why my dear boy, when I was leaving;—but there, never mind, Buckingham and Chandos was right. Never mind what they may say, Sir, Buckingham and Chandos was right as the mail." I replied that from the reports I had read of Buckingham and Chandos, I had no doubt whatever that he was all that could be desired by the most fastidious. Upon which Longbow favoured me with a history of B. and C. lending him £20,000 on his note of hand, and borrowing his dress waistcoat to dance at Rosherville Gardens. Before I left he volunteered to produce—some day when I wasn't busy—the Duke of Wellington's autograph letter, containing the celebrated recipe for devilled mushrooms, with a plan of the lines of Torres Vedras drawn on the back of it, and he would not allow me to leave him until he told me how Her Majesty had said, "Longbow, old man, sorry to lose you, but Australia's a fine place. Go in and win, my boy, and chance the ducks!" This last story was quite impressive, more especially as Longbow acted the scene between himself and Her Majesty, and—making the whisky-bottle take the place of the Duchess of Sutherland—alternated parts with himself as poor Jack Longbow, and himself as the first lord-in-waiting, crying, "Damme, Jack, come out o' that; she's going to cry, you villain!" I listened with approving patience, and never smiled until the very end of the story, where Longbow rushed frantically from the Presence, and knocked A. Saxe Gotha head over heels into the brand new coal-scuttle on the landing! "Oh! those were the days! D——— the colony, and pass the whisky!"

Opposite the " Royal Cobb " was the schoolhouse. It had four scholars, and the master was paid by results. He used to drink a large quantity of rum (to settle any symptoms of indigestion, arising from his plethora of funds, I suppose), and was always appealed to on matters of quotation. He was a very old man with a very red nose, and "had been a gentleman." There was never an up-country township yet that had not some such melancholy waif and stray in it.

When the schoolmaster got very drunk indeed, he would quote Aristophanes, and on one memorable occasion put Flash Harry's song—

"Oh Sally, she went up the stairs. and I went up to find her;
And as she stooped to buckle her shoe, I tumbled down behind her."

into Horatian alcaics. He quarrelled with the Visiting Inspector because he (the V. I.) said that wigs were not worn by the ancients, and our broken-down gentleman put him into his purgation with the case of Astyages as given by Xenophon. He confessed afterwards that setting your superiors right on matters of quotation is not politic, and that he wished he had let it alone. He was from Dublin University. How is it that the wittiest talkers, the most brilliant classics, and the most irreclaimable drunkards, all used to come from Dublin University?

There was a Post-office in Bullocktown, kept, if a post-office can be kept, by Mr. Rapersole aforesaid, who was regarded as quite a literary genius by the bullock-drivers. Mr. R. " corresponded for the paper "—*the* paper—and would loftily crush anybody who gave him cause of offence. If Rapersole lost a chicken or missed a pig, the world was sure to hear of it in the Paper. Rapersole, however, did not affect writing so much as speaking. " The platform for me!" he would say, as though the platform were a sort of untamed fiery steed, and he a rough-rider. However, nobody came forward with the article, and he did not "show." It was generally believed in Bullocktown, however, that if Rapersole once got his platform, the universe might consider itself reformed without further trouble.

GRUMBLER'S GULLY.

THE mining township of Grumbler's Gully is situated about twelve miles from Bullocktown.

There are various ways of approaching Grumbler's Gully. If you happen to be a commercial traveller, for instance, in the employment of Messrs. Gin and Bitters, and temporary owner of a glittering buggy and trotting mare, you would most likely take a tour by way of Killarney, Jerusalem, Kenilworth, Blair Athole, St. Petersburg, Maimaitoora, Lucky Woman's, and Rowdy Flat, thus swooping upon Grumbler's Gully by way of Breakyleg, Spicersville, Bangatoora, and Bullocktown. If you were a squatter residing at Glengelder, The Rocks, or Vancluse, you would ride across the Lonely Plains, down by Melancholy Swamp and Murderer's Flat, until you reach Jack-a-dandy, where, as everyone knows, the track forks to Milford Haven and St. Omeo.

If you were a Ballarat sharebroker, and wanted to have a look at the reefs on the road, you would turn off at Hell's Hole, and making for Old Moke's, borrow a horse, and ride on to the Hanging Rock, midway between Kororoot and Jefferson's Lead, this course taking you into the heart of the reefing country. You could jog easily from Salted Claim to Ballyrafferty, Dufferstown, and Moonlight Reefs, calling at the Great Eastern, and entering Grumbler's Gully from the north by way of the Good-morning-Bob Ranges and Schnilflehaustein.

The first impression of Grumbler's Gully is, I confess, not a cheering one. I think it was Mr. Caxton who replied when asked what he thought of his new-born infant, "It is very red, ma'am." The same remark would apply to Grumbler's Gully. It is very red. Long before you get to it you are covered with dust that looks and feels like finely-powdered bricks. The haggard gum-trees by the roadside—if you can call it rightly a roadside—are covered with this red powder. The white near leader seems stained with bloody sweat, and the slices of bark that, as you approach the town, fringe the track, look as though they were lumps of red putty, drying and crumbling in the sun. On turning the corner, Grumbler's Gully is below as a long, straggling street, under a red hill that overlooks a red expanse of mud flecked with pools of red water, and bristling with mounds, shaft-sheds, and wooden engine-houses. The sun is sinking behind yonder mighty range, under whose brow stretches that belt of scrub, and marsh, and crag that meets the mallee wilderness, and minor mountains rise up all around us. Grumbler's Gully is shaped like a shoe with a lump in the middle of it, or rather, perhaps, like

one of those cock-boats that children make with folded paper. It is
a ridge of quartz rising in the midst of a long valley surrounded
by mountains.

The place is underlined with "sinkings," and the inhabitants
burrow like moles beneath the surface of the earth. It is no disgrace
—quite the reverse—in Grumbler's Gully to wear moleskin trousers
stained with the everlasting red clay. There is, indeed, a story afloat
there to the effect that a leading townsman presided at a public dinner
in those garments, and was not a whit less respectable than usual. In
getting into the bar of the "Golden Tribute Hotel," you become
conscious that the well-dressed and intelligent gentleman, who, in the
whitest of shirt sleeves, handed you "Otard" (the brand then in
fashion in the Gully), and bid you help yourself, was a shareholder in
a rich claim, and could, topically speaking, buy and sell you over
again if he liked without inconvenience. In drinking the said
"Otard" you become conscious of a thumping vibration going on
somewhere, as if a giant with accelerated action of the heart was
imprisoned under the flooring; and getting out into the back yard,
where Mr. Merryjingle's pair horse and buggy is waiting for
Mr. Merryjingle to finish his twentieth last glass, you see a big red
mound surmounting the stable, and know that the engine is pumping
night and day in the Golden Tribute Reef.

But all the hotel-keepers of Grumbler's Gully are not as elegant
as Mr. Bilberry. There is Polwheal, for example, the gigantic
Cornishman, who lives in the big red building opposite the
Court-house. Polwheal considers his hotel a better one than
the "Golden Tribute," and swears largely when visitors of note stop
at Bilberry's.

For Polwheal's hotel is of brick, and being built in the "good
old times" cost something like a shilling a brick to erect, whereas
Bilberry's is but a wooden structure, and not very substantial at that.
The inmate of Bilberry's can hear his right-hand neighbour clean his
teeth, and can trace the various stages of his left-hand neighbour
going to bed—commencing with the scratching of a safety match, and
ending with the clatter of hastily deposited boots. When the County
Court sits at Grumbler's Gully, and the Judge, Crown Prosecutor,
and others put up there, it is notorious that Bilberry is driven politely
frantic by his efforts to put Mr. Mountain, who snores like the action
of a circular saw, in some room where his slumber will not be the
cause of wakefulness in others. It is even reported that a
distinguished barrister, after plugging his ears in vain, was compelled
one sultry night to take his blankets and "coil" on the wood heap in
order to escape from the roaring of Mr. Mountain's fitful diapason.
I, myself, tossing in agony three rooms off, have been enabled
to accurately follow the breathing of that worthy man, and to trace
how the grunt swells into a rumble, the rumble reaches a harsh,
grating sound, which broadens into the circular saw movement,
until glasses ring, roofs shake, and the terrified listener, convinced
that in another instant Mountain must either suffocate or burst,
hears with relief the terrific blast softened to a strangled whistle,

51

and finally die away in a soothing murmur, full of deceitful promises of silence.

Now at Polwheal's you have none of this annoyance, but then Polwheal's liquor is not so good, and his table is not so well kept. Now, often with the thermometer at 100, have I shuddered at a smoking red lump of boiled beef, with Polwheal in a violent perspiration looming above in a cloud of greasy steam! But Polwheal has his patrons, and many a jorum of whisky hot has been consumed in that big parlour, where the *Quartzborough Chronicle* of the week before last lies perpetually on the table. Then there is "Bosk-eyed Harry's," where the "boys" dance, and where a young lady, known to fame as the "Chestnut Filly," was wont to dispense the wine cup. Also Mr. Corkison's, called "Boss" Corkison, who dressed elaborately in what he imagined to be the height of Melbourne fashion, owned half the Antelope Reef, and couldn't write his own name. "Boss" was an ingenious fellow, however, and wishing to draw a cheque would say to any respectable stranger, "Morning, sir! A warm day! Have a drink, sir! Me name's Corkison! Phillip, a little hard stuff! Me hand shakes, sir! Up last night with a few roaring dogs drinking hot whisky. Hot whisky is the devil, sir." Upon the stranger drinking, and strangers were not often backward in accepting hospitality, "Boss" would pull from his fashionable pocket-book a fat cheque-book, and would insinuatingly say, "Sir, shall be obliged if you will draw a chick, for me (he always spoke of chicks) for £10, sir. Jeremiah Corkison. I will touch the pen. Sir, I am obliged to you." If the stranger was deceived by this subterfuge, "Boss" would waylay him for days, with the "chicks" getting bigger and bigger, and his hand getting shakier and more shaky. I may mention Tom Puffs' store, where one drank Hennessy in tin tots, and played loo in the back parlour; and the great Irish house, where you got nothing but Irish whisky and patriotism. I have no time to do more than allude to the "Morning Star," the "Reefer's Joy," the "Rough and Ready," or the twenty other places of resort.

Leaving hotels for awhile, let us walk down Main Street. Society in Grumbler's Gully is very mixed. I suppose that the rich squatters who live round about consider themselves at the top of the tree, while the resident police-magistrate, the resident barrister, the Church of England clergyman, and the Roman Catholic priest, and the managers of the banks sit on the big limbs—leaving the solicitors, rich storekeepers, and owners of claims to roost on the lower branches, and the working miners, &c., to creep into the holes in the bare ground. Of course the place is eaten up with scandal, and saturated with petty jealousy. The Church of England clergyman will not speak to the Presbyterian minister, and both have sworn eternal enmity to the Roman Catholic priest. The wife of the resident magistrate, and the wives of the bank managers, don't recognise the wives of the solicitors. If you call on Mrs. M'Kirkincroft she will tell you—after you have heard how difficult it is to get servants, and that there had been no water in the tank for two days—that shocking story, though, remember, only a rumour, of Mrs. Partridge and Mr. Quail from Melbourne, and how Mrs. Partridge threw a glass of brandy-and-water over Mr. Quail, and how Mr. Quail went into Mr. Pounce's office and cried like a child, with his head on a bundle of mining leases.

If you call on Mrs. Pontifex, she will inform you—after you have heard that there has been no water in the tank for two days, and how difficult it is to get servants—that Mrs. M'Kirkincroft's papa was a butcher at Rowdy Flat, and that M'Kirkincroft himself made his money by keeping a public-house on the road to Bendigo. Mrs. Partridge has a very pretty history of Mrs. Pontifex's aunt, who came out in the same ship with Mr. Partridge's cousin, who was quite notorious for her flirtations during the voyage; and Mrs. Partridge, who is a vicious, thin-lipped, little dark woman, pronounces the word " flirtation " as if it included the breaking of the seventh commandment seventy times over. You hear how Tom Twotooth ran away with Bessie Brokenmouth, and how old Brokenmouth took his entire horse, Alexander the Great, out of the stable in the middle of the night and galloped to the " Great Eastern," only to find the floods down below Proud's ferry, and the roads impassable. You hear how Jack Bragford lost over £600 to Dr. Splint, and how Jack drew a bill which was duly dishonoured, thereby compelling poor Sugman Sotomayordesoto, the wine and spirit merchant (who is as generous as becomes a man in whose veins runs the blood of old Castile), to impoverish himself in order to pay the money. There are current in Grumbler's Gully marvellous scandals respecting the parson, the priest, and the police-magistrate—scandals which, though they are visible lies, are nevertheless eagerly credited by dwellers round about. There are strong-flavoured stories—old jokes such as our grandfathers chuckled at—told concerning the publicans, the miners, and the borough councillors; and a resident of Grumbler's Gully would be quite indignant if you hinted to him that you had " heard that story before."

But come back to Main Street. The architecture is decidedly irregular. A bank shoulders a public-house, a wooden shanty nestles under the lee of a brick and iron store. Everything is desperately new. The bricks even look but a few days baked, and the iron roof of the Grumbler's Gully Emporium and Quartzborough *Magazin des Modes* has not as yet lost its virgin whiteness. The red dust is everywhere flying in blinding clouds. The white silk coat of " Boss " Corkison looking for the stranger is powdered with it; and the black hat, vest, trousers and boots of Jabez Hick—Jabez P. Hick he insists on signing himself—are marked with red smudges.

Mr. Hick is a very smart Yankee (there are one or two in Grumbler's Gully), and is the proprietor of the Emporium. He has also a share in the General Washington United, and has been down to the dam this afternoon to look at the small amount of water which yet remains there. The dust lies thickly on the hood of Mr. Salthide's buggy, standing at the door of Copperas, the ironmonger, and ruins the latest Melbourne toilets of Mrs. Partridge and Mrs. Pontifex, who continue to think Main Street Collins Street, and make believe to shop there daily from three to five. The peculiarity of Main Street is its incongruous newness. Around are solemn, purple hills, with their hidden mysteries of swamp and wilderness; and here, on the backbone of this quartz ridge, in the midst of a dirty, dusty, unsightly mud-patch, punched with holes, and disfigured with staring, yellow mounds, are fifty or sixty straggling wooden, iron and brick buildings, in which live people of all ranks of society, of all nations, of all opinions, but every one surrounded with his or her particular aureole of civilisation, and playing the latest music, drinking the most fashionable brand of brandy, reading the latest novels, and taking the most lively interest in the election for president, the Duke of Edinburgh, the Spanish question, the Prussian war, and the appalling fact that oysters in London are positively three shillings a dozen! A coach thundering and rattling at the heels of four smoking horses drops upon them twice a day out of the bush, and the coachman delivers his mails, skims a local paper, has a liquor, retails the latest joke (made in Melbourne, perhaps, twenty-four hours before), and then thunders and rattles away again through the lonely gum-tree forest, until he drops upon just such another place, with just such another population, at the next quartz out-cropping fifty miles away. Amidst all this there is no nationality. The Frenchman, German, and Englishman all talk confidently about "going home," and if by any chance some old man with married daughters thinks he will die in the colony, he never by any chance expresses a wish to leave his bones in the horribly utilitarian cemetery at Grumbler's Gully.

A word about this Grumbler's Gully Cemetery. It is close to the hospital, a fine building containing fifty beds, and supported by voluntary contributions; and the patients can see the grave of the man who died yesterday quite readily. Grumbler's Gully can see no reason why they should not see it. Sick people must die sometimes, of course. In the same spirit has the cemetery been built. It is a square patch of ground surrounded by a neat iron railing. Everything spick and span new, the railing not even rusted, the sordid red mounds not even overgrown with grass. No tenderness, no beauty, no association, no admirable place to hold the loathly corpses that were once human beings; a most useful graveyard and nothing more. Nothing more: save that near these ugly red mounds, unpolitical, untaught, ill-dressed men and women will sometimes linger, sparing an hour from the commonplace toil of the practical place to foolishly weep, thinking on the friends that are gone. The hideously excellent cemetery of Grumbler's Gully always seemed to me to realise the life of the colony —the stern, practical, laborious, unleisured life of a young country, a life in which one has no time to think of others until they have left us and gone Home.

Close beside the hospital is the church, and over against the church the chapel, and glaring viciously at both of them in an underbred way is the meeting-house. Religion, or rather difference of religion, is a noted feature in Grumbler's Gully. Formerly the inhabitants might have been divided into two classes, teetotalers and whisky-hot men. There was a club called the "Whisky Hot Club" at Polwheal's, each member of which was pledged to drink ten whiskys hot "*per noctem*," the qualification for membership being three fits of "*delirium tremens*"—but of late these broad distinctions have been broken down, and the town now boasts five sects, each of which devoutly believes in the ultimate condemnation of the other four. There is a Band of Hope at Grumbler's Gully, likewise a Tent of Rechab. The last has fallen into some disrepute since it was discovered by a wandering analytical chemist that Binks Brothers, who were affiliated Jonadabers in the third degree, and who supplied the camp with teetootal liquids, habitually put forty per cent. of proof spirit into the Hallelujah Cordial. There was quite a run upon Hallelujah Cordial for a few days after this discovery. The moving religious element, however, in Grumbler's Gully is a Mr. Jack. Jack was a cabinet-maker when yet in darkness, and did not get "called" until he had been twice insolvent. He was so near fraudulency the second time that it is supposed that his imminent danger converted him. Jack is a short, squat, yellow-faced, black-toothed, greasy-fingered fellow, with a tremendous power of adjective. When he prays he turns up his eyes until nothing but a thin rim of white is visible, over which the eyelids quiver with agonizing fervour. When he prays he is very abusive to his fellow-creatures, and seems to find intense consolation in thinking everybody around him deceitful, wicked, and hard-hearted. To hear him denounce this miserable world, you would think that, did he suddenly discover that some people were very hopeful and happy in it, he would suffer intense pain. He travels about the country "preaching the Word," which means, I'm afraid, sponging on the squatter, and has written a diary, "*Jack's Diary*, published by subscription," which sets forth his wanderings and adventures. Passages like this occur in that Christian work :—

"Nov. 28th.—My horse fell with me at Roaring Megs *(a claim to be understood, not a lady)*, and I could not get him to rise. After poking him with sharp sticks for some time in vain, I bethought me of lighting a fire beneath the beast ; this roused him, and I lifted up my heart in prayer.—Isaiah xix. 22."

"Nov. 29th.—Came to Bachelor Plains, and put up at the home station. The overseer, an intelligent young man, put my horse into the stable and gave him some oats, the which he had not tasted for many months. In the evening, after an excellent repast, I ventured to commune in prayer, but the overseer pulled out a pipe, and began to play euker with a friend. I felt it my duty to tell them of the awful position in which they stood, and upon their still continuing to gamble, to curse them both solemnly in the name of the Lord."

It will be seen by this that Jack is not averse to a little blasphemy. He is a self-seeking, cunning dog, who is fit for nothing but the vocation he follows, viz. :—that of "entering widows' houses, and for a pittance making long prayers." Yet he has a large following, and crowds the chapel when he preaches. The result is that all the rationalistic-going men in the township, and there are some half-a-dozen, disgusted with the hypocrisy and vulgarity of this untaught preacher, have come to consider all clergymen knaves or fools, and to despise all religion.

These enlightened persons hold meetings at the "Morning Star Hotel," and settle the universe quite comfortably. They are especially great at such trifling subjects as "The Cause of Poverty," "Our Social Relations," "The Origin of Species," "Is Polygamy or Polyandry best calculated to insure the Happiness of the Human Race," "Whence do we come," "Whither do we go," and so on. Indeed, Grumbler's Gully was at one time denounced by the opposition (Baker's Flat) journal as having dangerous tendencies to pure Buddhism. The local paper, however, retorted with some ingenuity, that the Baker's Flats were already far gone in the pernicious doctrines of Fo, and that it was well known that Hang Fat, the Chinese interpreter, held nightly "*séances*" in order to expound the teaching of Confucius.

A word about the local literature. The *Quartzborough Chronicle and Grumbler's Gully Gazette* is like all other country newspapers— whatever its editor chooses to make it. Local news is scare. Arrival of telegrams, a borough council riot, or two police-court cases, will not make a paper, and the leading article on alluvial diggings, Mr. Pagrag's speech on the Budget, Mr. Bobtail's proposition for levelling the Gippsland Ranges to fill up the Sandridge lagoon, or what not, or a written "cuttings" become things of necessity, and Daw, the editor, "cuts" remarkably well.

Daw is a capital amateur actor, and a smart journalist. His leaders can be good if he likes to put his heart into his work, and every now and then a quaint original sketch or pathetic story gives Grumbler's Gully a fill-up. Daw writes about four columns a day, and is paid £250 a year. His friends say he ought to be in Melbourne, but he is afraid to give up a certainty, so he stays, editing his paper and narrowing his mind, yearning for some intellectual intercourse with his fellow-creatures. To those who have not lived in a mining township the utter dullness of Daw's life is incomprehensible. There is a complete lack of anything like cultivated mental companionship, and the three or four intellects who are above the dead level do their best to reduce their exuberant acuteness by excess of whisky-and-water. The club, the reading-room, the parliament, the audience that testifies approval and appreciation are all found in one place—the public-house bar. To obtain a criticism or a suggestion one is compelled to drink a nobbler of brandy. The life of an up-country editor is the life of Sisyphus— the higher up the hill he rolls his stone, with more violence does it tumble back upon him. "You want an editor?" said a hopeful new-chum to the lucky job printer who owned the *Blanket Flat Mercury.* "I have the best testimonials, and have written largely to the English Press." The man of advertisements scanned the proffered paper. "Clever! sober! industrious! My good sir, you won't do for *me.* I want a man as is blazing drunk half his time, and who can just knock off a smart thing when I tell him." "But who edits the paper?" then said the applicant. "Who?" returned the proprietor, flourishing his scissors over his head in indignant astonishment, "Why, *I* do ! All you have to do is to correct the spellin', and put in the personalities!" It is remarkable that in this free colony, where everybody is so tremendously equal, the tyranny of cash is carried to a greater extent than in any other country on the face of the earth. Men come to Australia to get rich, and if they don't get rich they go to the wall. In Melbourne one can in a measure escape the offensive patronage of the uneducated wealthy, but in a mining township, where life is nothing but a daring speculation, the brutal force of money is triumphant.

But it is time to "have a drink"—the chief amusement of the place. If we cannot imitate these jolly dogs of reef-owners, who start from Polwheal's at 10 a.m., and drink their way to Bilberry's by 2 p.m., working back again to unlimited loo and whisky-hot by sundown, it is perhaps better for us, but we must at all events conform to the manners and customs.

To sum up the jollity of Grumbler's Gully in two words— "What's yours?"

ROMANCE OF BULLOCKTOWN.

MR. JOHN HARDY, the schoolmaster, was regarded with some degree of awe by the Bullocktown folks. As a general rule, Bullocktown stood in awe of nothing under or over heaven, believing utterly in the eternal fitness of things, and the propriety of its own existence. But Mr. John Hardy was a human being of a type so unfamiliar to Bullocktown, that for once in its life the township unwillingly did reverence.

The new schoolmaster was a tall, gaunt, angular man, with a mop of black hair, large bony hands, and black melancholy eyes. He arrived by the night coach with no more property than a small bag sufficed to carry, and asked Flash Harry if the schoolmaster's house was anywhere near. Harry pointed with his whip to the little hut which, embowered in creepers, stood on the hill, and the new comer at once tramped away to it, ignoring with provoking complacency the great business of "liquoring up" which was the commercial pursuit of Bullocktown.

Nor was he more sociable next day. Maggie Burns, who was "keeping" the schoolhouse, deposed that Mr. Hardy had asked her for a light, opened his bag, produced a small book, and read till daylight. At daylight he had gone for a walk, and returned laden with plants and ferns, just in time to open school. School being over, he went for another walk, and did not come back till 10 o'clock. This process of self-abstraction from the joys of Bullocktown was at first resented. It was the custom that every stranger should be made free of the place—receive the liberty of the city, so to speak—by at least one glorious bout of brandy. Intoxication in Bullocktown had become elevated into an art, and, as with other delights of a sensual character, *connoisseurs* studied to protract its enjoyment as long as possible. Rumours were afloat that Mr. Hardy was a scholar of eminence, a man of much erudition, whom "circumstances" had compelled to accept the appointment of a common schoolmaster. A report filtered through the common layers of society, as such reports mysteriously do filter, that Mr. Hardy had been a man well known in Melbourne, and that his name was not really Hardy, but something else. Now, Bullocktown, the best-hearted place in the universe, was ready to receive this unfortunate victim of unknown circumstances with open arms—was ready to clasp him to its manly bosom, and to initiate him into all the art and mystery of its profession of drinking. For the proper reception of such a stranger, Bullocktown was prepared to risk a present of insensibility and a future of trembling delirium. Had it been possible to set the kennels running with red wine, and have the fountain in the square spouting particular sherries, Bullocktown would have done it; but it was quite impossible for there were no kennels, no fountain, no square, and no red wine or sherries (worth mentioning), in Bullocktown. There was no lack of brandy, however: Henessy, Otard, and "Three Star" were all at command, and brandy would have flowed like water had the stranger wished it. It is not to be wondered at, therefore, that when Mr. Hardy declared that "he did not drink," Bullocktown considered itself slighted.

A sort of consultation was held at Coppinger's as to the course to be pursued with this extremely unsociable schoolmaster. Fighting Fitz said that not only had Mr. Hardy refused to drink with him, but that he had mildly but decidedly withdrawn from his company. Archy Cameron said that if he got "Good day," it was as much as he did get; for all that his three children were regular attendants at the schoolhouse; and Coppinger topped the chorus of complaints by relating that Mr. Hardy had not only declined to partake of the gentle stimulant afforded by brandy and bitters at 9 a.m., but that he had expressed himself astonished at the inordinate consumption of grog by the men, women, and children of the district.

"He flew into a tearing rage," said Coppinger, "and declared that drink was the curse of the country. I don't say that it isn't, boys, but I'm d———d if I'll allow any man to say so in my bar!"

So it was agreed that Mr. Hardy should be sent to Coventry. Strange to say, he did not seem to mind this decision in the least; in fact, his punishment seemed rather to amuse him.

One creature in the township, however, did not partake of the general feeling. Rose Melliship, the daughter of old Melliship, of the Sawpits, openly said that the conduct of Bullocktown was "mean and ridiculous." Now, had anyone but Rose said this, Bullocktown, with its Widow Grip at the head of it, would have arisen like one woman, and torn her to pieces; but Rose was privileged. It was known in Bullocktown that old Melliship had "married a lady," and this fact constituted the pale, quiet girl the constitutional sovereign of the little State. Nothing that Rose Melliship did could be anything but right; anything she said was received with the respect due to a Queen's speech ere yet Prime Ministers had acquired the art of writing. Rose Melliship herself did not disdain this humble homage. Whatever her parentage may have been, it was certain she owned a large share of that grace and intelligence which are presumed to belong entirely to the aristocracy. Rose Melliship, taught at a common school, with a few books, with no companions of similar tastes to her own, grown to womanhood among vulgar sights and sounds, was—well, let me put it plainly at once—the one woman for whom John Hardy felt he had all his life been seeking.

I do not know how their courtship began;—I fancy at some accidental meeting, at which a word or two on either side gave token to each of sympathy with the other; but no one ever knew. They met, talked, and parted. Rose, with feminine instinct of such things, knew the middle-aged man loved her, though he had never expressed to her his love as lovers in books were wont to express it. He was often absent-minded, always sad, sometimes impatient.

"You have some great trouble," said Rose once to him. "Tell it to me; I will try and comfort you."

But he angrily put by the question, and she said no more.

There was not much love-making at these interviews. It was enough for her to listen, to know that her thoughts were understood, that those speculations which she had imagined tremblingly were hers only, were common to many; that there was by her side a strong soul upon which she could lean and rest.

It seemed enough for him to have near him a tender-eyed woman, with soft voice, and bright perceptions, who comprehended without explanation, and read his griefs before he could utter them. It was to both of them, as though their souls, long divided, had mysteriously met. There was harmony between them.

Yet they had been many months acquainted before John Hardy spoke of marriage.

Old Melliship had a shrewd notion of the progress of affairs, and desired, in his worldly wisdom—which is, we know, so much superior to anything else in this world—to bring the schoolmaster to book. He told Rose he was going to send her to Melbourne on a visit to her uncle, the cooper. Rose told this to Hardy, and Hardy called on Melliship next day to try and dissuade him.

"You had better leave your daughter here, Mr. Melliship. She is just at an age when she should remain at home; and——we are reading French together."

"Look ye here, Mr. Hardy," returned old Melliship, "I think you read French a deal too much together, that's a fact."

"Sir," stammered Hardy.

"Oh, I don't think you mean no harm. You are a gentleman, I believe, and I can trust my girl anywhere; but——she'd better go to town a bit."

John Hardy slept less than ever that night, if Mrs. Burns is to be believed. According to her account, he walked up and down his schoolroom, as one in violent agitation, for some hours, and then dashed out of the house, hatless, into the bush. When the school opened, however, he was at his place, as quiet, though perhaps paler than usual, and after school he walked straight to the Sawpits.

"I have come to ask you to marry me, Rose."

She blushed a little—a very little—and looked away across the hills without answering.

"Do you love me enough to do so?" he asked, after a pause.

"I was thinking," said she, frankly, turning her head; and then—giving him both her hands—"Yes, I do. I will marry you."

It was his turn to look away and to keep silence. By-and-by he spoke in a laboriously controlled voice. "I have no fortune to offer you, no hopes of future grandeur to hold out to you. If we marry we must live here, or in some place like this, poor and obscure, until we die. Are you content?"

"Yes, dear, I am content."

He turned—suddenly and passionately—catching her in his arms, and devouring her face with his great eyes.

"Rose, do you love me enough, knowing me only as you do, to keep faith for me, to think always well of me, to remember that whatever happens—whatever has happened—I loved you, and will love you always?"

For reply, she gently unwound his arms, and took his hot hands in her cool ones.

"There is some mystery in your life. If you choose to tell it to me, tell it. But I do not seek to know, saving that I may comfort you. It is idle to promise that we will *always* love. How can we tell? I love you now, and you only, dear. of all men on earth. What does it matter to me what you have done, or may do?"

There was no passion in the tones, though, perhaps a taste of high-flown sentiment might not have seemed misplaced in a reply to such a wild appeal as his; but the simple truthfulness of the grave, sweet voice soothed and convinced the questioner.

"You are a woman who would meet death for one you loved, my Rose!"

"Death is the least of human ills," said Rose, smiling at him, "if your philosophy is to be believed. Ah, my love, my love, you need not doubt me."

      *   *   *   *   *   *

The township was more indignant than ever when it heard that "that d——d Hardy" was going to marry their pride and darling. Not only did the township receive a blow in the tenderest portion of its corporeal anatomy by old Melliship daring to give away his daughter at all, but it was highly offended by the fact that old Melliship had done this deed *propriâ motu*, and without duly lubricating that machine he called his mind, with brandy. The affair would appear to have been decided without even a "nobbler." In a township where the advent of a calf was the subject of alcoholic rejoicing, such a proceeding was simply monstrous. Moreover, by thus artfully placing himself under the protection of the township's pet, "that d——d Hardy" had escaped the usual penalty decreed by the jovial fellows at Coppinger's for bridegrooms. Had the schoolmaster married anyone else, the whole battery of Bullocktown wit and humour would have been turned against him. In accordance with the time-honoured practice, his door would have been nailed up, his chimney choked, his water-tank filled with the bodies of defunct township cats, and his wood-heap carted into the bush. A band of merry boys would have exploded in his back yard, and have banged kerosene tins beneath his wedding window. The jovial dogs might even have gone so far as to burn him in effigy— as they did Boss Corkison, of Quartzborough, at the back of the Church. But it was impossible that these jests should be indulged in when Rose Melliship, "whose mother was a lady," was to be the subject of them. So, with a sigh, Bullocktown saw the wedding morning of the schoolmaster arrive, and gave up all projects of midnight merriment.

The little Church by the river bank was crowded, and when Rose came out with her husband the cheers deafened her. Tears stood in her eyes. "How ungenerous she had been to despise these people. They had good hearts and loved her."

As the thought crossed her mind she looked up to John Hardy to compare him proudly with the others, and was astonished at his paleness. His mouth was firmly shut, but the lips quivered, and from time to time the muscles of the face relaxed as though weary with the strain put upon them. It was evident that the schoolmaster suffered strong emotion.

The Quartzborough and Seven Creeks coach, which passed through Bullocktown at noonday, made its appearance in a cloud of red dust from over the hill and swung heavily towards the Church. Flash Harry seeing the locked mass of buggies, carts, and horsemen which hung upon the tail of the bridal party, checked his unicorn team, and waved a hasty order to clear the way.

Fighting Fitz, spurring his buck-jumping ginger-coloured nag, beside the wheel, urged a parley.

"Curse ye man," cried Harry, savagely, "let me pass. Are they married?"

"Yes," says Fitz, "as fast as old Spottleboy can do it."

"God help him then! I'll break every bone in his body."

"Whose?"

"His!" returned Flash Harry, pointing to the bridegroom. "Let me pass I tell ye, man; we don't want a scene here."

But it was too late. The scene was over. There was no box-passenger on the coach that day, but it seemed that the bulging leathern curtains concealed somebody. They were parted with a wrench, and from them tumbled something that looked like a bundle of parti-coloured clothes, surmounted by a horse's tail. This object lying, groaning feeble oaths, at the very feet of the advancing pair, Coppinger caught hold of it, and dragging it upwards, discovered a being with tangled hair and dirty hands, and bloated lips murmuring blasphemy—a being that was obscene, drunk, and a woman.

The party paused, disgusted at this hideous intrusion into their midst, and Flash Harry felt constrained to say, "Come, get in again, mum, get in; I knew that last nobbler at the Cross Reefs would set yer off. Get in."

But the bemuzzled poor wretch, striking some frowsy hair out of her eyes, made reply by suddenly plunging at the bridegroom.

"Wha's all this, John?" said she, supported by Coppinger. "Don' ye know me?"

The face and attitude of the miserable schoolmaster answered more decidedly than words.

He had loosed hold of the bride's arm, and stood apart, haggard, wild, despairing. Presently he raised his head, and taking.

a step forward, indicated with a gesture, the drunken woman, and said, with a deliberate, level accent of disgust and despair on each syllable—"This is my wife."

Old Melliship clenched his fist, and stepped out to fell the man to the earth, but his daughter laid her light touch upon his arm and, restraining him by that single gesture, stood motionless, tearless, speechless,—looking at the hideous thing which had come to blight her life. The drunken woman, her intellects roused by the dramatic force of the scene, suddenly seemed to comprehend her husband's offence, and, breaking from Coppinger, rushed forward to pour forth a torrent of blasphemous reproach, until exhausted with her own violence, she fell prone before them all upon the Church steps, a spectacle to shudder at and to pity. Her husband raised her from the ground and placed her inside the porch. Then, averting his face, he seemed to wait until he should be left alone with her, and so standing, became conscious of a hand on his whose electric touch thrilled him. It was Rose. "How you must have suffered," she said, and kissed the hand she held.

There is much delicacy in the minds of the poor, and those who are forced to live face to face with nature. The rovers of the bush and the sea are seldom vulgar, for in the forests and on the ocean, are no meannesses, no vulgarities. Bullocktown felt that at a moment like this it was an intruder. Flash Harry flogged his horses, Fitz struck spurs to his pony, Coppinger made for his buggy, and in a few seconds the space in front of the Church was empty.

*   *   *   *   *

"You are a d———d villain," said old Melliship. "What could make you come into a quiet place like this to break my lass's heart?"

"I intended no wrong, sir; believe me. She will understand me, if you do not. But I was weak. You do not know, perhaps, what it is to have a drunken wife. Pray God you never may. Pray God you may never know what it is to come home, and find the mother of your children—oh, my God!—how can I picture what I have suffered! Night after night, sir,—for my business took me out,— have I found her there,"—(pointing with both hands to the floor)— "drunk, drunk, drunk! I have been rich; she has made me poor. I have had a good name; she dragged it through the dirt. I have had children; she let them die. I have been much to blame—of course, where is there a case of wrong in which one only is blame-worthy? But I am passionate; have tastes incompatible with dirt and shame; am cursed with too keen a memory, too feeble hope. I despaired."

The girl had drawn closer to him, and was now almost on his heart. Yet her father did not chide her. In the frightful incongruity of all things around them, it seemed natural only that she should be there.

"At last I left her. I had money, which I assigned for her. I thought I would seek peace in some harmless way of life, in some quiet place like this. I came here, and—and, for the first time met.

63

a woman whom I could love. Do not frown, sir. I do not think you understand your daughter nor me! That I have done wrong, I admit. I was weak, weary, suffering, alone; and love is very sweet to those who can taste it first in middle age. I thought myself so far removed from chance of discovery that no shame could come to your daughter by my act; and my way of thought led me to see for her no sin where there was no shame. Enough—I have been punished. Good-bye my Rose; this is the calamity I feared."

The old man made in silence for the door. Turning then for his daughter, he saw her clinging to John Hardy's breast, and heard her last farewell to him. "Good-bye, my love, my love! When first I knew you, I used to think it no desert in me to love a man so worthy, and have wished, in foolish dreaming, you might do some terrible act for which all the world would spurn you, and so make my love of value. Good-bye, my——. You must go back— you *must!* Good-bye. Nay, I have nothing to forgive, nor you to regret. Time may cripple us with sorrow, or with suffering, but it cannot change our loves—cannot, at least, destroy the memory, that we have known each other. Good-bye!"

So she left him, and his last look of her showed him a sweet face, smiling sad hope, and streaming with silent tears.

The next morning he returned to Melbourne and fate, with his unhappy wife.

* * * * * *

"But did they meet again, and does she love him still?" Ah, these are the questions always asked.

HOW THE CIRCUS CAME TO BULLOCKTOWN.

WHEN it became known that the Circus was coming to Bullock-town there was much excitement. Anything in the shape of amusement was so eagerly seized upon—even a pound sale was considered a joyous occasion—that the news of a circus within cooey, as one might say, almost took away the breath of the inhabitants.

The intelligence was brought by 'Arry the mail boy, who, riding at Grogmore and Brandyvale twice a-week, had on his last journey fallen in with the Circus, camped (quite condescendingly) by the Muddy Waterholes. 'Arry's description of the regal magnificence of the proud proprietors of this travelling raree show fired all the youth of the township, and juvenile Bullocktown burned for the arena. As has been hinted at, juvenile Bullocktown did not often get a chance to do anything but burn. Bullocktown did not offer any vast attractions to the itinerant showman, and even the Wizard Oil Man, daring beyond his compeers in exploring of "untrodden ways," drew the line at Quartzborough, and turned off to Grogmore by the way of St. Omer and Whisky Flat. Two "performances" had indeed been given in the biggest parlour of the "Royal Cobb," but they were not eminently successful. One of these was a "lecture," and the other an "entertainment." I witnessed both, and until I saw the entertainment, would have ventured to wager large sums that nothing in the way of amusement could be more dreary than the lecture.

The "Siege of Sebastopol," with illustrations, is, one would think, a subject which could be rendered interesting, if not instructive, but it wasn't. In the first place, the illustrations were not all they might have been. A comic set of magic lantern slides representing Chinamen seized by sailors, rats entering the practicable mouths of sleeping miners, and marvellous men in red garments chasing anatomically alarming youths in blue, does not give one a very accurate idea of the Russian Campaign. Moreover, the lecturer was afflicted with what he was pleased to term "whisky in the hair," and was uncertain in his movements. Bullocktown grew bewildered when informed that, "'ere they saw the 'Eurilas' twenty-eight guns as hengagin' the Rooshan frigate 'Chokemoff,' 181 guns (to the left Hadmiral Sir C. Napier standing on the foretops'le sheet-blocks)," and were presented with a portrait of the Vale of Pempes, by moonlight, instead. Jack Harris, the son of the butcher, asked the lecturer in an unsophisticated way to "bung out his blank Sebastypool and get on," and when the lecturer wobbled in his speech, and hiccoughed solemnly during the Bombardment of Cronstadt, told him that "he'd never buy the child a new frock," and advised him to "knock off and have a smoke." Eventually the lecturer appealed to Longbow, who made a little speech, in which he stated that if his respected friend, Miss Burdett-Coutts, could by any possibility have heard the ungentlemanly observations of Mr. Harris she would "never get over it," as though *it* was a five-barred gate to be taken at a fly with a bad take off and an uncertain landing. Mr. Patrick Rafferty (senior-Constable Rafferty the *Quartzborough Chronicle* called him) cut the gordian knot by locking Jack Harris in the stable until the "lecture" was concluded.

The "entertainment" was given by Mr. and Mrs. Montacute, late of the Theatre Royal and Haymarket, Melbourne. The biggest table in the "Royal Cobb" was the stage, and Mrs. Montacute ran laughingly up a pair of steps on the left hand to meet Mr. Montacute, who bounded gracefully from the vantage ground of an inverted bucket on the right. The curtain was a horse-cloth, and the orchestra a piano, played by Tom Patterson, the overseer at Mount Melancholy, who had an ear for music, and who, being in the township on a matter of post-and-rail fencing, most generously volunteered his services. I am afraid that the artistic position which poor Mr. and Mrs. Montacute occupied at the Theatre Royal and Haymarket had not been the most exalted one, but they did their best, and were received with rapturous applause. Indeed, when Mr. Montacute, clad severely in a dressing-gown of Longbow's (given him, of course, by his "intimate friend, the Marquis of Doon"), rolled his eyes, and asked in a terrible voice, "Who has been opening oysters with my razor?" the peals of laughter were deafening. This was the more complimentary to the comic powers of Mr. Montacute, for none of the "born inhabitants" of Bullocktown had ever seen an oyster in all their lives.

But to resume. Riding along the bush road to Grogmore the day after the deliverance of 'Arry's budget, the traveller of the guide-books would have observed that the gum-trees were here and there "blazed" with posters—"Buncombe's Imperial Yanko-American Circus!" "The most complete Stud in the Australias!" "The Boneless Brothers of the Blazing Beet!" "Mademoiselle Zepherina, the Fairy Equestrienne!" "Feats in the Haute Ecole!" "Mr. Stanislaus Buncombe, the Machiavelian Clown!" and so on; while the pictures of the Brothers distorting their boneless limbs, the Machiavelian Clown roaring with laughter at his own jests, and Mademoiselle Zepherina performing her feats in the Haute Ecole, were calculated to appal the stoutest beholder. By mid-day Bullocktown shook to its foundations—the Circus had arrived.

Most of us have seen that inexpressibly melancholy spectacle—a "Triumphal Entry by Circus Riders." We know the paint and powder, and long hair, and fillets, and piebald ponies, and big drums. We are familiar with the lovely damsels who are not lovely, and the spirited steeds that are not spirited, and the golden car that is not golden, and the sham and pretension of the whole business. We know how cold and wretched the Bounding Bucks look in their silk tights at mid-day, and how singularly bony are the Boneless Brothers.

We sympathise with the dusty team of sixteen creams that comport themselves with such preposterous affectation of suddenly making for their native postures, and dragging at their fiery heels the fragments of the Triumphal Car. We observe even the bulged and blackened stocking-knee of the Famed Equestrienne, and bethink us how many times it has knelt in vain to the murderous marauder, who, bestriding three steeds at once, would fain bear off the pearl of the Haute Ecole across his triple saddle bow. All this we have seen, and have commented on in our various methods : some parsonically, with hints of burnings in store for the abandoned folk : some cynically, as betokening a condition of sham and humbug typical of much in humanity : some kindly and cheerily, with knowledge of good fellowship and friendship displayed among these hard-working holiday-makers that might put better dressed and more respectable people to shame. But I doubt if it has fallen to the lot of many of us to see the strange sight which this eighth wonder of Bullocktown presented when contrasted with its surroundings. The sordid little wooden stores, the grey, grim gum-trees, the staring public-house, the unmetalled roads, the dispiriting " newness " of the whole place, and in the midst of this position of unreal heroes, mock marauders, motley clowns, and pasteboard knights-in-armour.

Three times did the Circus encircle the township, and then it coiled itself gradually into the back yard of the " Royal Cobb," to be seen of men no more until night. By-and-by certain cadaverous, greasy-haired people came into Longbow's bar, and condescendingly drank with the inhabitants. In the bar congregated at once the rank and fashion of the township.

Mr. Bluffem was there ; also Mrs. Bluffem, called by her affectionate husband " Ize Betsy," and popularly known as " Bluffem's Pet." Flash Harry, the coachdriver, was there, in breeches of appalling tightness and loose spurs that jingled highwayman-like as he walked. There was also little Potkins, the owner of the adjoining run of marsh-mallows ; and numerous horses—" mokes " as their owners termed them—were hanging at various degrees of neck extension to the rings on the " Royal Cobb " verandah-post. By-and-by the Boneless Brothers, attended by an admiring crowd of township children, marked out a sort of free selection on a piece of waste ground, between McTaggart the blacksmith's and the school-house, and in the course of an hour or so a wondrous erection of poles and canvas, to which the tent of the Fairy Peri Barron (so celebrated in Eastern story) was but a shanty in comparison, rose into being. On the top of this canvas mushroom flew in the hot wind an enormous flag. The " Circus " had become a fact.

During the afternoon the world and his wife trooped into Bullocktown. Stockmen were abundant, and riding their own horses for the day, behaved with that reckless disregard of life and limb which characterises stockmen on such occasions.

The yard of the " Three Posts " presented a curious appearance. Hans Kolsen, the " cranky shepherd," was expatiating on the mystery of the mallee to a crowd of bearded fellows, who alternately ridiculed and "shouted" for him. Sandy McDonald fought a pitched battle with Andy O'Brien ; and that one-armed hero, old Niel Gow, the boundary rider ("shepherd ranger" he loved to term himself) bent pewter pots and held up strong men in his teeth, and achieved other feats for which he had become celebrated throughout the district. The fiddles struck up fast and furious in the "long room," the tobaccoed brandy circulated freely, and before sundown, had the traveller before-mentioned paused for an instant at the bridge, he could not have failed to have come to the conclusion that Bullocktown was in the primary stage of intoxication.

The Circus was to open at half-past seven o'clock, and shortly before that hour the crowd around the "Royal Cobb" increased in density. Mr. Patrick Rafferty—his whiskers blazing with a sense of duty—exerted himself to the utmost to preserve order, and with patriotic disregard of expense, dressed himself defiantly in full uniform. The avenues and passages of the "Royal Cobb"—not too many nor too wide—were choked with enthralled inhabitants. The Equestrienne was eating in an adjoining apartment. Rumour, with its thousand tongues, even hinted that Stanislaus Buncombe himself had, with Machiavelian Clownishness, ordered steak and onions. Great thought! The dish rose in the estimation of Bullocktown from that hour.

The violet darkness of a moonless summer night had fallen on the tent when the canvas flap was lifted to admit the multitude. Prices did not rule high—one shilling to the pit, one shilling and sixpence to the boxes, and sixpence to all other parts of the house,. were the advertised charges ; and Bullocktown, on pleasure bent, thronged to the pit. It was rumoured that three shillings had been charged in Quartzborough for a seat in that locality, and that so high were the notions of the Circus proprietors that but for the necessity of "spelling" their horses they would not have performed in Bullocktown at all, but gone straight to Grogmore. It was pleasant to see how Bullocktown appreciated the honour done it, and lavished its shillings on pit seats.

The aristocrats—that is to say, Little Potkins, Tom Patterson, Dick Stevens of the Gash, and other wealthy squatters, occupied the boxes, and tapped their boots with the thong-ends of their Sunday riding whips with much dignity. Meerschaum pipes obtained about this part of the house, and young Sholtz (learning colonial experience), who was generally supposed to devote his existence to the colouring of these articles, had mounted the most gigantic specimen in his collection in pure honour of the occasion. Tom Patterson, the rogue, ogled the two township belles, and even dared to cast the eye of flirtation on pretty Mrs. Ballantine, the poundkeeper's lately achieved bride. Potkins sucked the German-silver head of his whip, and looked knowing, while Stevens, who was in "society" when in town, leant against the post and assumed a "blasé" air.

A moment of anxious expectation, and the Machiavelian One himself leapt into the ring.

I believe that the Machiavelian One was a good clown. I have seen his memoirs, penned by my versatile "hic-et-ubique" friend, Bob

68

Jingle, bound in green covers, with a pensive portrait of the humourist himself on the back of it, and been alarmed at his violent predilection for jesting. I am willing, even now, to believe that the M.O. has turned fifteen double somersaults in succession, peeling and eating an orange during the process, and that as a " jumpist," so to speak, he is without a rival. But candour compels me to admit, on this occasion, he was not sparkling. I have heard funnier jests than those that fell from his Machiavelian lips, and have witnessed acrobatic feats quite as dangerous as those which horrified the Bullocktown public on this particular evening. But perhaps the day's journey had fatigued him, or perhaps—and this supposition is not an improbable one—he did not care about wasting his best jokes upon a Bullocktown audience.

It was well that he did not, for from the instant he entered a storm of noises shook the canvas. All the powers of bullock-driving " *badinage* "—seldom elegant—were put in force to drive him from the ring. The good folks thought he *was* the fool he feigned to be, and laughed at him, not with him ! When the ring-master, chosen, I imagine, for that exalted office on account of the peculiar breadth and beauty of his whiskers, lashed the clown, the audience solemnly applauded him ; and when poor Stanislaus, in ecstasies of melancholy laughter, upset and trampled upon the ringmaster, the audience cried "shame" at the unmanly action. It was evident that they regarded the jester as the one serious blot upon the amusement of the evening !

This being the unexpected conclusion, haste was made to bring in the Equestrienne, who was graciously received. Mademoiselle Zepherina sat gracefully on the tail end of her fiery charger—a Roman-nosed animal of sedate and wise appearance who seemed to be rather ashamed of his capers and caparisons—stood upon one leg, smiled beamingly, and leapt through hoops and bounded over silk scarfs (falling upon her knees with tremendous accuracy) until Bullocktown would have died for her fair sake to a man. Three times was she compelled to re-enter and kiss her fingers in acknowledgment of the homage of her subjects ; and in the last grand act, where her sailor-lover (having torn off his trousers and flung them to the wind) stripped off so many costumes during his rapid flight that blushing matrons, unused to daring acts of equitation, wondered alarmedly how deep he meant to go, the applause was deafening. The lover peeled to the last tight, waved his breathless thanks, and sank exhausted on the pad of his foaming piebald. As the flap closed on the pair the tumult was a hurricane, tempered by hiccups.

At this entrancing instant a pattering sound was heard. One of those violent sudden showers which sometimes burst upon up-country townships was about to descend on the tent. The ring-master paused in the midst of a whip-crack, and the Machiavelian jester had need of all his diplomacy to assume a jocular appearance. All faces turned simultaneously to the roof, and some half dozen men were observed to rush past the ticket-taker and vanish into the now cloudy night. The entrance of the Boneless Brothers recalled us to revelry. No event of less importance could have availed to do so.

The boneless pair were certainly very startling. The way in which they defied the anatomists, by putting their heads where their feet ought to be, and tying themselves into knots of the most gristly description, was perfectly perplexing. Longbow, who, amongst other professions, owned that of a surgeon, said that the cartilaginous formation was extraordinary; only equalled, indeed, by that of his poor dear friend, Lord Herbert of Cherberry, who *had* (upon Longbow's soul) the most remarkable development of muscle ever vouchsafed to man. But when the B.B. bent themselves into a triumphal arch, of which their heads were the keystone, and walked upon their hands twice round the arena, even Longbow felt compelled conscientiously to admit that Lord Herbert of Cherberry was, in comparison, cartilaginously nowhere.

As the brothers rose, empurpled from this feat, a hideous yell resounded, and the canvas, after swaying ominously, bulged into the centre.

The tin-hoop chandelier, with its wreath of flaming tallow-dips, dropped rattling into the " boxes," and amid a wild shriek of dismay the whole fabric collapsed upon us. Those merry fellows outside had cut the ropes!

The cries of women pierced the canvas, and a running accompaniment of strong language testified that male Bullocktown was not at ease.

It is not a good thing to be suddenly swamped into a sea of dirty canvas, and for a few moments suffocation seemed imminent. Longbow, however, who was next to me, suggested a remedy.

" I've got a knife in my trousers pocket," said he, in semi-stifled tones, " and if you can get it out we'll cut the canvas. *My* arms are immovable."

Painfully conscious of the immediate and oppressive presence of " Ize Betsy," I made shift to grasp the desired weapon, and plunged it into the blinding mass above me. With a sound like that emitted by a tearing sheet the tent split in sunder, and we wriggled out. The momentary glimpse we got of the chaos out of which we had escaped was not calculated to reassure us. The centre tent-pole alone remained. Grimly upright, it protruded from a heaving desert of dirty white canvas, upon which the gathering rain fell patteringly. This canvas was here and there bulged with heads and pinnacled with feet.

Indistinct growlings and groanings escaped from it, and at the slit from which we had emerged peered one forlorn face.

It was that of Stanislaus Buncombe himself.

Longbow extended his hands which had been pressed so many times in friendship by F.M. the Duke of Wellington, and dragged the Machiavelian one gasping in the air.

" Oh my !" said he, " here's an almighty slide."

He spoke truly. It *was* an almighty slide, and looked like nothing so much as a dirty avalanche that had lost its way in a London fog, except perhaps a monster bundle of clothes split on their course to a Titanic wash.

The clown surveyed the scene with emotion, but at last the driving rain, filling his clownish pockets with water, compelled him to cease meditation. Around us, on the edge of this overturned Circus riding, were several figures who appeared from their gestures to be on the point of expiring in convulsions of laughter. These were the merry dogs who had perpetrated this exquisite jest. Stanislaus seized upon two of these as volunteers, and borrowing the knife that had done such good service, he rapidly cut the cords that bound the canvas to the tent-pegs.

For an instant it appeared as though the vast sheet would be twisted into a ball by the struggles of the creatures beneath, but Buncombe catching one end of it, and Neil Gow the other, they " skinned " it from the corporate body beneath. Rending as it ran, into its various sections, the emblazoned tent was pulled from the *élite* of Bullocktown. Squirming, struggling, gasping, fighting, there lay the best blood of the township, the human bottles that held what Daw, the editor of the *Quartzborough Gazette*, so euphoniously termed the " vital fluid of the colonies."

Despite all one's knowledge of their misery and discomfort, one could not forbear a laugh at the appearance of the " audience." It was as though we had overturned a huge stone that covered a snug family of earth worms. Though not a head was visible, I never fully realized the truth of the saying " that man is but a forked radish with head fantastically carved " until then. Stanislaus was a modest man, and he turned away his face with a gasp of dismay.

In a few minutes, however, all were upright, and then was confusion worse confounded than before. Several friendly fights, begun under the obscurity of the canvas, were concluded above ground ; women wept over crushed bonnets and torn dresses. " Ize Betsy " urged her lord to execute instant vengeance upon the whole troupe of circus-riders, and catching sight of poor Stanislaus, made at him like a lioness. Not all the diplomacy of Machiavel was equal to the occasion, and feebly uttering " My good woman !" the proprietor of the Yanko-American Circus turned and fled. " I'll good woman you," screamed Mrs. Bluffem. " Wait a minute, you dog ! wait a minute."

But Stanislaus had no such intention. Bounding over the fallen patriarchs of the village, he ran like a deer for the "Royal Cobb," and reaching his bedroom a hand's breadth in advance of " Ize Betsy,' locked the door, and vanished from view. Mrs. Bluffem, foiled in her vengeance, and wet to the skin, screamed " Fire !" at the top of her voice, and, falling into strong convulsions, was only to be got round by still stronger brandy and water, administered scalding hot in the biggest tumbler the house afforded.

By-and-by, however, the first flavour of alarm having gone off, it was found that after all the affair was a most excellent jest, and merited drinks all round. So more dark brandy was consumed, and Bullocktown agreed in the parlour, passage, and what not of the " Royal Cobb " that it had not enjoyed itself so much for years, and that the true way to see a circus performance was to cut the ropes at the earliest opportunity.

This conclusion having been amicably arrived at, and the Yanko-Americans pledged bottle deep in liquor—which they drank suddenly and silently, as though they were not quite satisfied at the hilarity of their hosts—it was discovered that there was yet more excitement. A Mysterious Beast and a Knife-Swallowing Boy were exhibiting in a small booth which had escaped the general overthrow, and sixpence was the price of admission.

The Mysterious Beast was certainly very mysterious. He was a clean-shaved, melancholy animal, with a collar of gray fur round his neck, and a chain round his body. He sat on his hind legs in a corner, and moaned plaintively, shaking his miserable head from side to side as though he would exclaim against the wickedness of the world and the intolerable vanity of circus-riders. The only creature I had ever seen that resembled him in the slightest degree was a worthy pastor at Aberdeen that preached there to me on the Sabbath upon " Balwin' oop the trumpet i' the fool moon," and did so with just such a woebegone expression. It was evident that the Mysterious Beast was weighed down by the consciousness of his mystery. He felt the loneliness of genius.

The Knife-Swallowing Boy was, however, of a most cheerful character. He was stupendously fat. (I am indeed of opinion that he was in training for greatness in that profession, and burned to eclipse Lambert). His eyes were of pale blue, and his cheeks a sodden white. His tights were stretched to their utmost, and rolls of adipose tissue hung down over his spangled boots. If he swallowed nothing but knives, cutlery must have agreed with him wonderfully.

He commenced operations by a snack of pebbles. Handing round some good sized pieces of quartz upon a plate, he informed us that he was in the habit of consuming these delicacies in prodigal profusion, and that he found they were eminently satisfying and agreeable. Having said this he swallowed—or seemed to swallow—five or six in rapid succession, and made a low bow. The audience thrilled with delight, and one gentleman, in an ecstasy of admiration, swore with surprising energy for several minutes.

The boy, however, took this compliment as his evident due, and disdainfully spat into his hand. A lean man in the corner, who acted as showman to this exhibition, said as solemnly as though he really believed it, " He eats ten o' them every morning afore breakfast. It is supposed by physicians that the flints striking fire with the steel, enables him to better digest this remarkable repast." The boy sniffed contemptuously at this, and pretended not to know that everybody was looking at him.

" He will now swallow a sword," said the lean man. " 'And it round Master Merryweather ! 'and it round !" So the sword was 'anded round, and everybody felt it and weighed it, looked knowingly over it, and tried if it would go into the handle, and if it was real steel, and winked their eyes mysteriously, or affected to pass it by with a placid smile, as though they had seen it habitually from boyhood, and knew the man who made it.

During this process I got a little closer to the boy, and observed that he was standing on a platform, around the bottom of which was a legend to this effect:—

> "JOHN LAMBTON MERRYWEATHER,
>
> "Age fourteen and a-half years, born in the County of Grant. He swallows knives, swords, and all sorts of old iron. He eats pebbles, and is passionately fond of chalk.
>
> "AUSTRALIANS !
> "PATRONISE NATIVE TALENT !
> "PRICE 6d."

By the time I had read it over, the sword had been returned, and the swallow was about to commence. Stretching his legs very wide apart, the boy flung back his head until the Adam's-apple in his throat protruded in a dangerous manner, and then holding the sword very straight in the air, he allowed it to slide into his gullet. To the horror of all of us, the hilt rested upon his teeth, and the blade consequently fifteen inches deep into his stomach. After remaining in this position for an instant, the boy rapidly stretched out his arms, and the lean man, mounting on a chair, dexterously drew the weapon from its human sheath, and handed round the reeking blade to be admired.

During the awe-stricken silence which followed upon this feat a wild shriek was heard. It proceeded from little Potkins, who, tormenting the Mysterious Beast, had been bitten severely for his pains.

"Go it!" says the lean man. "Wot der want to hirritate him for?"

"I wasn't irritating," says Potkins.

"Yes yer were, I sor yer," says the boy. "You was a rokin' of him."

"Yer carn't expect beasts to be quiet when folks rokes 'em."

Flash Harry scented a riot.

"Shut up, you young quartz-crusher," said he. "Who asked for your opinion."

The boy solemnly advanced.

"Hold on my pipkin," he said. "Wait till I get up with yer, and we'll see whose quartz 'll get crushed."

"Come on young stoneworks," says Harry. "Roll up here and show yer muscle."

The crowd parted like water, and in another minute Harry and the boy were at it hammer and tongs. I'll do Harry the justice to say that he fought well, but he was nowhere against the boy. That corpulent infant had been apparently bred to the science of self-defence, and the precision with which he planted his fatal left upon

the nose of the horsebreaker was, as Longbow declared, beautiful to
see. After the third blow of this sort, which induced Harry's nose to
spurt burstingly beneath the fat fist, as though it had been a suddenly-
quashed gooseberry, the fight was virtually over, and the boy withdrew.
Harry was removed by Potkins, and harmony seemed again restored,
when a terrible accident was found to have taken place—the
Mysterious Beast had vanished. Taking advantage of the confusion,
the captive had escaped. It would be "roked" no more.

The lean man was violently wroth at this, and preposterously
accusing Neil Gow of having concealed the marvellous animal
about his person, was promptly knocked head over heels by that
gigantic worthy.

The boy came to the rescue, and the row, for it deserves no
better name, became fiercely general. The booth was uprooted, and
the knife-swallower ran some danger of annihilation. But help was
nigh. The Circus-riders came down upon us in a compact mass, and
cut into us like a wedge. Hemmed in and separated from our
companions, Longbow and I surrendered at our discretion, but the
others, madly drunk, fought until they could fight no longer. The
place where the Circus had been was the arena of one of the freest
fights I remember. The Circus men were terribly sober, and in most
unpleasant "condition." They had evidently made up their minds
to avenge the destruction of their tent, and they did so most com-
pletely. I did not see much of the combat, but in about half-an-hour
the Yanko-Americans returned, and ordered whiskies hot. Their
coats were torn, and their faces badly cut, but not a Bullocktown man
showed in their wake.

One of the Bounding Brothers was kind enough to ask me for a
light, and I took the opportunity of enquiring what had become of
my companions.

"Guess we kinder squelched 'em," said he. And I guess they
kinder had, for not another resident showed his nose that evening.

Having thus celebrated their victory, the Yanko-Americans began
to look about them for amusement, and strange to say they found it
ready at their hand.

Curiously enough that very evening had arrived at the "Royal
Cobb" that teetotal lecturer whose eloquence had formerly moved
Bullocktown to repentance and sodawater. The name of this distinguished man was Barclay, and he had with him a teetotal friend, who,
by one of those laughable coincidences which so often occur in life,
was named Perkins. These two were sworn friends, and hunted in
couples. The low-backed shandy-dan—half buggy, half go-cart—in
which they rode was well-known in the district, and with its full
freight of lecturers and lecturers' wives, had been dubbed "Barclay
and Perkins Entire." This shandy-dan was now resting in Longbow's
back-yard, and the four eschewers of the evil of strong drink seated in
Longbow's best parlour.

Mrs. Barclay was a tall, thin, and aristocratic lady ; Mrs. Perkins
was podgy, short, and plebeian. Mrs. Barclay was severe in demeanour;
Mrs. Perkins was merry with all. Mrs. Barclay read serious books ;

Mrs. Perkins affected novels of the Percy B. St. John type. They both, however, agreed on the subject of alcholic liquors ; for the matter of that they might have been twinned in teetotalism. It was rumoured that Mrs. Perkins had been heard to express more than friendly admiration for Mr. Barclay, and that Mrs. Barclay had owned to a tender respect for the noble character of Mr. Perkins. As for Barclay and Perkins, they were both like brothers. To see them you would think Cato and Hortensius were not more unselfishly affectionate.

Plump upon this happy quartette did Stanislaus Buncombe, creeping down the passage in mortal terror of " Ize Betzy," fall.

"A thousand pardons."

"Pray ! come in," said Mr. Perkins, with a sigh. "It may chance that we win another soul to grace."

This blessed utterance was heard by the troupe, and expecting fun, they blocked the doorway.

"Come in, me Keristian friends," says Barclay, with a sigh that seemed to rend his vitals. "Oh ! come in !"

Mr. Perkins in the meanwhile addressed himself to Stanislaus with a smile. "Do you drink, sir ?"

"Thank you," says the bewildered Machiavel, expectant of liquor, "I do." "I thought so," returned Mr. Perkins, throwing himself back in his chair. "Dorothy ! my dear, just look at this unhappy man !"

Mrs. Perkins tittered (in a pious way) and looked. "Is he not a miserable spectacle," asked Perkins, with deep sorrow in his tones. "Oh why do the heathen thus furiously rage together,"

Stanislaus began to see how the land lay, and with Machiavelian sharpness, winked at his joyous band. " Ize Betsy " had departed, and he felt himself a man again. "My dear sir," he said, "do you know that your teetotal cordials are more pernicious than any quantity of ardent spirits."

Barclay waved his hand to Perkins, as who should say, "here is another benighted heathen. Hark at him !"

"I was not aware of it," says Perkins, "I have heard the argument many times before. It is a favourite one with the children of Beeelial."

"It's a tact," says Stanislaus. "Mr. Longbow, bring me some stomach bitters."

Longbow brought them.

"Drink this," said he, "and tell me your candid opinion."

Perkins drank and handed the bottle to Barclay. The bitters were good, for the holy men smiled a pleasant smile.

"It is comforting," said Barclay.

Stanislaus pretended to be astonished, and drank himself. "Upon my word," he cried, "it *is* not bad. I half begin to believe your doctrines. "Sit down, my friend," cried Barclay, "and I shall expound them yet further into thee."

"The ladies," says Stanislaus, "if they will forgive a poor player, but discussion is weary, and—may I suggest lemonade "

75

Mrs. Barclay iced herself at once, but Mrs. Perkins bowed a gracious assent, and the lemonade was brought.

I have not now space to give the sermon that was preached by the pair, but it was a good one, and one of these days I may repeat it. Suffice it here to say that we all sat down and listened, and that the two holy men applied themselves to the stomach bitters between whiles. Speaking was dry work. The evening waned, and Stanislaus gallantly ordered more lemonade. We drank a good deal of lemonade, and then the ladies retired to a sort of cock-loft bed-chamber suite of their rooms that were built upon the upper storey.

"The bitters are empty," said Stanislaus. Another bottle. Your discourse has impressed me."

Some more bitters were brought, and more lemonade, and presently I began to feel unaccountably drowsy.

A glance through the open door explained the mystery. Longbow, doubtless by that villain Stanislaus' directions, had been putting gin into the lemonade, and brandy into the cordial.

What need for further explanation. Perkins began to wander in his speech, and Barclay to get unsteady on his legs. Babbling peacefully of teetotalism, they were soon as happily drunk as the most confirmed toper of us all. Stanislaus, triumphant, called for a "health," and filling up a cordial glass to the brim with brandy, he handed it to Perkins.

"Water for ever," cried he.

"Wah! wah! water for—egh," says Perkins, draining the brandy, with a dreadful splutter, and suddenly awakening to the consciousness of the trick that had been played upon him. "Why you oul, oul villain, I'm t-t-t-tight!" Here his speech failed him, and he fell exhausted on the carpet.

Then came our task to convey him to bed. With wondrous exercise of mechanical ingenuity, we bore him up stairs, and opening the doors of their rooms, bundled him in and retreated. But when half way up the stairs a wild cry arose, and two white figures rushed at each other on the landing.

"Jeerusalem!" says the leader of the Yanko-Americans, "but we've put 'em into wrong rooms."

It was even so. Mr. Barclay had enraded the chamber of Mrs. Perkins, and Mr. Perkins that of Mrs. Barclay. 'Twas like a scene from Smollett. The two ladies, each thinking that she had discovered her husband's infidelity, flew at each other with deadly fury. Barclay, holding on by the bannister, denounced them both, but Perkins, too drunk to stand, clapped his hands feebly, and said with the last flicker of expiring sense, "Gug-go it Kak! Kak-Karoline!"

*　　*　　*　　*　　*

Who is it says that nothing is more gratifying to the gods than the spectacle of a good man struggling with adversity!

But I am not a god, so let me draw the veil.

THE ROMANCE OF LIVELY CREEK.

CHAPTER I.

"GREEN BUSHES."

THE township of Lively Creek is not the sort of place in which one would expect a romance to happen; and yet, in the year 18—, when I accepted the secretaryship to the Mechanics' Institute, occurred a series of circumstances which had in them all the elements of the wildest French fiction.

The unwonted impetus given to social relations, which was affected by the "opening up" of the Great Daylight Reef, brought together those incongruous particles of adventurous humanity which are to be found floating about the gold-mining centres of Australian population, and in six months the quiet village—up to that time notorious for its extreme simplicity—had become a long street, surrounded by mounds, shafts, and engine-houses, and boasting a Court House, a Mechanics' Institute, half a dozen places of (variously conducted) religious worship, and some twenty public-houses.

The thirst for knowledge which attends upon worldly success soon made my office a laborious one, for, in addition to my duties as Librarian, I was expected to act as Master of the Ceremonies, Conductor of *Conversaziones*, Curator of a Museum of Curiosities, and Theatrical Manager. The Committee of Management were desirous that no attraction which might increase the funds of the institution should be passed over, and when Mademoiselle Pauline Christoval (of the Theatres Royal, Honolulu, Manilla, Singapore, and Popocatapetl) offered a handsome rent to be permitted to play for six nights in the great hall, I was instructed to afford every facility to that distinguished actress.

Mademoiselle Pauline was a woman of an uncertain age—that is to say, she might have been two-and-twenty and was not improbably three-and-thirty. Tall, elegant, self-possessed and intelligent, she made her business arrangements with considerable acuteness, and, having duly checked all items of "gas" and "etceteras," announced that she would play the *Green Bushes*, as an initiatory performance. "I always act as my own agent," said she, "and my Company is entirely under my own direction."

Upon inquiry at the Three Star Brand—where the Company were lodged—I found this statement to be thoroughly correct. Miss Fortescue (the wife of Mr. Effingham Bellingham, the "leading man") had already confided to Mrs. Butt, the landlady, several items of intelligence concerning the tyranny exercised by the lady manager. Mr. Capricorn, the "juvenile man" (husband of Miss Sally Lunn, the charming *danseuse)*, had hinted vaguely, with much uplifting of his juvenile brows, that Mademoiselle was not to be trifled with, while I found that old Joe Banks, the low comedian (the original "Stunning Joseph" in the popular farce of *My Wife's Aunt*), had shaken his venerable head many times in humorous denunciation of "the artfulness of Christoval."

There was much excitement in the bar-parlour of the "Main Reef Hotel" at the dinner hour. So many reefers took me mysteriously behind the door, and begged me to bring them casually behind the scenes during the performance, that it was evident that, for the first night of the six, at all events, the improvised theatre would be crowded. The only man who manifested no interest was Sporboy— Sporboy, the newly-arrived; Sporboy, the adventurer; Sporboy, the oracle of tap-rooms; Sporboy, the donor of curiosities to our Museum; Sporboy, the shareholder in the Great Daylight; Sporboy, the traveller, the narrator, the hot whisky swiller:—Honest Jack Sporboy, the richest man, the hugest drunkard, and the biggest liar in all Lively Creek.

"I've seen enough of them sort o' gals," said he. "I'm getting old. My hair's grey. Pauline Christoval, of the Theatres Royal, Manilla, and Popocatapetl, eh? Bosh! Hot whisky."

"But, Captain Sporboy, your influence—— "

"Oh, yes! All right. I've been in Manilla. I've eaten brain soup and *basi* in Hocos, my boy. *Human* brains. Devilish good, too. Ha, ha! Another lump of sugar."

"Human brains, you old cannibal!" cried Jack Barnstaple. "What do you mean?"

"Just what I say, dear boy," returned the old reprobate, wagging his Silenus head. "When I was in Pampalo we made a trip to Pangasinan, and assisted at a native feast. The Palanese had just achieved a victory over the Quinanès, and seventy-five heads were served up in my honour. Gad, gentlemen, the fellows cracked 'em like cocoa-nuts, and whipped out the brains in less time than you would take to disembowel a crayfish!"

"But a theatrical entertainment, my dear Captain Sporboy, merits your patronage."

"Seen 'em all, sir. Tired of 'em. N'York, Par's, London. No! Jack Sporboy, sir, is tired of the vanities of life, and prefers the noble simplicity of hot whisky. I had the Theatre on Popocatapetl myself once, and lost 4,000 dol. by a *mêtis* that I hired to dance the tight-rope. Fine woman, but immoral, gentlemen. She ran away with my big-drum-and-cymbals, and left me to support her helpless husband. Never trust a half-caste; they are all treacherous."

So we left the virtuous old gentleman to the enjoyment of his memories, and went to the hall. My anticipations were realized. The *Green Bushes* was a distinct success. Joe Banks, as "Jack Gong," was voted magnificent, and for the "Miami" the audience could not find words enough in which to express their admiration.

Mademoiselle added to the attractions of her flashing black eyes, streaming black hair, supple figure, and delicate brown hands, a decided capacity for the realization of barbaric passion, and her performance was remarkably good. The *Lively Creek Gazette*, indeed, expressed itself, on the following morning, in these admirable terms :—"Mademoiselle Christoval's 'Miami' was simply magnificent, and displayed a considerable amount of dramatic power. She looked the Indian to the life, and her intense reproduction of the jealous wife rose almost to mediocrity in the third act. Indeed, in the delineation of the fiercer emotions, Mademoiselle Christoval has no equal on the Colonial stage, and we have no hesitation in pronouncing her a very nice actress." After the drama was over, I took advantage of my position to go "behind the scenes," and, while Joe Banks was delighting the public with the "roaring farce" of *Turn Him Out,* to compliment the lady upon her triumph. I found the door of the improvised dressing-room beseiged by the male fashion of the township, who (having made Lame Dick, my janitor, drunk) had obtained introductions to the eminent *tragedienne.* Foremost amongst these was Harry Beaufort, the son of Beaufort, of Beaufort's Mount.

"Ah," said I, "are you here?"

"Yes," said he, blushing, "I rode over to-day from Long Gully."

"Mr. Beaufort and I are old acquaintances," said the soft tones of the lady, as emerging, cloaked and bonneted, from the rough planking, she melted the crowd with a smile, and turned towards me, "Will you join us at supper?"

I looked at Harry and saw him blush again. It struck me that he was only two-and-twenty; that his father was worth half-a-million of sheep, and that Mademoiselle Christoval was not a woman to marry for love.

"Thank you," said I. "I will."

We had a very pleasant supper, for though I was evidently a skeleton at the banquet, the actress was far too clever a one to let me see her uneasiness. Harry sulked, after the manner of his stupid sex, but the lady talked with a vivacity which made ample amends for his silence. She was a very agreeable woman. Born—so she told me—in the Phillipines, she had travelled through South America and the States, had visited California, and was now "doing Australia," on her way to Europe. "I want to see Life," she said, with extraordinary vigour of enjoyment in her black eyes, "and I must travel."

"Why don't you take an engagement in Melbourne?" I asked.

"Can't get one to suit me. I don't care about sharing after everything a night but the gas. Besides, I only want to pay my way and travel. I should have to stop too long in one place if I took a Melbourne engagement."

"And don't you like to stop in one place?" asked Beaufort.

"No," said she, decidedly. "I am an actress, and actresses, like fine views, grow stale if you see them every day."

"But did you never think of leaving the stage?" asked the young man.

"Never. I was born in a theatre. My mother was a ballet dancer. My father was an actor. My grandfather was clown in a circus. I have played every part in the English language that could be played by a woman. I could play "Hamlet" to-morrow night if the people would come and see me. Why should I leave the stage?"

"True," said I, "but you may marry."

Oh! the vicious look she gave me!—a dagger sheathed in a smile.

"I never intend to marry. It is growing late. I am an actress— the people will talk. Good-night."

We parted with mutual esteem; and, as she shook hands with us, I saw, lurching up the passage, the whisky-filled form of the Great Sporboy. His eyes, attracted by the light from the room, fell upon us, and—surprised, doubtless, at the brilliant appearance of Mademoiselle Pauline—he started.

Mademoiselle Pauline grew pale—alarmed, perhaps, at the manner of the intoxicated old reprobate—and hastily drew back into her chamber.

"Go away. You're drunk!" said Harry, in a fierce whisper.

"Of course I am," said Sporboy, advancing diagonally, "but that's my business. Who's that?"

"That is Mademoiselle Pauline," said I.

"Ho!" cries Sporboy, his red face lighting up as if suddenly illumined by some inward glow. "Ho! Ho! That's she, is it. He, he! A fine woman. A fair woman. A sweet woman." It was a peculiarity of this uneducated monster to display a strange faculty for mutilated quotation.

"Ho, ho! I wish ye joy o' the worm. So a kind good-night to all."

CHAPTER II.

THE MYSTERY

BUSY all next day, I found in the evening that the *tragedienne* had been indisposed, and had kept her room. Harry Beaufort, who informed me, said that she had intended to throw up the engagement, and quit the town, but that he had persuaded her to remain. "I do not want her to do anything that may appear strange," he said. Then, sitting in the little room off the bar, underneath the picture of the Brighton Mail, he told me the truth. He intended to marry Mademoiselle Pauline. "But," said I, "do you know anything about her? I will tell you frankly that I don't like her. She is a mystery. Why should she travel about alone in this way? Do you know anything of her past life?

" No."

"So much the worse. One can always obtain the fullest·
account of an actress's life, because she is a notable person, and the
public takes an interest in the minutest particulars concerning·
notable people. If, as she says, she is the daughter of an actor, fifty
people of the stage can tell you all about her family. Have you·
made enquiries ?"

"She came from California," said he. "How should they·
know her ? Come, let us go into the theatre."

I went in, and saw, to my astonishment, the cynical Sporboy·
seated in the front row, applauding vehemently, and sliming " Miami "·
with his eye as a boar slimes a rabbit it intends to devour.

"Capital !" he was exclaiming, "Capital ! What a waist !·
What an ankle ! What a charming devikin it is ! Black blood·
there, boys ! Supple as an eel. Ho, ho ! Good ! Our Pauline
shall receive the homage of her Sporboy in the splendid neatness of·
a whisky hot !"

The stage, being of necessity but three feet from the front seats,
these exclamations were distinctly heard by the actress, who seemed
to shiver at them, as a high-bred horse shivers at the sight of some·
horrible animal. But she never turned her flashing black eyes to·
where the empurpled vagabond wheezed and gloated. She seemed,
I thought, rather to avoid that fishy eye, and to feel relieved when
Sporboy went out for that "splendid neatness," and did not return.
I complimented her—in my official capacity—upon the success of
her performance, but she seemed tired and anxious to get to the
hotel. I offered to escort her, and when on the steps was met by
Sporboy.

He lifted his hat with a flourish which made the rings on his fat·
hands flash in the gaslight. "Introduce me !—Nay—then, I will·
introduce myself. John Sporboy, madam, late of Manilla, 'Frisco,
Popocatapetl, and Ranker's Gully. John Sporboy, who has himself
fretted his little hour upon the stage, and has owned no less than ten
theatres in various parts of the civilized world. John Sporboy craves·
an introduction to Mademoiselle Pauline Christoval."

She paused a moment, and then—probably seeing that opposi
tion might expose her to insult—said to me : " Pray introduce your·
friend, if he is so desirous."

"Spoken like a Plantagenet," cried Sporboy. "Mademoiselle,
I kiss your hands. If you will permit me, I'll sing the songs of other
years, of joyful bliss or war, and if my songs should make you weep,
I'll touch the gay guitar !"

"Pray come upstairs," said she, coldly ; "all the people are
staring at us."

The Great Sporboy was never greater than on that well-
remembered evening. He talked incessantly, and when he was not
devoting himself to the "elegant simplicity of whisky hot," he was·
singing Canadian boat songs to his own piano accompaniment, or
relating anecdotes of his triumphs in Wall Street, his adventures on·
the Pacific Slope, or his lucky hits in every kind of speculation.

"I have been through fire and water, I know most things. I have been up some very tall trees in my time, and looked around upon some very queer prospects. You can't deceive me, and my advice is, don't try, for, if you do, I'm bound to look ugly, and when I knock a man down, ma'am, it takes four more to carry him away, and then there's five gone! Tra-la-la! Pu-r-r-r!" And he ran up and down the keys with his fat fingers.

"I think Mademoiselle Pauline looks tired," said I.

"Oh, no," she returned, uneasily. "Not at all. Captain Sporboy is so amusing, so vivacious—so young, may I say?"

"You may, Mademoiselle," said Sporboy, "say what you like."

To lovely women, Sporboy was ever as gentle as the gazelle.

"Pray"—suddenly wheeling round upon the music-stool and, liquorishly, facing her—"have you heard lately from your sainted MOTHER, ma'am?"

They say that a creature shot through the heart often leaps into the air before it falls dead. Mademoiselle Pauline must have received at that instant some such fatal wound, for she leapt to her feet, standing for an instant gazing wildly at us, and then sank back into her seat, speechless and pale.

"What do you mean? I do not understand you," she gasped out at length; and then, as though her quick intellect had assured her that deceit was useless—"I have not seen my mother since she left me, seven years ago, at St. Louis."

"As she left *me* once before!" said Sporboy, with savage triumph in his bloodshot eyes. "I thought I knew you, Miss Mannelita. 'Should old acquaintance be forgot?' eh? I hope not."

I rose to go, faltering some lame excuse, but Sporboy stopped me. "Nay, my young and juvenile friend (as I used to say in Chadband), be not hasty. This lady and I are old friends. 'We met, 'twas in a crowd;' and I thought she would shun me. Ho, ho! Let us drink to this merry meeting! For 'when may we three meet again?' I will order Moet and Chandon."

"I think, Sporboy, that you have drunk enough." (She was sitting motionless, waiting, as it seemed, for the issue of events.) "Let us go home."

"Home. It's home I fain would be—home, home, home, in my ain countree! Eh! Miss Pauline, 'I'd be a butterfly born in a bower.' EH?"

"If you have anything to say to me, sir," (the dusky pale of her cheeks illuminated by two spots of crimson) "you had better say it."

"I, my enslaver? No, not I, not I, not I! Was it Vestris used to sing?" (humming it) "' I'll be no submissive, wi-fe, no, not I, no, not I!' Would you like to be a submissive wife, ma'am? God help the man who gets you! Adieu, adieu! 'Hamlet, r-r-remember me!'"

"Good heavens, Sporboy," said I, when I got him outside, "what on earth did you go on in that way for? What do you know of her?"

"Ho, ho!" chuckled Sporboy, with thickening utterance. What do I know of her? Tra-la-la! Tilly-valley! No good, you may depend."

"Tell me what you do know then. Young Beaufort wishes to marry her."

"I know," said Sporboy, with another chuckle; "he told me. He's gone to Melbourne by the night coach to make arrangements."

"When will he be back?"

"The day after to-morrow. Tra-la-la! Oh haste to the wedding, and let us be gay, for young Pauline is dressed in her bridal array. She's wooed and she's won, by a Beaufort's proud son, and Pauline, Pauline, Pauline's a lady."

"But, Sporboy, if you know anything absolutely discreditable about her, you ought to tell me."

"Not to-night, dear boy. To-morrow! 'To-morrow, and to-morrow, and to-morrow, creeps on this pretty pace from day to day, and all our yesterdays have lighted fools away to dusky death.' Where's the brief candle, to bed!"

All night I tossed uneasily. The strange mystery of this handsome and defiant woman affected me. Who, and what was she? What did the profligate old adventurer know of her? Was she innocent and maligned, or a guilty creature to be unmasked and abandoned to her own fortune? The hot morning steamed into my window, and woke me from some strange dream, in which such conjectures as these had taken visible shape to torment me. I sprang up and opened the window. Presently I heard voices approach the lattice-work, and distinguished the tones of Sporboy and Mademoiselle Pauline.

"Why do you wish to persecute me?" said she. "I am not interfering with *your* schemes. This boy is not a friend of *yours*. I have not seen you for years."

"No, my charming child, you have not. You thought me dead, eh?"

"I had *hoped* so often," said she, slowly.

"But we don't die young in our family, my dear," he laughed. "'We live and love together through many a changing year'—ay, and *hate* together! Ho, ho!"

"What do you want to do then?"

"To make you suffer for your mother —for your infernal wretch of a half-bred, Spanish-blooded, treacherous devil of a mother—my young lamb."

"How?"

"By waiting until your lover comes back with his licence in his pocket, and then telling him as much of your history as I know, and as much more as I can invent."

She fell upon her knees.

"O, no, no! You will not do this. I will go away to-night, to-day, this hour. I never injured *you*. If you knew the life I have led. I am weary, weary. This boy loves me. He is honest, and, and——"

"And *rich*, my Manuelita?"

"I cannot marry a poor man. You should know that. I have suffered poverty too long."

"But have you not your Profession? Are you not an eminent *tragedienne?* Do not the diggers throw you nuggets? I am ashamed of you, my Manuelita," and he began to whistle as though intensely amused.

She rose to her feet. "My profession! I hate it! hate it! hate it! I never wished to belong to it. I was forced into it. Forced by my mother, and by you——"

"And by others, my pigeon!"

"When I was thirteen you sold me. When I was fifteen I was a woman. I am thirty now, and do you think that fifteen years of sordid cares and desperate strifes have led me to love my art—as you call it? An art! It *is* an art. But you, and men like you, have made a trade of it—a trade in which bare bosoms and blonde hair fetch the highest prices."

"Gently, sweet Manuelita! Tra-la-la-la! Tum-tum! Tra-la-la-la!" And he stopped his whistle to hum, beating time with his hand on the verandah-rail.

"All my life I have been told to get money — money — money — money. Good looks are worth — money. Health is worth—money. I am taught to sing, to play, to dance, to talk, that I may bring— money. Well, you have had your profit out of me. Now, I am going to sell myself for my own benefit!"

He stopped whistling and caught her by the wrist.

"I tell you what you are going to do. You are going to do just as I tell you, until this time to-morrow morning. You are going to stop acting, for I won't let you out of my sight. (Don't start; I will pay the salaries of your people.) You are going to remain with me all day. We will visit the claims, the shops, the museum, the places of interest, and this time to-morrow your lover will arrive, and I shall have the honour of relating to him the particulars of your lively career in the United States, Mexico, California, and the Great Pacific Slope."

"I will not obey you. Let me go."

"Does my Manuelita wish that I relate her history to the world, then? That I print it in the local paper; that I tell my friend Craven, the police-magistrate and warden that——" and he approached and whispered something in her ear which I could not catch.

There was silence for a moment, and then the sound of suppressed sobs. Sporboy had conquered, for he walked away humming, and in a few minutes I saw him pass out of the door below me, and—with no trace of the debauch of last night upon him—call out to the waiter, "Mademoiselle has asked me to breakfast, Chips. When the heart of a man is oppressed with cares, the mists are dispelled when a woman appears! Rum and milk, Chips."

·CHAPTER III.

THE SUMPITAN.

I WENT about my business that morning rather more satisfied than I had been. It was evident that, however infamous, from a moral point of view, might be the behaviour of Sporboy, the woman was an adventuress who merited exposure, and that the action proposed would liberate my foolish friend. I resolved to wait events.

The first event was the arrival of Sporboy to pay me for the Hall. "Our charming friend—I knew her poor dear mother in 'Frisco—is unwell and cannot play. Genius, dear boy, is often a trying burden. I have taken upon myself to show her about the township, to take her for a drive to the dam—to amuse her mind in fact. Is that whisky in that bottle? No? Ink! Ah, I will not trouble you. Till we meet, dear boy! Ho, 'let me like a soldier fall.' Tum, tum! Te, tum! Tum, tum!"

The second was the report started at the "Main Reef Hotel," that Sporboy was going to marry Mademoiselle Pauline, and that he was taking her down his claims to show her his wealth.

The third was the appearance of the pair themselves in Merry-jingle's new buggy, to "look at the Museum." "We have done the dam, seen the claims, been down shafts, and exhausted nature generally," said Sporboy. "Ma'amselle is almost expiring."

In truth she looked so. She was very white and nervous, and glanced about her with the stare of a hunted animal. Knowing that which I did know, I thought that Sporboy might esteem himself fortunate in not having been precipitated down a shaft by the little hand which so nervously twitched at the magnificent shawl of Angora goat's hair, which had been the envy of Main Street for the last three days. I almost pitied the poor creature.

"Show us the wonders of the Museum," cried the vivacious Sporboy (smelling strongly of the elegant simplicity of hot whisky). Let us see your fossils, your emu eggs, your Indian shields, and your savage weapons of war! Ho, ho! Here is a canoe, Ma'amselle. How would you like to be floating in it away back to your native land? Here we have a model of the Great Lively Creek Nugget. How would you like to have that now, and live in luxury all your days?"

If this was the method of torment he had put in practice since morning, she must have had more than human patience to endure it in silence.

"Here we have a club from New Caledonia, How nice to cleave the skull of your enemies! Our charming friend, Pauline, if she *has* enemies, might long to be able to use so effective a weapon! Or this spear! Adapted even to a woman's hand! Ho, ho! Miami, would you like to draw this little bow, and spit your foe with this arrow? By the way, how goes the time?"

It was two o'clock, and I told him so.

"The coach for Melbourne passes at three; would you like to go by it?" he asked her. "But no, I would not recommend it. And yet the company is paid a week in advance. They would not stop you. Shall we make a trip?"

She turned to him half hopefully, as though deceived by his tones, but catching the malignant glance of his eye flushed and turned away.

Skipping from case to case like an overgrown bee, he paused at last.

"Ho, ho! What have we here! Oh! *my gift. The Sumpitan, or blow-pipe, the weapon of the natives of Central America, presented together with a case of poisoned arrows, by John Sporboy.* Tra-la-la! Observe this :—The fellow takes one of these little wooden needles stuck into a pith ball, puts it into the pipe, blows, and puff!—down falls his dinner!"

He commenced capering about with the long reed to his lips, swelling out his cheeks as in the act of blowing, and looking—with his big belly and tightly-buttoned coat—like a dissipated bullfrog.

Mademoiselle seemed roused to some little interest by this novel instrument.

"But how can they eat poisoned meat?" asked she.

"The poison does not injure the meat," I replied, with the gravity proper to a Secretary. "It is the celebrated Wourali poison, and effects no organic change in the body of the animal killed by it. You fire at him; he feels the prick of the needle, and, as Captain Sporboy says—puff—he falls dead in a few minutes!"

"Ho, ho!" cries the exhilarated Sporboy from the other end of the room. "See me slay the Secretary with his own weapons," and wheeling about, he blew at me a pellet of paper, propelled with such force that, narrowly missing my face, it struck and knocked to the ground a little Indian figure, which shivered into fifty pieces.

The gross old villain was somewhat sobered by this incident, and taking the quiver from the hands of Mademoiselle, replaced it, together with the reed in its accustomed rack.

"I am an ass," he said. "Let us return to the hotel and see the coach come in. We may have news of absent friends, who knows? My Pauline, thy Sporboy awaits thee!"

Paler and colder than ever, she allowed him to lead her away, and they departed. The manner in which Sporboy treated the wretched woman whom he had vowed to unmask disgusted me. It was unmanly, cruel. That she should be prevented from ruining a young and wealthy fool was right and necessary, but there was no need to torment her, to play with her as the cat plays with the mouse. Surely the best thing to do with her would be to let her go her own ways back into the great world out of which she had come. I determined to see Sporboy, inform him of that which I had overheard, and beg his mercy.

At four o'clock, the hour for closing the Museum, I went down to the hotel. At the door I saw Stunning Joe Banks.

"I was coming to see you," he said; "I want to take the Hall."

"Oh certainly, but I must see Mademoiselle Christoval first."

"She's gone!"

"*What?*"

"Gone to Melbourne."

"When?"

"By the three o'clock coach. It's all right. *We're* all square." ··

"But," said I bewildered, "what about Sporboy?"

"Which?" asked Joseph, with one of those fine touches of humour for which he was so distinguished. "What?"

"Excuse me a few minutes," I said. "There is something strange here," and I hastened down Main Street. "Captain Sporboy in?" I asked Chips.

"He was here this afternoon, sir."

"When did Mademoiselle Christoval leave?"

"She came down with the Captain in his buggy, and went upstairs with him. Presently she rang the bell and told me to take her passage by the coach. She paid her bill, sent down her boxes, and was O.P.H., sir."

"And was not Captain Sporboy with her?"

"No. sir. Didn't see him after he went upstairs with her. P'raps he's in his room."

I went upstairs and knocked at the Great Man's door. No answer. I opened the door, and nearly fell over Sporboy's body. He was lying on the floor, just inside his room—DEAD!

"My hurried summons filled the room with people in a few seconds. We lifted the corpse from the ground. There was on it no mark of violence, save that in falling the dying man had struck his nose against the floor, and the blood had slightly spotted his shirt front, and that his right hand doubled under him was bruised and discoloured.

"I wonder," said the Coroner, taking his "Three Star" afterwards in the bar, "that a man of his habits was so apparently healthy. He drank whisky enough to have killed a regiment of dragoons. Those sort of subjects almost always die suddenly."

Suddenly, indeed, when he was last seen by Mr. Butt, in perfect health, shaking hands with Mademoiselle Christoval at the threshold of the room that was his death-chamber.

The romance of Lively Creek was over, buried in the grave of the friendless adventurer. No one ever knew the nature of the secret which bound the Great Sporboy to the travelling actress, for when Harry Beaufort returned by the morning coach, he found a letter awaiting him, containing three lines of farewell from the unworthy woman he had hoped to marry, and who disappeared into the unholy mystery out of which she had emerged.

*   *   *   *   *   *   *

Was it accident or murder which removed the profligate prosecutor of Pauline or Manuelita so opportunely and so suddenly from her path? In common with the rest of the world I believed the former—until yesterday.

Despite the strong motive for the crime, the absolute absence of all testimony, medical or circumstantial, against her had compelled me to adjudge her innocent of the deed. I thought so then—I hope so now—but the reason I have recalled upon paper the details of this unfinished history is, that upon taking down yesterday, for some official purpose, the Sumpitan quiver, which had hung upon its accustomed nail for the last ten years under the noses of all the world, I found that the tiny, poisoned, thorn-point of one of the wooden needles had been broken off, and caught by a splinter in the little cane ring which sustained the mutilated shaft was a fine white thread—the hair of the Angora goat.

KING BILLY'S TROUBLES; OR GOVERNMENTAL RED-TAPEISM.

"IT is perfectly monstrous," said I, "this is the ninth pair he has had since shearing. Buckmaster himself would be ruined at this rate."

"My love," suggested Mrs. Tallowfat, "he can't go about without them."

I made some pettish observations about the "poor Indian" and "beauty unadorned &c.," but Mrs. Tallowfat said "stuff" in a tone which precluded argument. "The Bellwethers are coming up to the station next week" said she "and to have a black fellow walking about—Oh, it's not to be thought of."

"Budgeree, climb tree" says King Billy, turning his dilapidations towards us with the elegant simplicity of the savage. "Slip down long o' 'possum. Big fellow hole that one."

There was no disputing it.

"Well my dear" said I, "he'll get no more from me I'll—I'll write to the department."

His Majesty King William the First was the chieftain of the Great Glimmera blacks, and carried on his manly breast a brass label inscribed with his name, date and title. He was general knock-about-man" on the station, and as I had been idiot enough to allow myself to be made a corresponding member of the Board for the Protection of Aboriginals, William imagined that he had a right to demand from me unlimited clothing. The Board liberally supplied the few blacks who yet survived the gin bottle with a blanket per year (by the way, the storekeepers who gave rum in exchange vowed the quality was most inferior); by some accident the blanket intended for the monarch had been captured by some inferior aboriginal, and had never been replaced. William indignantly demanded to be clothed, and to quiet his outcries I gave him a pair of pantaloons. The gift was so highly appreciated, that when the blanket did arrive, His Majesty declined to wear it. "What for you gib it that." "No good," said he, with profound contempt, and continued to eat, drink, sleep, ride, and climb trees in my pantaloons.

"Mrs. Tallowfat," said I, "I will write to the department."

I did write—a forcible, and I flatter myself, even elegant letter, setting forth the poor savage's yearning for civilisation, begging that the Board would take the matter into their favourable consideration, and supply the dethroned monarch with one pair of moleskins a year. A week passed, and I received a letter from the secretary.

8796
B.

BOARD FOR THE PROTECTION OF ABORIGINES.

JULY 27TH, 186—.

SIR,—I have the honour to acknowledge your letter of 20th inst., requesting that the aboriginal named in the margin may be supplied with one pair of moleskin trousers annually by this department, and in reply have the honour to inform you that I will lay the letter before the Board at their next sitting, and communicate to you their decision on the subject.

I have the honour to be, Sir,
Your most obedient humble servant,
JOHN P. ROBINSON,
Secretary to the Board.

To Tityrus Tallowfat, Esq., J.P.,
Cock-and-a-Bull Station,
Budgeree Flat, Old Man Plains, Great Glimmera.

This, so far, was very satisfactory, and I triumphantly snubbed my wife, who had ventured to hint that I should find my application treated with *nonchalance*. Weeks, however, rolled away, Billy wore out two more pairs of trousers, and the Board did not write. I sent another despatch; no answer. Another; no answer. A third; still no reply. I got angry, and penned a sarcastic note. "Am I Briareus?" asked I, sardonically, "that I should keep a hundred pairs of breeches on hand." My sarcasm had the desired result. It provoked an answer.

No. 11,289
C.

28TH SEPTEMBER, 186—.

SIR,—I have the honour, by the direction of the Board for the Protection of Aborigines, to acknowledge the correspondence cited in the margin, and to inform you in reply that the Board have given your application their fullest and most complete attention. The practice, however, of supplying breeches to black fellows is one which has not hitherto obtained in this department, authorised, under *Act Vic.* cxxii., *Sec.* 4001 to provide blankets and petticoats only. I am directed, however, to inform you that the Board will again consider this somewhat important matter, with a view to bringing it under the notice of the Hon. the Chief Secretary at an early date.

I am further instructed to say that your observation on the subject of "Briareus" is not only incorrect, but considered by the Board to be quite uncalled for.

I have the honour to be, &c.,
JOHN P. ROBINSON.

I was staggered. What vast machinery had I not set in motion. Good gracious! I had no desire to trouble the Chief Secretary. I would write to him and apologise. Like an ass, I did so.

In three months I received back my letter, marked in red ink, in blue ink, in green ink, minuted in all directions, and commented upon in all kinds of handwriting.

"Noted and returned, W.P.S." Not on the business of this department, O.P.G." "Refer to the Paste and Scissors Office, M.B." "Apparently forwarded in error, L.B.O." Across the right hand bottom corner of this maltreated document was written, in fine bold hand, with which I afterwards became hideously familiar. "Communications on the subject of Clothing of Aboriginals must

90

be made to the Hon. the Chief Secretary through the Gunnybag and Postage Stamp Department *Only*, O.K."

This was decisive, though who "O.K." was, and what the Gunnybag and Postal Stamp Department had to do with the Clothing of Aboriginals (who wore neither Gunnybags nor Postage Stamps), I could not tell. However, I was not yet beaten. I wrote to the Hon. Silas Barnstarke, then Comptroller General of Gunnybags, enclosed the returned letter and begged that he would use his influence in the proper quarter to procure a pair of moleskins for King Billy. The Hon. Silas Barnstarke was an official by nature, and he replied after six months accordingly.

$\frac{8024}{8749}$ 362 B.

GUNNYBAGS AND POSTAGE STAMP DEPARTMENT.

3RD JULY, 187—.

[OFFICIAL.]

SIR,—In reference to your note of 24th January last, I have the honour to inform you that no official cognisance of blackfellows' breeches can at present be taken by this Department.

I have the honour to be, &c.,
SILAS BARNSTARKE,
Comptroller of Gunnybags.

———

[SEMI-OFFICIAL.]

MY DEAR SIR,—I have to regret that I am unable to comply with your very reasonable request.

Yours faithfully,
S. BARNSTARKE.

———

[PRIVATE.]

DEAR TALLOWFAT,—I can't do anything about this confounded blackfellow.

Yours,
S. B.

In the meantime King William wore out three more pairs. I wrote again to the Board, and, after waiting the usual time, received the following reply :—

$\frac{3684}{X.}$

9th October, 187—.

SIR,—I have the honour by direction of the Board, to inform you that they cannot at present move in the matters named in the margin.* The subject of the Clothing of Aborigines in general has occupied the gravest attention of the Board for the last six months, but, after mature consideration, they fail to see how your request can be in any respect complied with, unless by the direct authority of His Excellency the Governor-in-Council.

I am instructed to suggest, that perhaps in the meantime, as the case seems urgent, and His Excellency is in Adelaide, a kilt might meet the difficulty.

I have the honour, &c.,
JOHN P. ROBINSON.

"A kilt meet the difficulty! No, nor half of it." In indignant terms I wrote to this half-hearted Robinson. "No one but an idiot,"

---

* Blackfellows' Breeches.

said I, "could make such a preposterous suggestion." The phlegmatic creature replied (after three weeks) as follows :—

3784
———
X.

1ST NOVEMBER, 187—,

SIR,—I have the honour to acknowledge your communication of 12th October last, in which you inform me I am an idiot, as per margin, and in reply thereto, I beg to inform you that on that point a difference of opinion exists in this Department.

and he had again "the honour to be."

This seemed a fatal blow to my hopes, but I wrote again, begged to withdraw the offensive expression made in the heat of the moment, and to request that the Board would condescend to take my petition into earnest consideration. Mr. Robinson replied in a temperate and forgiving spirit.

The "Board" he observed, in the most elegant round-hand "are most desirous to promote the welfare of Aborigines in the minutest particular, and I am directed to state for your information that a proposal to amalgamate the votes for flannel petticoats and patent revolving beacons will be made to the Government, which amalgamation will enable the Board to issue one pair of moleskin trousers, as per Schedule B., to every three adult aboriginals in the colony. I am directed to ask if you have any suggestions to offer with regard to cut, number of buttons, flap or fly, &c."

I could not see how one pair of breeches between every three adult natives would "meet the difficulty," as Mr. Robinson elegantly put it, nor did I understand why the votes for flannel petticoats and patent revolving beacons needed amalgamation, but I replied thanking the Board, and wrote to my friend O'Dowd, member for the Glimmera, to beg him to make a "proper representation" on the subject. O'Dowd was at that time "in opposition." I saw in the *Peacock* that "the hon. member for Glimmera gave notice that he would ask the hon. the Comptroller of Gunnybags, on the following Thursday, if he was aware of the particulars attending the case of an aboriginal known as King Billy."

My hopes rose high, when, on the following Thursday, O'Dowd delivered himself of a terrific speech, in which he accused the Government of the most wanton barbarity, and drew such a terrible picture of the trouserless monarch hiding in the dens and clefts of the rocks, that it brought tears into my eyes as I read it.

Barnstarke, however, who had kept two clerks at work night and day, copying the correspondence replied in his usual calm and dignified manner. "The attention of the Government had already been called to the lamentable condition of the aborigines in that wealthy and populous district, where the hon. member who had just sat down owned such extensive property, and he might inform the hon. member that the Government had taken steps to remedy, in some measure, the effects of the apparent parsimony of the inhabitants of the Glimmera district, by a method which he was convinced would fully satisfy every intelligent and liberal member of that House."

O'Dowd was muzzled, but, as luck would have it, little Chips, the leader writer to the *Peacock*, was in the gallery and wanted a "subject." "Monstrous case about that blackfellow," said he to the editor later in the evening. "I should like to do a smart little thing on old Barnstarke about it."

There was nothing better going, and the article was written. I forget it now, but I know it was vastly clever, quoting Horace twice, and comparing poor Barnstarke to Le Roi Dagobert. In fact, it was full of as much withering scorn as Chips could afford for £2 2s., and Chips was liberal.

Thus encouraged by the support of the Press, O'Dowd moved for a Commission to inquire into the subject of Aborigines' breeches, with power to call for persons and papers.

The Commission was granted, sat at the Parliament Houses for nine mortal weeks, examined 300 witnesses, ordered "plans and specifications" of all the breeches since the original fig-leaf, and at a cost of £2000 published a Report of 1000 pages, containing a complete history of the development of breeches from the earliest ages.

This Report contained my correspondence in an appendix, and advised that all the Aborigines throughout the Colony, male and female, should at once be provided with three pairs of broadcloth pantaloons a-piece.

In the meantime King Billy wore out four pairs of mine.

Elated, however, by the successful issue of my labours, I gave him the garments, and waited for my revenge. I waited for three months.

It was nearly the end of the session, and I had almost begun to despair, when I received a large packet from Mr. Robinson, enclosing a copy of the Report, and asking for a "return of the number, height, age, and weight of all the Aborigines in the district." I set to work without delay to furnish this return, and had the gratification of seeing by the papers that "In reply to a question by Mr. O'Dowd, the Comptroller of Gunnybags informed the House that the Report of the Blackfellows' Breeches Commission had been referred to the Board for the Protection of Aborigines, who would give the recommendation of the Commission their best attention."

It seemed that we had come back to the place whence we had started.

Nothing was done, of course, during the recess, but when the House was about to sit, I saw that the *Peacock* was "informed that the Special Report of the Board for the Protection of Aborigines, which, we understand, will be shortly laid on the table of the House, contains some startling revelations on the subject of blackfellows' breeches, and proves beyond a doubt the necessity for an Absolute Freetrade Policy for this Colony."

The Ministerial journal (the *Peacock* was always in opposition) hinted that it was the intention of the liberal and intelligent

Government, to further Protect the Native Industry of the Colony by placing a tax of 4½d. a leg on every pair of imported moleskins—a proceeding which cannot fail to redound to the credit of that Government, whose fiscal policy we have always upheld through the medium of our advising columns." It was not to be expected that the *Peacock* could allow such a gross fallacy to pass unquestioned, so it inquired sarcastically the following morning if " its Little Bourke Street contemporary was aware that America had been plunged into Civil War in consequence of the bloomer movement, which deprived thousands of hard-working negroes of their nether garments. "The Imports of the United States during the year 1862, when a freetrade policy prevailed," said the *Peacock* "reached a total of $8,936,052·18. In 1863, when Henry Clay, a member of the notorious Pantaloon-and-gaiter-Ring, levied a tax of one red cent. on every article of clothing that came below the knee, the Customs returns showed a deficit of $18,000,000,000. This fact speaks for itself."

At it again went the protectionist paper, and proved entirely to its own satisfaction that the only way to make mankind happy, was to encourage the growth of breeches industry by severe protective duties. " It is rumoured " said the protectionist paper " that an effort will be made by the soft goods faction to import the 200,000 pairs of breeches required for our aboriginal population. *Quem deus vult perdere, &c.* Such an act would blur the blush and grace of modesty. We trust that a patriotic Government will look to it. We have imported too long. Our short-sighted and venal contemporary, not satisfied with importing its Sparrows, Rabbits, Bulls, and Editors, must needs attack the country in its most vital point— stab it in its very seat of honour. We are confident that Sir Ossian M'Orkney, however much he may have appeared to lean towards the unholy condition of Flinders Lane, will draw the line at breeches."

The controversy was highly interesting, but in the meantime King Billy wore out four more pairs—leathers. I wrote to Barnstarke informing him that while the great question of Freetrade or Protection yet remained unsettled, my wardrobe was becoming absorbed into the surrounding forest, and that unless something was speedily done, I would send the monarch breechesless to Melbourne, marked "This side up with care," and let his country deal with him.

Barnstarke replied that "while deprecating the indiscreet haste which I had displayed in the treatment of a matter of so much importance, he was willing to do everything in his power, and after consultation with his colleagues, had given instructions to the Chief Commissioner of Police to forward an old pair of regulation cords, which would perhaps satisfy me. No cords came, but a very large letter from the Chief Commissioner, in which he regretted that all the regulation cords of the Department being in constant use, he was unable to comply with the request of the Hon. the Comptroller of Gunnybags, but that he had forwarded my letter (forwarded to him *through* the Department of the Hon. the Chief Secretary *by* the Hon. the Comptroller of Gunnybags) to the Commandant of the Local Forces, with a request that he give the matter his immediate attention.

Three weeks passed, and I received a letter from the Commandant of the Local Forces, who, in a military "memo" in red ink, begged to forward me copies of the correspondence between the Hon. the Comptroller of Gunnybags, the Chief Commissioner of Police and himself, and to attach a list of the articles with which "it was in his power to supply me through the usual official channel." The list was five folio pages of close print, and contained, I believe, every article under heaven except the one I desired. I replied by marking a few dozen, convinced that nothing would come of it, and wrote again to Barnstarke. Barnstarke sent me a parcel with a private note.

[PRIVATE.]

DEAR TALLOWFAT,—I don't see how to please you, but as the matter will be brought before the House shortly, and those confounded fellows in the Opposition will be sure to make a handle of it, I have begged a personal interview with the Governor, stated your case, and asked him as an old friend of my cousin, Lord Lofty, to help me. His Excellency, in the kindest and most delicate manner, has sent me an old pair of "plush," discarded, I believe, by one of the vice-regal domestics, and placed them entirely at your service. For goodness sake, my dear fellow, keep the matter dark, for I sadly fear that so irregular a proceeding will result in some confusion in this Department.

Yours,

L. B.

P.S.—I rely as ever on your powerful support in case of a General Election.

We clothed King Billy in the Vice-Regal Plush, and for some months he was happy. The papers having got hold of a Divorce Case, were engaged (in the cause of morality) in commenting on the particulars, and I had hoped that matters would not rest. But I had forgotten one thing—"The Audit Commissioners."

Early in the following spring, Tommy, the boy who rode for the mail to Bullocktown, informed me that there was a packing-case at the Post Office, marked "On Her Majesty's Service," and addressed to me. I sent a bullock-dray for it, and it proved to be a bundle of papers from the "Audit Commissioners," accompanied by a note from Barnstarke.

[PRIVATE.]

DEAR TALLOWFAT.—I knew that we should get into a mess about those confounded breeches. It appears that they had been reseated by the Government contractor, and that no requisition had been sent into this office. The result is that the Commissioners of Audits (among other queries) desire to be "informed" about this "gross irregularity." The whole of the accounts of this Department are in arrear in consequence. Can you tell them what they want to know?

Yours,

L.B.

I rose every morning at daylight for the space of a month, and read away at the bundle. It contained some tolerably rough reading. All the accounts of His Excellency's household were then noted and commented upon in the most acute and accurate manner. The Audit Commissioners were continually "dropping down" upon His Excellency, as thus—His Excellency's valet desires a water-bottle for

Excellency's bedroom, and is informed in a brief note from the Chief Clerk of the Water-bottle Department of the Government stores, that he "must requisition for it in the usual way." He does so, and sends in the bill "in the usual form." A voluminous correspondence then occurs between the Government Storekeeper, the Commissioners of Audit, and the Contractor, as to whether "cut-glass bottles" should or should not be charged for at a certain rate. This question satisfactorily settled, the Contractor applies to the Government Storekeeper to apply to the Commissioners of Audit to "pass the account through the Treasury," and is informed contemptuously that "the number of pints not being stated in the voucher, the Commissioners of Audit are unable to forward the account in question." This causes another correspondence with the Treasury, and, just as I had worked myself into a fever of expectation, imagining that the money *must* at last be paid, the Treasurer triumphantly encloses a copy of the Registrar-General's certificate of the death of the applicant, and refers the whole matter for adjustment by the Curator of Intestate Estates.

I stumbled also upon an exciting chase after an item of 2¾d. overcharge for farriery, which at last proved to have been paid for a threepenny drink to the smith, less the "usual discount on Government contracts," but I found nothing bearing upon my breeches, or His Excellency's breeches, or King Billy's Breeches, or, to speak more correctly, and in accordance with official exactness, the "one pair of double-plush extra super small clothes, the property of Her Majesty the Queen of Great Britain and Ireland, Fid. Def."

With bewildered brain, I returned the bundle to Barnstarke, and begged him to settle it anyhow. He replied that the only thing to do was to *at once* return the breeches to the Government Storekeeper "for," said he, "if this is not done, we must move the Treasurer to put a sum of 5s. 4d. on the Supplementary Estimates, and such a course will naturally cause great inconvenience to this Department."

I sent him down a blank cheque, begged him to fill it up for any sum he pleased, and settle the matter at once. Alas! little did I know the wisdom by which the world is governed. Barnstarke was most indignant.

"Not only," said he in his reply, "is the course you propose most improper, and utterly opposed to all the traditions of official business, but it would put the Department to the utmost inconvenience to entertain, even for an instant, such a monstrous proposition. You will, I trust, excuse me speaking thus plainly, when I inform you that, to enable me to receive the sum of money you so rashly proffer, I should require a special vote to the House. If it is absolutely *impossible* for you to return the breeches, the Treasurer must be moved in the usual way." What could I do? The breeches were torn to shreds by this time, and fragments of them gleamed derisively from several lofty gum-trees in the vicinity of the station. There was evidently no help for it. The Treasurer, poor fellow, must be "moved in the usual way," whatever that might be.

In the Supplementary Estimates for 187— accordingly appeared the following item :—

COMPTROLLER OF GUNNYBAGS:

"Division, 492 ; Sub-division, 8.

"His Excellency the Governor-General and Vice-Admiral of the Colony of Victoria.

"For re-seating one pair of extra plush small clothes, 5s. 4d."

It was thought there would have been a row. The Treasurer trembled when he submitted the fatal item to the House, and an ominous silence reigned. "I would ask the Hon. the Treasurer," said Mr. Wiggintop rising, "if this piece of wanton extravagance is to be paid for out of the Imperial or the Colonial Funds."

"The Colonial funds of course," says a rash member from the Government benches. Wiggintop sat down quietly, and those who knew his antipathy to Downing Street, trembled for the fate of the Ministry.

The next morning the *Daily Bellower*, a paper that went in for economic democracy, laughed bitterly. "So then *this* is the way in which the Victorian taxpayer is robbed to support the liveried myrmidons of an effete and palsied aristocracy. The representative of Downing Street, not contented with gloating over the Victorian artisan from Toorak, must needs clothe his footmen out of the proceeds of the hardy miner's toil. The rogue wants his breeches re-seated, does he ! Pampered menial."

There was no standing this. The Ministry resigned, and Wiggintop was sent for. He formed a Ministry in twenty-four hours, and went to the country with the breeches metaphorically nailed to the mast-head of his future policy. "It shall be my business," said he at an enthusiastic meeting of his constituents, "to see that every half-penny of that 5s. 4d. paid is out of the Royal Exchequer." When Parliament met, Wiggintop called for "*all* the correspondence connected with this gross case of Imperial tyranny" (the report of the Blackfellows' Breeches Committee, came in as an appendix this time), in order that he might lay it on the table of this wronged and outraged House." He did so, and, to the triumph of the Colonial Progress Party, it was resolved by an overwhelming majority that the question should be immediately referred to the Privy Council.

I imagined that all was over. But by the return mail, Wiggintop received the gratifying intelligence that a Royal Commission had been appointed, who would examine personally the witnesses in this most important case. A few days after the *Bellower* informed the public that the first blow had been struck, the "pampered menial" had gone home in the "Great Britain" to give his evidence.

By the following mail was transmitted a list of witnesses who were required to be examined before the fourteen noblemen and gentlemen of the Royal Commission. Of course, I was one, but my blood was up now, and I resolved that I would not shrink from my duty. I left orders with my tailor to supply King Billy, and started. With my gained experience of the celerity of officialdom, I spent a couple of months in London sight-seeing, and then thinking it about time to attend to business, wrote to the Secretary to the Commission, but received no answer. I waited two months more, and then having primed myself with names, called at Downing Street. It was the "silly season," and London was empty. A messenger was elegantly lounging on the steps of the Colonial Office, however, and to him I addressed myself.

"Is Lord Lofty within?"

"No, His Lordship is in Greece."

"Mr. Chicester Fortescue?"

"Gone to Norway."

"Mr. Washington White?"

"In the South of France."

"Mr. Fritz Clarence Paget?"

"Rusticating in Boulogne."

"Good Gracious," said I, "is there no one to look after the interests of these two million of colonists?"

"I think you'll find a young gentleman upstairs," said the messenger, carelessly."

I went upstairs, and after some investigation found the young gentleman who looked after the colonies. He was very spruce and very small, with his hair cut very short, and wore a rose in his coat and a glass in his eye. He stared at me as I entered, as one who should say, "What the deuce do you mean coming into a Government Office in this way."

"Mr. Crackelly Jenks?" said I.

"Quite so! What can I do for you?"

"I have called about the Breeches Commission!"

"Ah! door B., first on the right, third turning to the left! Not here! Mistake."

"Pardon me! sir, I have called there, and they referred me to you."

"Oh, did they," says Mr. Crackelly Jenks. "Ah! Well, what is it?"

"I wrote some time ago to Mr. Washington White, who acts as Secretary to the Commission."

"What Commission?"

"The Breeches Commission!"

"Oh! Ah! Is there such a thing! Quite so! Didn't know! Beg your pardon! Go on!"

"My name is Tityrus Tallowfat." I am an Australian! sir, and have come 36,000 miles!"

"All right! Marrowfat! sit down. Never mind the distance! every Australian tells us that. So you're from Victoria Island! Eh?

"Victoria! sir! Capital, Melbourne."

"Oh! ah! yes, stupid of me, but the Vs. are not in my department, don't you see! I take the Bs., Bermuda, and so on; but, however, never mind, I daresay we shall get on. You want to see White?"

"Well, no!" said I, "I want to know——"

"Hadn't you better put it in writing, Marrowfat? Put it in writing now!"

"There is no occasion for that," said I, taught by bitter experience, how futile was such a course; I have already written to Mr. White."

"Ah!" says the young gentlemen at once relieved." Why didn't you say so before? Tomkins bring me Mr. White's letter-book." Tomkins brought it, and Mr. Jenks perused it.' You must be under a mistake, Marrowfat," he said at last. "There's no letter mentioned here."

"But I wrote one sir," I ventured to remark.

"I rather think *not*, Marrowfat," said he. "You must be in error, Marrowfat."

"But my dear sir ——"

"But my dear sir, the thing's as plain as a pikestaff. We register all our letters of course ; now there is no letter mentioned *here*, so we couldn't have received one. Don't you see!"

"Perhaps it might have escaped you," I hesitated again.

He smiled a patronising smile. "My dear Mr. Marrowfat, our system of registration is perfect, simply perfect ; it *couldn't* have escaped us."

Just then, the door was burst open, and there entered another gentleman with a letter in his hand.

"Hullo!" said Mr. Jenks quite unabashed. "Here it is!" Egad that's strange. Thanks my dear Carnaby, thanks. Now, sir," (to me severely, as if I had been in fault) "perhaps you can explain your business."

A bright idea struck me! I would inquire as to the probable result of my inquiries.

"That letter, sir, fully explains my business. May I ask you what will become of it?"

"Become of it! It is the property of the office, sir."

"But what will be done with it."

"It will go through the usual official course, I presume," said Mr. Jenks.

"And what is that, may I ask."

"Oh! said the young man, waving the letter as he spoke, Mr. White will hand it to Mr. Paget, who will minute it, and send it on to Mr. Fortescue. He will pass it through his department, and then it will, in the usual official course, reach Mr. Secretary Landwith ; he will send it to the Commissioners."

"Oh! and what then!"

"Well, the Commissioners will have it read and entered in their minutes, and, then, unless they choose to sent it to the Privy Council, they will return it to us in the usual course."

"As ——"

"From Mr. Secretary Landwith to Mr. Fortescue, from Mr. Fortescue to Mr. Paget, from Mr. Paget to Mr. White, from Mr. White to me!"

"And what would you do with it?'

"I should hand it to the Chief," said Mr. Jenks.

"And what would become of it then?"

Mr. Jenks admired his boot, gloomily, and said at last:—

"'Pon my life, Marrowfat, I don't know. The Chief is rather absent, and—between ourselves—when once a document gets into his hands, 'gad, there's no telling *what* he may do with it."

"Sir," said I in a rage!" I wish you good-morning."

"Good-morning, my dear Marrowfat," said Mr. Jenks, with perfect affability, anything we can do for you, you know, d'lighted I'm sure."

I did not pause to ask what would become of my letter in the alternative of the Commission choosing to hand it to the Privy Council, but left the office. Outside were some thirty or forty of the cloud of witnesses. "Ha! Ha!" they laughed, "here is Mr. Tallowfat. He can tell us all about it. Where is the Commission, Tallowfat, we've been all over London looking for it."

"Gentlemen," said I, "it may be in the moon for all I know of it. If I don't go home and go to bed, I shall be a subject for Bedlam."

I waited in London ten months, and, hearing nothing of the Commission, returned to Melbourne. King Billy had cut the Gordian Knot by dying, and as, according to the custom of his race, he was buried dressed; he took my fifty-third and last pair of breeches with him to his long home.

The Commission is still sitting, I suppose, for we hear the most flourishing accounts from the Agent-General, of the wonderful progress they are making with the collection " of the vast mass of interesting evidence, which I shall have the honour to transmit to you in the usual official course."

"But if ever ' I write to the Department ' again I'm ——— "

HOLIDAY PEAK.

T was dusk when we reached the flat, for, determined to make the most of my brief holiday, I had wandered with Wallaby Dick all day among the ranges.

Wallaby Dick was a lame man, with a face like one of those German toys called "nut-crackers." He was very old, and had lived in his bark hut under the Bluff for the last fifteen years. Wallaby could shoot or snare any living creature that bred, and boasted that he knew every mountain-path, track, and gully between White Swamp and Mount Dreadful. So mighty was the prowess of his gun, that men from the stations round about, spending a barren day stalking the scrub, would aver that Wallaby had discovered the track which led to that legendary Land of Plenty existing on the inaccessible summit of the ranges, and was wont to withdraw from his kind to hunt there.

*   *   *   .*   *   *

There is an indescribable ghastliness about the mountain bush at night which has affected most imaginative people. The grotesque and distorted trees, huddled here and there together in the gloom like whispering conspirators. The little open flats encircled by boulders which seem the forgotten altars of some unholy worship. The white, bare, and ghastly gums gleaming momentarily amid the deeper shades of the forest. The lonely pools begirt with shivering reeds, and haunted by the melancholy bittern only. The rifted and draggled creek-bed, which seems violently gouged out of the lacerated earth by some savage convulsion of nature; the silent and solitary places where a few blasted trees crouch together like withered witches, who, brooding on some deed of blood, have suddenly been stricken horror-stiff. Riding through this nightmare landscape, a whirr of wings, and a harsh cry disturb you from time to time, hideous and mocking laughter peals above and about you, and huge grey ghosts with little red eyes hop away in gigantic but noiseless bounds. You shake your bridle, the mare lengthens her stride, the tree-trunks run into one another, the leaves make overhead a continuous curtain, the earth reels out beneath you like a strip of grey cloth spun by a furiously flying boom, the air strikes your face sharply, the bush, always grey and colourless, parts before you, and closes behind you like a fog. You lose yourself in this prevailing indecision of sound and colour. You become drunk with the wine of the night, and, losing your individuality, sweep onward on a flying phantom in a land of shadows.

"The moon will be up in an hour, my lad," said the old man. "Keep all the left-hand tracks, and you'll pull the Long Waterhole," and then, whistling to his dog, he turned.

"But where are *you* going, Wallaby?"

"O, *I'm* going up the ranges," said Wallaby, with what appeared to me in the dusk to be a fiendish grin, "for a holiday."

When I drew bridle, the moon flung my shadow on the turf. I had gained the little plain which divides Mount Barren from Mount Scar, and the panorama of the valley lay below me. Mile after mile stretched the dusky grey tree-tops. Here and there a link of the chain of water holes which connected the Great and Little Styx flashed white beneath the moon, and from time to time the level surface of the forest was broken by the spectre-like upstarting of some huge gum-skeleton grasping at air with his crooked and ravenous claws. From out this valley, brooded upon by big blue and floating mists, uprose a mysterious murmur composed of crackling twigs, falling leaves, rustling wings, lapping water, and stirring breezes—the breathing of the sleeping bush. Above me to the right and left towered, steel-blue in the moonlight, the twin peaks of Mount Mystery, and between them, far up the gap that led, no one knew whither, a red light gleamed.

The plateau on which I stood bore an evil reputation. It had been in old times the camping-place of the blacks, and upon the largest of the three gigantic stones, which disposed in the form of a triangle, seemed to point to the triple peaks of the triform mountain, human sacrifices had been held, and horrible banquets celebrated. The earth, pawed by my impatient horse, was black and rich—strangely black and rich when compared with the surrounding soil, and the three enormous trees that overshadowed the three altar-stones seemed to own roots fed with fat food, so vigorously had they upsprung from out the rock. The gloomy glamour of ancient barbarism was upon the place. Standing there alone, a usurping white man within the mystic temple of a dead and forgotten creed, I seemed to realize for an instant the whole horror of the ancient worship. Again the skin drums resounded, again floated up to the full moon the wild chant of the women, again the furious fires blazed high, again the people in the valley of the peaks shouted to their savage divinity, again the painted and naked priest reared high the thirsty knife and flung himself—blood-red in the fire-glow—upon the panting victim. What mysteries might not have been celebrated in this forest, haggard and grey with age and storms? Those savage priests, those leaping warriors, might be administering a right primeval, recalling in their wild dances the mystic worship of Egypt, and completing, in their ignorance, the magnificent allegory of that ancient Faith, which, through all the world's history, remains still the hope of thousands. Here in this lonely spot, among the frowning hills, where the pious Christian cries to his risen Lord, might sacrifice have been done to Mithra the virgin-born, to Isis the virgin-mother, to Osiris stretched upon his cross, or to Tammuz the slain for our sins, and re-risen from the dead to save us. Here might the trembling neophyte have prostrated himself before a barbaric Hyphon —that terrible genius of darkness and of doubt, that great Serpent Tempter of the ancient mysteries! In Mexico, in Africa, amid the snows of the Himalayas and the deserts of Central Asia, dwells this ancient worship. The mighty monuments which frown in bewildering grandeur from out the virgin forests of Darien, the legends of the sacred islands of the South, the wild rites of Papua and the Marquesas, give token of the mystic lore of Egypt and the East. Its symbols are used equally by Jew, Turk, and Christian, and now, in this strange and barren land, long deemed worthless to the tread of white feet, did I meet again the traces of the old religion.

As these speculations held me, methought that the mysterious light in the mountain cleft moved higher, and that it was joined by another light. My mare snorted and wrenched at her bit, as though eager to leave the spot of ill omen. The first light twinkled, went out, beamed forth again, and, impelled by one of those sudden resolutions which seemed like inspiration, I rode down the side of the rise, and made towards it. The flats between the gorge and the mount were marshy, and bestrewn with fallen timber. Belts of impenetrable scrub intersected the numerous water-courses. The air grew cool, and a heavy dew began to fall. The moon had risen high, and was riding serenely in a wine-dark and cloudless heaven. A stillness reigned, the mysterious lights moved steadily onwards, and before me fluttered from tree to tree, swooping in upon me from time to time, as though to lure me on, a huge grey bat, through whose transparent wings I could almost see the sparkle of the coldly-gleaming stars. I pressed forward, and the two lights were joined by a third. The second light twinkled and went out, as the first had done, but to be again re-lumined; and then, not a hundred yards before me, the three moving points of fire beamed forth bright and clear. Another instant, and my snorting horse dashed the pebbles under her hoofs, and, rearing with terror, came to a sudden pause before three men who barred the rocky roadway.

"Hullo, Wallaby Dick!" I cried, "is this your holiday?"

But no answer came from the grey lips of the old man, who, facing about, with glassy eyes, thrust forth his flaming torch of mountain pine, as though to forbid my progress.

I turned to his companions, and a species of ludicrous terror seized me. One was Dombie, the blackfellow, the other Ah Yung, the Chinaman. All three—European, Australian, and Mongol—were naked to the waist, each carried a blazing pine-torch, and on the face of each sat that hideous expression of death in life which caused the yellow fangs of the old wallaby hunter to glisten like the teeth of a skeleton.

"Whither are you bound?" I cried, controlling, with difficulty, my terrified horse.

Dombie raised his lean black arm, and silently pointed to the extremity of the gorge. I looked, and saw from behind a huge boulder upshoot a pillar of fire. As though this illumination had been some well-known signal, from all parts of the mountain burst forth the red glare of torches. Above, around, and below burned innumerable spots of fire. The gorge seemed to swarm with fire-flies, the mountain-side to be honeycombed with glow-worms, while in the valley I had left, an immense multitude pressed onward and upward, their torches tossing wildly as they came. Bewildered and alarmed, I rubbed my eyes to see if I was dreaming; but no, I was wide-awake, and conscious that it needed all the strength of my muscles to sit my now maddened horse.

"What foolery is this?" I cried. "Ah Yung! Dombie! speak." But they turned abruptly and breasted the mountain, singing a wild chant as they went. I was forced to follow, for on all sides pressed the multitude. Perhaps from the glare and smoke of the torches my brain had become stupified, or my vision impaired, but it seemed to me that the persons who surrounded me were of all nations and colours. Mulattoes, Blacks, Chinese, Yellow men, and Red men, all the barbaric nations of the South came hurrying onwards: walking, riding, crawling—old men, women, and cripples— as they swarmed along the mighty mountain-side like travelling ants. The fire behind the boulder, fed fast by the gigantic shadows, shot high up into the night its threefold flame. I turned, and lo! the moon, mounted to her zenith, flung down the hill I had left the triple shadow of the three altars! The murmurous prelude to the hymn already began to tremble over the valley, and the multitude, pressing nearer to the sacrificial fire, carried me along with them. I looked round in vain for escape,—no, not in vain; at the very instant when another plunge of my mare would have flung me beneath the feet of the crowd, a young girl, riding on a white mule, pointed to a narrow cleft in the wall of rock on my right. I comprehended her, and wheeling my horse, forced myself clear of the press. A sharp salt wind blew in upon me, and in another instant the strange multitude and the mysterious fire faded behind me, and I was galloping up the gorge in the teeth of a driving storm.

  *   *   *   *   *   *

You, reader, who have known what it is to ride hard all night in an Australian mountain tempest, will appreciate the delight with which I hailed the glorious outburst of a sunny morning. I could not but think my vision of the night a dream, born of my own thoughts and the mysterious influence of the moonlit forest; and in the pure bright air of morning I laughed my follies to scorn. One thing was certain, however, in my dream or my stupidity, I had galloped up the ranges, and by some strange chance had struck that long-sought-for path which led to the mysterious and legendary land behind the mountains. Dismounting, and leading my weary horse by the bridle, I followed a sort of track along the top of the range, and looked, as I went, upon the scenery of the new country in which I found myself. The path wound in and out among the crags, and I soon lost all glimpse of the semi-civilised land I had left. I saw at my feet what seemed at the first glance to be a little township embosomed in encircling gardens. As I drew nearer, however, I

.saw what I had taken for a township was really a collection of buildings, apparently belonging to a large, white, low-roofed house, which stood on the edge of a slope of vineyard. It was evident that some settler, more adventurous than his neighbours, had penetrated the mysteries of the mountain, and had set up his abode in this fertile and charming valley. Wallaby Dick had indeed discovered a pleasant place in which to spend his holidays! Descending the track, which soon widened into a broad and well-kept road, I pulled the hanging handle of a bell which was suspended from a lofty wooden gateway before a huge and nail-studded door. The echo of my summons had not died away when the door was flung open, and Wallaby Dick himself appeared, his face no longer wrathful or ill-humoured, but beaming with smiles of welcome.

The appearance of the old man made me start. "You here, Wallaby? Why, what mystery is this?"

"No mystery," said Wallaby, with the merriest laugh I had ever heard from his lips. "I have arrived before you, that is all. Come in; you are expected."

"Expected! Then what place is this?"

"It's got a lot o' names," said Wallaby. "Some calls it one thing, and some another. I call it Holiday Peak, because I comes here for my holidays; but it's known to many folks as Mount Might-ha-been."

"Many travellers stop here, it appears?" I enquired.

"Oh yes," said the old fellow, hobbling off with my horse. "Most people passing this way stop here for a night, at all events, especially about the beginning of the new year. However, you go in, and I'll show you round by-and-by."

I went through the court-yard, and up the broad stone steps into an open space or square, in the midst of which a fountain played. Ah Yung was standing at the door of a queer little pagoda. No longer the greasy Chinaman cook, he was dressed with great splendour in the fashion of his country, and, bowing, invited me in. The house was wonderfully furnished. A Chinese woman, of pleasing countenance, sat on a low cane-chair, nursing a baby, and a domestic squatted on his hams in a corner of the verandah, filling the bowl of Ah Yung's capacious pipe. Through the open lattice-work I saw spreading paddy-fields, and could catch the monotonous song of the stalwart river coolies as they propelled their heavily-laden barges up the river.

"All this is mine!" said Ah Yung, embracing with one sweep of his hand the furniture, the matron, the fat baby, the opium-pipe, and the paddy-fields.

"All yours! But if you own so fine a property, why do you work as cook in the men's huts?"

"Cook in the men's hut! What do you mean?" returned he with a pitying smile. "Me no cook. Me Chinee gentleman. Me *mightabeen* cook if me run away on board ship, and go fool my money in lottery!"

I turned away bewilderingly, and found myself face to face with my old college friend, Jack Reckless.

"Jack Reckless!" I cried, astonished at this new apparition. "Why, man, I thought you were——"

"Don't be afraid of saying it," said Jack, cheerily, though a touch of sadness caused his voice to quiver. "You thought I was in gaol for forging Huxtable's name to a bill. No, thank God, my boy! *I might have been*, but instead of yielding to the devilish temptation, I told my dear old father all about my debts and duns, and a year or two of economy set all right. You shall come over by-and-by, and see my wife. You remember little Lucy?"

"Little Lucy! Yes;—but wasn't that dreadful story true?"

"True! No. She saw through the scoundrel's pretended affection, and as I was out of debt, and in a fair way of doing well, married *me* instead of running away with *him*. But I must go to the farm now," he concluded, pointing to a picturesque roof that nestled in a pretty English landscape; "I call for you to-morrow."

I walked up the lime-tree avenue which led to the Old Manse more bewildered than ever. Then the terrible story of sin and shame which had wrecked two homes was but a fiction after all? My spirits rose with the thought; indeed, gazing on that lovely garden, stretching terrace after terrace, away to the crystal river, it was difficult to harbour thoughts of sorrow or of suffering, and I felt, as I drank in the pure clear air of the mountains, almost as vigorous as Dombie, who, no longer blear-eyed and palsied with excess of tobacco and rum, but young, healthy, and hopeful, dashed past me with a "Hulloa!" making hard for a flock of emu yonder.

Passing by an old house which stood back from the others in the terrace, my attention was caught by a crimson scarf trailing from one of the upper windows. "An artist lives there," was my first thought, for nowhere in the world but in the pictures of Prout do we see bits of colour floating about in that fashion. "Yes, you are right," said a young man emerging from the well-dressed crowd which throngs in spring the steps of the Academy.

It was Gerard! Gerard, my boy friend, who fled from Oxford to Stonyhurst, and embraced the discipline of Loyola.

"Gerard, what means this?"

"Dear old fellow," said he, putting his arm round my neck in the fond old schoolboy fashion, "it means that I thought better of my resolve, and followed out the natural bent of my talents. My picture, the 'Death of Alcibiades,' is the talk of the year. I shall soon be as famous as you."

"As I. You jest. A poor devil banished to Bush Land, tied neck and heels in debt, soon slips out of the memory even of his friends."

"So you persist in that dream out Australia! Surely you know that the fortune was recovered, and that your year of poverty but served to correct your boyish extravagances, and that in easy circumstances you banished Poins and Pistol, and settled down to the career you chose!"

"Gerard, you are laughing at me!"

"Come into your house, then, and be convinced," said Gerard.

My house, it appeared, was a villa at Richmond. The railway-station was sufficiently near to take me into town when town-talk was needed, and yet the cottage in its charm of park and river was sufficiently far away from London smoke to suffer one's soul to breathe freely.

"I wonder," said Gerard, "that with the horses you keep, you *ever* travel by the train?"

"My horses, then, are considered good?"

"Horses and books are your only extravagances. It is lucky that your income is not sufficiently large to suffer you to indulge a taste for pictures. You had better put down your yacht, and buy my 'Death of Cromwell.'"

"No, no," said I, dreamily, accepting this novel position; "I always had a taste for yachting;—but come in and let us converse."

"You dine with Carabas to-night, remember," said Gerard; "Ballhazar Claes and Byles Gridley will be there. I know you affect to dislike dinners, but the marchioness is a good soul, and you must not disappoint her."

"True," said I, "she is; and after presenting my eldest daughter too. I shall certainly come."

"The *Superfine Review* has cut up your book as usual," remarked Gerard, turning over the papers on the horse-shoe table; "but to an author whose readers are counted by millions, and to whom Bentley gives £5,000 a volume, a sneer in the *Superfine* is not of much consequence."

"No, indeed," I replied, feeling much as if someone had taken away my head and left me a bubble of air in the place of it. "Besides, I write for the *Slaughterer*, and the two papers are at daggers drawn."

"Ah! lucky fellow," said Gerard, throwing open the window to inhale the perfume of my rose-garden. "How different things *might have been* if you hadn't taken your uncle's advice."

"You are right," said I, "but help yourself to wine, and let us walk somewhere. To tell you the truth, my head feels a little queer this morning."

"That is often the case," returned Gerard, "when first one comes to Holiday Peak, but you will soon get used to our mountain air. Order your horses, and we will go and call on Mostyn. He didn't marry the widow after all, and is still the same jolly fellow as of old."

"Aye, I remember how he used to take me up from Aldershot in the baggage-train, and introduce to my schoolboy eyesight the wonders of London at midnight. Pray, are the Armida Gardens still existent?"

"I don't know what you mean. Mostyn never took you to London with him. You were never in the Armida Gardens in all your life."

"Thank goodness, Gerard! Are you sure?"

"Quite certain. You *might have* wasted your youth in such places, and got into no end of mischief, had not your father kept such a strict and friendly eye upon you."

"Ah," said I, "you are right. Let us, then, remain at home to-day. Mostyn can wait."

"As you please," said Gerard. "Here is the end of *Denis Duval.* Have you read it?"

"The end of *Denis Duval!* Why, poor Thackeray died before he finished it."

"Nonsense! He is as hearty as you or I. I met him at Dickens's (they are great friends now, you know) the other day, and he never looked better. If it had not been for his excellent constitution, and the attention of Dr. Lydgate, however, he might have been dead long ago."

"Gerard, my dear fellow," said I, rising. "I—I feel a little confused; leave me for a while. We will meet at dinner."

"Very well," said Gerard. "I will take Constantia for a drive."

"Constantia! What, not the girl we——"

"The same, dear old fellow."

"And she did not marry Count Caskowisky?"

"Count Caskowisky be confounded! No; she married me. We have three children. *Sans adieu!*"

I fell back in my easy chair, *my* easy chair, stupefied. I must be dreaming! But no, the well-bred presence of my Swiss valet, as he laid out my dress clothes, was too palpable a reality!

＊   ＊   ＊   ＊   ＊   ＊

The most noble the Marquis of Carabas lived at Grosvenor Gate, and it seemed to me that my five-hundred-guinea horses had never accomplished the distance in so short a time. Scarcely had I entered the carriage when I was sitting beside the marchioness, and pulling Julie's silken ears with all the freedom of an old acquaintance. Vivien Grey and I were the only persons allowed that privilege, but since his marriage with Violet Fane, he had resided principally abroad.

"So you have returned at last," said the marchioness. "You and the count have the reputation of being the most erratic pair in Europe.

The tall, thin, pale man, with the wonderful eyes, bowed slightly.

"The Countess of Monte Christo," said he, "has ordered me to give up travelling."

"And you obey?"

"Yes. I am tired of having my own way," said Monte Christo. "Omnipotence becomes wearisome. Moreover, I have pensioned Bertuccio and sold my island."

'Indeed? To whom?"

"To an Australian wine-grower. He finds the rick admirably suited to the growth of White Ivanhoe, and he has turned my cavern into cellars. Faria and he are planning a press on a new principle."

"Then M. L'Abbé recovered from his attack?" I enquired.

"Certainly. A few seconds after I had taken that involuntary leap into the sea from the summit of the Chateau D'If, the gaoler returned, gave my poor friend another dose of the cordial, and revived him to rejoice in the pardon sent by the Emperor. He is the tutor of my eldest son, Morcuf Villefort Danglars. Ah! Marchioness, if you could only see our little family circle, you would deem me the happiest man in Christendom. Dear Danglars! How I long to press his honest hand once more! Poor fellow, what enemies we *might have been* had the story Dumas chose to invent been true."

Lord and Lady Byron sat opposite to me, Balzac being between them.

"It is needful that some man of sense should separate so absurdly affectionate a pair," benevolent Lord Steyne whispered to me, "for they cannot keep from cooing even at dinner. By the way, Mrs. Crawley, I visited your orphanage to-day, and must congratulate you upon the excellent use you have made of poor Miss Crawley's fortune."

Sweet Becky lifted her guileless eyes, and smiled. "Ah, Lord Steyne, it is Rawdon whom you should praise—not me. He has quite a genius for charity."

"I will bet fifty guineas that Steyne has been giving another cheque," whispered the Rev. Henry Foker; "that man's charities are unbounded."

"I thought ——" I stammered.

"I know," said Archdeacon Castigan, "you thought Wenham's confounded story was *true!* Ah me, dear sir, what is, and what might have been are two very different things. For instance, Newcome yonder might have married Miss Mackenzie—that is the present Mrs. Foker—had not Lady Kew insisted upon dowering Ethel with her fortune, Sir Barnes, and Lady Highgate begged me to carry her compliments to Lady Clara. I discharge my duty!"

Good simple-minded Sir Barnes smiled. "Tell Highgate I am angry at his absence. He never comes to Newcome now."

At the other end of the table they were talking of the unfortunate condition of Prussia.

"I am told had it not been for the French subscription, whole families would have perished of hunger," said Steerforth. "And yet think how different things might have been had Bazaine been defeated," returned Sir Montague Tigg.

"Might have been! yes. The 'Anglo-Bengalie' *might* have been wrecked, with other institutions of a similar character," laughed Bishop Prindie in the ear of Indiana.

"But M. Teeg is such a financier! My husband thinks him unequalled."

"But your husband is so well-bred a gentleman, madam, that he thinks well of everyone."

＊　　＊　　·　＊　　＊　　＊

The conversation made my head ache, and I seized the earliest opportunity to escape.

"Come to the club," said Warrington, "and smoke a cigar. Laura is away on a visit to Mrs. Pen, and I am a bachelor."

"Did you marry Laura, then? I thought that ——."

"That I had married someone else. No, thank God; I was very near it, though."

The club was full. Fermer and his crony Romaine, as usual, were the life of the smoking-room. George Gentle (of Fen Court), was playing Mr. Cassaubon at billiards, Major-General Hinton and Colonel Lorrequer betting on the game.

"So Monsoon has turned trappist," said Prince Djalma to Admiral Cuttle, K.C.B. "Who would have expected such a thing?"

"*L'homme propose, mais Dieu dispose*," returned the Admiral.

"For which overhaul your conversations-lexicon. Jack Bunsby became a local preacher."

The Prince puffed his cigar meditatively. "A fine woman the Macstinger," said he, "I don't wonder that *ce cher Bunsby* broke his heart at her refusal of his hand. But, then, who could resist Fosco."

"Save Quilp, I seldom met a more fascinating man," said Guy Livingstone. "He is too fond of violent exercise though, for *my* taste. I detest your muscular heroes."

"Who does not?" said Kingsley, from the little table where he sat with Dr. Newman and Swinburne. "Algernon, we're four by honours?"

"And the odd trick," interjected Antonelli. "I decline to take advantage of an adversary."

"Surely," I thought, punching myself violently. "I *must be* dreaming."

"Then do not strive to awake my friend," said a gentle-voiced little gentleman, sucking a Trabuco. "It is good to dream."

"Who is that?" I whispered to Singleton Fentenoy, as we descended the steps.

"Pio Nono. The Baptists allow him one hundred and fifty pounds a year, and he lodges over a hatter's in Piccadilly."

•   *   •   *   *

Fentenoy and I strolled down the Haymarket, and the familiar faces passed and repassed us. There is but little variety, after all, in life. We had both been absent from England during twenty years, and here the same music was resounding, the same eyes glittering, the same laughter ringing. There was, however, a strange reality about it all that saddened me.

"Singleton, do you remember when you thought that tawdry ball-room a palace, those silly fellows yonder the most daring of rakes, and those poor half-educated, good-hearted girls the equals of Ninon de L'enclos, and Faustina Imperatrex? Let us go away ; I am memory burdened."

We walked onwards, and by-and-by found ourselves near Notting Hill. Singleton paused at the gate of a little villa, and pointed to the windows. The blinds were drawn up, and I saw, seated in a pleasant drawing-room, a young lady—it was Jenny—

> "Lazy, laughing, languid Jenny,
> Fond of a kiss, and fond of a guinea.

Her face brought back to me a strange dream of boy-and-girl folly, of a merry, thoughtless flight by train and boat, made dishes, French wines, babble, kisses, tears, and no pocket-money.

"But I thought Lord Dagon had discovered in my funny little friend a *bonne* worthy of his purse."

"*Your* funny little friend! What do you mean? She married the respectable grocer, and never heard of Lord Dagon except in the newspapers. It was fortunate that you went to Scotland as you intended though, for there might have been mischief."

"Good heavens!" I said, "am I then to believe that everything has happened as it should have happened, and that I have no regrets."

But Singleton had gone, and I was alone above the broad terrace above the moon lighted garden.

* * * * *

Tier upon tier swept upwards to the castle-crag the busky slopes of verdure. Pierced with alleys of bloom, gleaming with statues, musical with fountains, the marvellous gardens of the palace lay sleeping beneath the moon, even as they had slept when the Fairy-Prince leapt the briar-hedge to win with daring kiss his enchanted bride. The mellow lights in the pavilion of the Arabian jeweller shone in the waters of the lake. I heard the silvery laugh of Noureddin's Persian, and could distinguish the gilded barge of the great Caliph, as, encompassed with barbaric music, panoplied in Eastern pomp, he moved towards the mysterious city. There, crowded with the misty halo of its myriad lamps, the great Babylon lay beneath me in the valley. At the white-stone breadth of the quay swung the rising tide of a hundred argosies. All of squallor, misery, and sin was hidden, and the majestic angel on the doomed summit of the great cathedral seemed to plume his shining vans for upward flight into the clear cold purity of the star-sprinkled heavens.

This, then, was the world of which I had dreamt, and that other sordid one in which I had lived so long was but a dream! How often a truant schoolboy, in depths of summer woods, garlanded with cool hyacinth, and couched on rustling fern, had I not seen this fair world! How often lying awake, while the breeze piped shrill across the coldly tossing sea, had I not beheld these glories of land and lake, of spired city and embattlemented rock. How often weary and hot with folly or with toil, had not that magnificent moon swum up into heaven to soothe and comfort me. Here, then, was Atlantis, here the Fortunate Isles, the Valley of Avilion, the true El Dorado—the wondrous Land of Might-have-been!

As one entranced in waking slumber, I moved through the portal, where frowning in war-like steel, sat ready horsed for combat the guard of Barbarussa. Charlemagne and Arthur had come again, and Duraudel gleamed once more in the grasp of risen Roland. The mighty laughter of the heroes shook the hall, and the smile of happy Metaine was reflected in the lips of gentle Aude. Yes, it was true! —chivalry lived still, and smug tradesmen, rejoicing in the science of money-breeding, had not beaten honesty and love to death with their yard-measures. All around me were beauty, truth, and honour, and serene in the midst of great and noble souls, I felt my spirit

111

strengthened and sustained. At length, above a door of ivory, half hidden by a purple curtain, I saw, perched upon the bust of Pallas, the mocking figure of a raven. The door yielded and I entered. I was in a long apartment, going on a balcony open to the night; as I entered, a lady clad in white came towards me. I knew her at once. It was the Lady Lenore.

Lenore! The lost Lenore. She who forever waits and forever eludes our passionate arms. Dante called her Beatrice, Petrarch Laura, Burns knew her as Mary, Byron as———— but why multiply names? She is for all of us, this impossible woman. Name her yourself, dear reader, lounging on the club sofa, wiling away an hour before dinner with this silly story. You are very cynical and pleasant now, and worship your stomach complacently. But there *was* a time, was there not, when "you were young, and songs were sung, and love-lamps in the casements hung," when something might have been that was not and never will now be? Or will *you* name this little figure with the sad sweet eyes—are they brown or grey for you? Oh! prosperous and well-dined merchant, musing with your fond children round your knees, and your faithful wife smiling cheerily at the end of the table? You love your wife and children, but, but—was there not—is there not—an ideal somewhere in your heart, albeit shut up and locked down, and the Family Bible laid at the top of it? Yes, she exists; here, in the land of might-have-been, call her by what name you will.

"Lenore!"

She gave me two cool hands and kissed me.

"At last, then! At last. Lenore! The Raven prophesied falsely. Our pain and sorrow, our 'strange, unsatisfied longing,' are over, and at last—oh, other half of my soul—I have and hold thee!"

She did not speak, but her eyes said more than words, and her slight figure trembled in my arms.

I drew her to the window, and with brain and blood on fire, pointed to the vessels at anchor at the quay.

"Whether this strange land be a land of shadows, I know not; but I know that *thou* art real. Come my love, come; see the boat lies below. Let us leave this place."

She raised her head from my shoulder, and looked around. In the far east, where the waves tumbled white upon the shore, trembled the dawn. The moon was fading, the city, the river and the enchanted gardens lay lapped in a mysterious light—alas!

"The light that never was on sea or land,
The consecration and the poet's dream."

"Come," I repeated; "stern Heaven is kind at last, and we have met, why should we part again?"

But even as I pleaded, in tones that had perhaps too much of earth in them for that fair spirit, she seemed to withdraw from me. One glance, sad and tender, pitying and hopeful, thrilled me, a farewell kiss, pure as fire, light as a falling rose-leaf hushed my lips, and—I was alone.

Alone upon the triform hill whose mysterious altars reddened in the risen dawn. My holiday was over.

*   *   *   *   *   *   *

Little Nelly (*to the story-teller*)—"But Mr. Marston, did you not go back to Holiday Peak?"

Marston—"I did not know the way, my dear."

Little Nelly—"But there must *be* a way. If so many people stop there, a coach should go near the place."

Marston—"There is a coach that goes to the very door, little one—a coach by which we must all travel one of these days—a black coach drawn by black horses. Some day they will take me when I am sleeping soundly, and put me into a big box, nail me up, and put on the lid a neat brass plate :—

'JOHN MARSTON,

' ÆTAT —,

'FOR HOLIDAY PEAK. WITH CARE.

' *This Side Up.*'

"GOOD-NIGHT."

"HORACE" IN THE BUSH.

THE coach had broken down at Bullocktown, and we five—that is to say, O'Donoghue, Marston, Tom Dibdin, McTaggart and myself—were partaking of eggs, bacon and whisky at Coppinger's.

"I fear I shall be late," said classic Marston, a professor at the Melbourne University, who had been holiday-making with us, "the examinations are on Tuesday."

"Time eneuch to harry the puir deevils," said compassionate M'Taggart, the squatter, of Glenclunie.

"Hould yer whist," interrupted O'Donoghue, "the professor's thinkin' of how he'll bamboozle the bhoys. If he wasn't quoting Aristophanes in the coach, I mistook the jolting o' the vayhicle for the full-mouthed sintences o' that roarin' ould haythen."

"O'Donoghue, you are personal. I never quote Greek."

"Widout book, ye old imposthor ! Marsthon, I dispise ye.

'εἴ σὲ μὴ μισῶ, γενοίμην ἐν Κρατίνου κώδιον,
καὶ διδασκοίμην πρόσᾳδειν Μορσίμου τραγῳδίαν.'

Ev I don't hate ye may I be cut up into copy-paper and have *Argus* leaders scribbled upon me."

"In truth," returned Marston, lighting his pipe with a fire-stick, "I was thinking rather of the Latin than the Greek."

"It is much the same," said I rashly, "the Latins prigged their good things wholesale."

"No, by the mass ! "

"Look at that elegant robber Horace. The '*O sæpe mecum*' ode is a calm theft from Alcæus."

"Pardon me, sir," said a voice at the door, "You do the friend of Virgil an injustice. He is rather sinned against than sinning."

We turned and saw the box passenger, a comfortable, well-dressed fellow with blear eyes.

"Do you mean to say," cried Marston, fired at the interruption, "that Horace did not copy from the Greek ? Why, that elegant Epicurean was swaddled in Greek literature. The classics of his day were birched into him by old Orbilius. He was Greek even in his politics, first a republican, and then a monarchist."

"He has been copied even in that," said the new comer ; "there is nothing like free land selection to make your radicals conservative. If the Ministry will give me a Sabine farm I'll cultivate my dried olive, sit under my preserved fig-tree, and vote for them in all particulars."

"Horace was a mean man," said M'Taggart, "for I've heard that he wrote mony a screed against old Mecænas before he got his patronage."

"The rumour is untrue," says the stranger. "You mean that nonsense about the trailing gown, I presume? The charge was never proved sir."

"I admit it," said the professor, "'twas a calumny."

"He was jist a weathercock," cries M'Taggart," a time-serving rogue, blown aboot wi' every blast o' doctrine."

"He began life as a patriot."

"A youthful indiscretion," said the urbane intruder. "He afterwards repented, and went —— to his villa."

"Faix, he jist sold himself for a Government billet, like many an honest man before and since," laughed jolly O'Donoghue.

"The *res angusta domi*, and being in debt to the butcher, will do much to change a man's opinions," returned the stranger. "What says the bard himself! ' *Aurum per medios ire satellites.*'

> ' Danae grim-guarded in her brazen tower,
>   With dogs and double-doors 'gainst those who sought her,
>   Fell a sweet victim to this mighty power
>   Of half-a-crown bestowed upon the porter.' "

Marston started.

"You seem familiar with the poet," said he.

The stranger smiled sadly.

"Sir," he answered, "I have spent my life in exposing plagiarisms from my—from Horace's writings. It is melancholy to see how the so-called 'original' writers have pilfered from the ancients."

"Sit down, sir, and join us!" cries Marston, fairly astride his hobby. "What will you take?"

"You have no Massic?" asked the guest, seating himself.

"To be sure we have," says honest Dibdin. "Coppinger, hot whisky to the gentleman."

The stranger smiled and proceeded. "The moderns are thieves."

"They are," said Marston. "I agree with you. Tennyson owes his being to Theocritus."

"Keates smacked of him."

"No, *his* plagiarism was unconscious genius. 'Hyperion' might have been a fragment of Æschylus, and yet the doctor's boy was ignorant of Greek."

"I don't think," said I "that our Australian writers can be accused of plagiarising from the Latin. I have observed that quotations printed or spoken are mostly wrong."

"Cynic."

"Your Australians are not plagiarists!" cries our guest, swallowing his whisky at a gulp. "'Ye powers that smile on virtuous theft!' But two days since the editor of the *Dead Horse Gully Tribune* inserted the following as original poetry. You will see that the idea is stolen from Horace, the ninth ode of the first book beginning—

> ' Vides ut altâ, stet nive candidum
> Soracte.'

The fellow had the impertinence to call it ' The Squatter's Advice to his Nephew,'" and helping himself to another jorum, our visitor warbled—

" (Air—" *Rosin the Beau.*")

" Come, Jack, draw your rocking-chair nigher,
  Mount Macedon's white with the snow ;
Pitch another pine log on the fire,
  And tip us ' Old Rosin the Beau.'

I ne'er saw the bush look so barren
  (When I rode out this morning with Sam),
And last night—so I'm told by M'Claren—
  There's something like ice on the dam.

Let it slide. To us all heaven's handy,*
  To the cold ground we one day must go ;
In the meantime—that's Hennessy's brandy
  Sit down, lad, and rosin your bow.

Who knows what may happen to-morrow,
  What lot is our ultimate fate ;
There are some who rejoice to court sorrow—
  I d rather be courting of Kate.

God gave lasses and glasses to men, Jack—
  'Twould be wrong not to use them, you know ;
When you're bald as a bandicoot, *then*, Jack,
  'Twill be time to be solemn and slow.

CHORUS.

In the spring time, life's music was playing,
  Do we pause in the melody's flow ;
In the winter—the cause for delaying
  Is, of course, Jack, to rosin the bow ! "

" Euge ! Euge ! " cried Marston, " but the last verse is *not a* paraphrase on the original."

" True," said the stranger, " the last verse contains an allusion that likes me not. The ' *risus ab angulo*,' the ' laugh from the corner' might be thought to hint at Ballarat and its Stock Exchange."

" By the mass " says O'Donoghue, " but the strain is worthy of Trinity. ' *Leonum arida nutrix.*' Mac, ye spalpeen, I feel my heart big within me, and could break your head for the honour o' ould Ireland on the sloightest provocation."

" True indeed for—

> ' Baktrion epi tauton me gar de melathalainon.
> Poluphlois ketikimboun, kai kikety rolopoloios,' "

said I.

---

* Heaven is above all.—" Cassio.

116

"If that's not Homer, it's mighty like him," cries O'Donoghue. 'Ah, ye deceaver, it's gibberish you're talking. Marston, hand me the impty bottle that I may throw it at him."

"Brawling in your cups, gentlemen! Fie! that is but barbarian at best. As Horace says—

> 'Natis in usum lætitiæ scyphis,
> Pugnare Thracum est,'

or, as a countryman of your friend's has translated it—

> 'To foight over punch is like Donnybrook fair,
> When an Irishman, all in his glory, is there.
> Hould your whist! see the combatants, Bacchus between,
> With that sprig of shillalagh, his Thyrsus so green!'"

"Sir," said O'Donoghue, in great heat, "you wrong the illustrious composer of that ancient melody. The janius o' Paddy Macguire never stooped to copy. But you don't drink; the whisky is with you."

"*Non sum qualis eram, bonæ sub regno Cinaræ,*" said the red-eyed stranger. "I am not the man I was when I supped with Lola Montes. I have poor and unhappy brains for drinking. I mingle my liquors with water, and one amphora of Reisling will set my brain-pan bubbling."

"This is a quaint fellow," whispered Marston to me. "Let us draw him out. Though he avows himself a model of sobriety, there is a twinkle in his eye that speaks an application for grape-juice. I hate your dry talks. Coppinger! another bottle of whisky! Sir, I salute you."

"I looks towards you, sir, and likewise bows."

"The whisky will open his heart," said Marston.

> 'εἶτα δ' ἔνδοθεν
> τὴν γλῶτταν ἐξείραντες αὐ-
> τοῦ σκεψόμεσθ' ἐν κἀνδρίκῶς
> κεχηνότος
> τὸν πρωκτὸν, εἰ χαλαζᾳ.'

"We'll drag out his tongue, and while the sinner gapes, look for spots of plagiarism in his entrails!"

"Steady!" cried M'Taggart, "the chiel hasna proved his case! That the Southern pooets may grab frae Horace, I mak' nae doot o'; but the Scotch! Eh, man, whar's your plagiarism in Rabbie Burrrns?"

The stranger tossed off a mutchkin o' Glenlivet, and smiled a ghastly smile. "Rabbie Burns," said he, in a strong Scotch accent, "was just the biggest leear and thief extaunt. Leesten to this, mon," and again he sang—

> "MY NANCY O!
> "I've lately lived amang the girls,
> And fought not wi'oot glory O!
> But now nae mair they tug my curls,
> My pow is getting hoary O!

Hang up my staff o mickle micht,
  My pipes fa' tapsalterie O !
Hang up my lantern, by whose licht,
  I clambered to my deary O !

O Venus, dear, I'm fidgin' fain,
  Come down and ease my fancy, O !
O' a' the girls I lo'e but ane,
  Ah, leeze me on my Nancy O !"

"Now, sir," said the songster, "if that is not an impudent transcription of '*vixi puellis nuper idoneus*,' the twenty-sixth ode of the third book, bray me in a mortar, and daub the walls of a printing-house with me. *Retro Sathanas!*"

"Sir !" cried the Scotchman, amid the laughter of the company, " Rab never wrote those lines. I defy you to prove him a plagiarist. May I never sup parritch again if Rab was not a genius of Heaven's ain makin'. He combined, sir, the antitheses o' Pope, wi' the tenderness o' Herrick. Byron only surpassed him, in his love deeties and ——"

"Horace, in his moments o' leesure," interrupted the stranger. "Stuff, my good sir ! '*Fœnum habes in cornu.*' You have a bannock 'o barley meal skewered tae yer bonnet. I'll sing ye a mair rantin' melody, *a carmen seculare*, a ditty not fitted for churchgoers. (Alas ! *parcus deorum cultor et infrequens*, I have only been twice to the new Scotch Kirk since I came to Melbourne), and I will ask you to judge calmly. Horace's ode begins '*Vitas hinnuleo me similis Chloe.*' 'Tis the twenty-third of the first book, as I need not remind you. The impertinent gauger paraphrases it thus :——

    " To Peggy.

" Hoot ! why like a cantie heifer,
Skippin' at each breathin' zephyr,
  Bonnie Peggy, fly me !
Though but rough my manners be,
They're no sae rough tae flechter thee ;
Peggy, lassie, gang wi' me—
  Sonsie Peggy, try me !

I'm nae bleth'rin, rantin' laddie,
But thy bairns maun hae a daddie ;
  Bonnie Peggy, try me !
Thy mither says 'tis time to wed ;
Mithers must be no gainsaid—
Come and mak' thy weddin' bed,
  Bonnie Peggy, by me !"

"Maist indecent, sir," said M'Taggart. "I'll no believe it o' Rabbie. And yet I confess that the similes are unco alike."

Marston burst into Homeric laughter.

"*Virginibus puerisque canto*," said our guest with a blush. "I'm singing-master at the common school, and am not used to such warmth of language—save on occasions."

"Faith, then, this is one of them," said O'Donoghue. "There's Dibdin half-seas-over already. It takes an Irishman to drink whisky.

Your English brains sop beer like sponges, but the thrue nectar of the gods intoxicates their dull sowls."

"The gentleman has b—bowled you all out," said Dibdin, huskily, "but my grandfather, poor Ch—Charles, is at least spared. He was n—no p—p—plagiarist."

"Dibdin!" cried the stranger, leaping to his feet with an agility which in a person *teres atque rotundus* was simply marvellous. "Charles Dibdin! The most unblushing scoundrel of them all! That '*O sæpe mecum*' ode of which you were speaking when I entered has been transferred bodily to Dibdin's pages in the following infamous travistie :—

"JACK JUNK'S RETURN TO WAPPING.

"Jack Junk, my old comrade, what fortunate breeze
    Has blown you to Wapping and me?
Jack Junk, with whom often I ploughed the salt seas,
    When Blake sailed to Trincomalee.

Jack Junk, by the Lord, lad, how often we've sat
    In the fok'sel in boisterous weather,
And greased our pig-tails with the primest o' fat,
    And swigged at the grog-can together.

D'ye mind how I fared, Jack, at Spirito Bar,
    When the Portuguese boarded the wreck,
And, o'erpowered by numbers, full many a tar
    Gasped his honest life out on the deck?

It was touch and go, Jack, for my heart was grown soft,
    And thumped at my ribs like a knocker;
But that sweet little cherub that sits up aloft,
    Snatched Tom Pipes from old Davy Jones' locker!

I've been in a few stiffish fights in my life,
    But in that one I own I felt queer,
Though I chiefly regret that I left poor Poll's knife
    In the ribs of that bloody mounseer.*

I got my discharge, Jack, and warped into port,
    And the glass of life's fortune set fair;
But you—you old sea-dog—who by my side fought,
    Must needs ship in the old 'Temeraire.'

Shove your wooden leg under the table, my lad!
    The egg's fresh, the rasher is flaky;
Here's a quid of tibbacky, the best can be had,
    And a can of right rousing Jammaiky!

So bouse round the bowl! Fill again! Damn my eyes,
    To get drunk with a shipmate is proper!
I drink first! No! Well, lest a dispute should arise,
    We'll decide it by skying a copper.†

Now wet t'other eye, man! Poll, lass, me old wife,
    It ain't often I get on the spree;
But if ever I mean to get sprung in my life,
    It is now! with Jack Junk home from sea!"

---

* "Poor Poll's knife." How different in tone from the graceful *Relicta non bene parmula.*
† A most impudent rendering of the elegant original. *Quem Venus arbitrium dicet bibendi.*

"Hear ! hear !" roared the Professor, banging on the table,
"*Habet ! Habet !* He's got it, by Hercules ! A delicate paraphrase,
if ever there was one."

But Dibdin snored unconscious.

"Another strain, O most musical of strangers ! No ? Another
drink then ! "

"We won't go home till morning," roars O'Donoghue, "*dum
rediens jugat asthra Phaybus.* Till the early milk froightens the cats
from door-step. Hurroo ! *Nunc pede libero pulsanda tellus.* Now's
the time to shake a loose leg, boys ! "

"Let us batter down a door," cries M'Taggart.

"Or filch a sign," says Marston.

"There's the barber down the street," hiccups the classical
stranger. "*Obsceno ruber porrectus ab (hic) palus*, with a thundering
great red pole stuck out of his dirty little shop window ! Let's have
that ! "

"*Quo me Bacche rapis tui plenum*," exclaimed I, feeling the
whisky impelling me to recklessness.

"Another song, a classic ditty !" cries Marston. "Tip us a
stave of modern Roman, my jovial, pot-walloping blade ! "

"*Absit somnus !* Let slape quit me for iver if I go to bed this
night.

' οἶαν δίκην τοῖς κύρεσι δώσω τήμερον.'

Och, Stony Stratford's a fool to Coppinger's."

Dibdin, waking from his slumbers, began to sing—

> " I'm bound to win, when I go in,
> Tommy Dodd ! Tommy Dodd !
> Heads or tails, I'm bound to win,
> Hurrah for Tommy Dodd ! "

"Peace, wretch !" roared our guest. "Insult not the *manes* of
the dead ! That ditty was Marcus Tullius Cicero's, and while *I*
live shall be sung in the original. Come, gentlemen, a chorus—

> "'Civis nam Romanus sum,
> Cicero ! Cicero !
> Ergo semper Vinco, quum,
> Ineo ! Ineo !
> Sortem spargant aleæ,
> Gaudeo ! Gaudeo !
> Seu Venus, seu Caniculæ,
> Evoé ! Cicero ! ' "

Dibdin did not show in the morning; but I, having a slight head-
ache, went down to breathe the fresh air, and take a brandy and soda.

At the bar were M'Taggart and Marston consulting Coppinger.

"Went away in a buggy at six this morning to Quartzborough,"
said Marston. "Who can he be ? "

All were silent.

"Don't *you* know the stranger's name, Coppinger," said I.

"Mr. Flack, I think he said," replied Coppinger.   "'Q. H. F.' was on his portmanteau."

We stared at one another.

QUINTUS HORATIUS FLACCUS.

"It's impossible!" cried I.

"It's totally prepostherous!" said O'Donoghue.

"It's a metempsychosis!" suggested Marston.

"It's just whusky!" concluded M'Taggart.

SQUATTERS PAST AND PRESENT.

YESTERDAY afternoon, when reading the remarks of our latest critic, Mr. Anthony Trollope, upon Australian life and manners, I received almost simultaneously a letter from my old friend, Robin Ruff, of the Murrumbidgee, and a visit from my young acquaintance, Dudley Smooth (nephew to Lord Lytton's friend), of "Scott's Hotel." Both were squatters, both about equally wealthy, both good fellows in their way, both occupied nearly the same position in society, both were alike—and yet how widely different !

Robin Ruff, writing in a shaky hand, with honest independence of spelling, and hearty contempt for necessary doubling of consonants, sent a message to his grandson, and would I see Wether and Weaners' people about "them yowes." Robin Ruff is an old man. He is nearer seventy than sixty I should say ; but he is as erect as a dart, and can ride a long day's journey, or do a hard day's work, with many a younger man. He is six feet high, his hands are knotted and brown—mottled with sun, and hardened with labour. His shoulders are broad, his head well set on, his eye confident. His head is white, and his beard is white also, save that brown patch round the mouth that looks as if snuff had been spilt on it. In appearance he is not elegant. His coat is too big for him, and his hat is not of the fashionable mould. His boots are clumsy, and have thick soles, which creak as he walks. He carries a big oak stick, and wears a big silver watch. He looks very fierce indeed, and not at all a "lady's man ;" but people who know him well like him, and little children run to him at first sight.

Robin Ruff came to this colony in 1836, the year before Mr. Latrobe was made Superintendent. He had been squatting in Sydney before that, but hearing much of the "new colony," came over to better his fortunes. Old Ruff—long since put away comfortably in the kirkyard—had kept a little shop in a little Scotch town, and had saved a bit of money, but Robin, adventurous lad, wearied of the big grey hills and the quiet old straggling street, wearied even of his uncle's farm, with its dull round of ploughing, and sowing, and reaping, determined to seek his fortune. The old father advised, and the old mother wept beneath her horn spectacles, but Robin would go   Wise bodies at market assembled, predicted "nae guid" of the lad—(he rebuilt the market-hall the other day, with good Aberdeen granite)—and it was generally prophesied that he would bring his parents' grey hairs with sorrow to the grave.

For the first ten years of his Australian struggles he seemed likely enough to fulfil the worst of their prophecies. It was a hard fight, and little to get for it. But by steadiness and industry he got a little money together at last. The marvellous virtue that lies in sheer hard work brought him through after ten years, and made him independent. Arrived in the Port Phillip wilderness, up the country he went. Land was to be had easily enough in those days, and being his own bullock-driver and stockrider, and shepherd, and farmer and cook, Robin Ruff soon made a home for himself. He began to be looked upon as a " warm " man. Jolly boys carousing in Melbourne town, at the foundation of Prince's Bridge, spoke of Ruff's luck and cursed their own in genial fashion. By-and-by the great crash came. Sheep and cattle were worth nothing, and Ruff's luck seemed gone. But it turned again. He had bought land with his saved money, and when the " diggings broke out " (like an eruption, one would think), had recovered his losses.

He is an old man now, and people ask him why he doesn't " go Home and live ; " but he knows better. His daughter is married here, and his grandchildren are here too. He has his station to occupy his mind, his trips to Melbourne, his rubber, his pipe, his club, and his chats with other jolly old boys. How the old fellows chuckle as some quaint nickname, springing up in the conversation, recalls some hearty piece of jollity in the "old days ! " He did go home once, but he didn't like it. London was so lonely. He didn't like to pull out his old clay pipe in his dapper nephew's smoking-room, and when his niece talked French to him, and asked his opinion of the *mise en scène* at the opera he felt uncomfortable. He went to his native town, but his father and mother were dead, and he could remember nobody. A railway bridge spanned the burn where he paddled in his boyish days, and the Telegraph Office had been built where stood the tree on which he cut little Jeanie's name with his clasp-knife forty years before. He gave money to the local charities, and rebuilt the market-house, and for that the Town Council got at him and gave him a dinner, and a fat cheesemonger, with a turn for oratory, made speeches at him all the evening. Sickened, tired. and disappointed, he took his passage for Melbourne, and, smoking his pipe in the " Port Phillip Club," on the night of his arrival, with the old faces round him, inwardly vowed he would go home no more. He is not a brilliant fellow to talk to ; he is not aristocratic, nor even deistical ; but he is a fine, honest, kind-hearted old man, and has not been without his use in this brand-new go-ahead colony of ours.

As I looked up from his letter, I saw Mr. Smooth in the doorway. He was a very different stamp. Mr. Smooth was a very young gentleman. His hands were brown but well-kept, and his whiskers were of a fine yellow floss-silk order, like the down on a duckling. He had but lately come down from his station, but was arrayed in the most fashionable of fashionable garments. His trousers were so tight, that his legs looked as if they had been patented by some mono-manaic player on the flute, as cleaning machines for that instrument of music. His waistcoat yawned like a

123

whited sepulchre. He wore half-a-yard of black satin tied round his neck, or rather his shirt collar. His feet were encased in shoes of that high-heeled class affected by step dancers, and the suddenly expanded trouser-ends flapped around his ankles—entwined like two barber's poles, by the red stripes of his silk stockings. In addition to a gold hawser that swung heavily from buttonhole to pocket, and fluttered—so to speak—with lockets and charms, as though it were a clothesline on which such trinkets had been hung out to dry, he was spotted generally with jewellery. His manly breast was like nothing so much as Biddy's canvas-covered trunk studded with brass nails, and at his throat, and on his wrists, gleamed gigantic plates encircled with his name and date—I mean his crest and bearings. The crest of the Smooths is two flat-irons rampant, and from every available portion of my young friend's body gleamed golden repetitions of those time-honoured weapons. He wore a hat which seemed to have been made by an eccentric hatter, who in the midst of an attempt to imitate the head-covering of a sporting coal-heaver, had been stricken with remorse, and finished his handiwork with a haunting sense of the beauty of the episcopal broad-brim. His manner was affable and easy, he smoked a very strong cigar, and cursed only to that extent necessary and becoming in a man of fashion.

"Well, you melancholy old cuss," exclaimed this Arcadian youth, "how are you? Got any soda and B.? I was so dooced cut last night! Went knocking round with Swizzleford and Rattlebrain. C'sino, and V'ri'tes. Such a lark! Stole two Red Boots and a Brass Hat. Knocked down thirteen notes, and went to bed as tight as a fly!"

This and more he tells me—sitting the while on the end of my sofa, swinging his flute-cleaning legs, and puffing with his cigar, at an angle of forty-five degrees. His language is ornate and redundant of adjectives. Anything he doesn't like is "Beastly" or "Loathsome;" anything he does like is "Festive," "Sportive," "Ripping." He calls his father "a cheerful swell," or a "festive cuss," and when he goes to the theatre with his family, has been heard to allude periphrastically to his mother as a "square party in the boxes."

Mr. Smooth's papa—Dudley has been named after his uncle, for whom the family entertain a profound respect, as a man moving in good society,—came out here fifteen years ago and made his fortune by lucky speculation in land. He owns several stations, has a house in the hottest and most uncomfortable part of South Yarra, and is a most respectable person, with a stake in the country, and a tendency to stomach. He has placed Dudley on the Murriowooloomoolooneriangtrotolong station—he likes the fine old native names,—and that young gentleman is "managing" it at a fine rate.

Dudley is a great man on the Murrio, &c. He is called the "——boss," and lives in the "house," in contradistinction to the "hut." He also keeps his horses habitually in the stable, and feeds them with "oats"—tremendous achievement! He has a buggy and a trotting mare. Nobody says anything to him if he "coils" in the front parlour all the afternoon, and when he rides over to the little public-house and is condescendingly blasphemous towards the publican, the best brandy—*without* the Barret's twist at the bottom of the cask—is brought out in his honour. At mustering time he is in his glory—for, to do him justice, he can ride hard enough—and when he gets drunk at night, his stories are voted exceedingly humorous. He is, in his way, a sort of Epicurean. He despises the vanity which prompts honest John Strong of the Plains to jump over a hurdle with a fat wether under each arm; but he is very particular about the brightness of his stirrups, and is the only man on the station who has his boots cleaned every morning.

When he comes down from the country, he makes, as it were, a foray into an enemy's country. He does not enjoy himself during the day—the time hangs heavily. Having paid a visit to his father and mother, if they are in town, he "looks up a friend," and the two loaf aimlessly about the town. They may be seen "knocking the balls about" at "Scott's" or the "Port Phillip," or drinking "soda and b.," or "sherry and bitters," at any decent bar in town. If it is a "selling" day, you can meet them at Kirk's Horse Bazaar, lounging against the wall as though they owned so many blood-horses themselves that the sight of anything on four legs was wearisome. But it is at night when they enjoy life. What with the theatre and the café they feel quite like old *roués* by midnight, and stroll down to the Varieties or the Casino like a twinned Alcibiades in the Agora,—only they have never heard of the Alcibiades. There they drink, and smoke, and bask in the smiles of beauty. By two o'clock it is time to "knock round," and having supped at Cleal's, and the night Hansom having been duly chartered, Dudley and his friend take a tour in the provinces. It is possible that in the course of their peregrinations they meet Swizzleford and Rattlebrain, and then it is, ho, for the breakage of lamps, the carrying away of signs, the pretty larceny of gilt hats and wooden boots! Dudley is under the impression that his dancing society is much sought after by ladies, and behaves to those poor creatures in a tyrannically fascinating way, putting his name into their programmes with a tender violence that is quite affecting. He dances a little wildly, but with much vigour and height of action. He doesn't sing, but he can eat a great deal, and is fully alive to the fact that a tip to the waiter will secure a cool bottle of champagne for himself and friends, long after the general run of the guests are wearied of seeking refreshments and finding none. He plays billiards fairly, and is proud of his skill at pool. He makes a book on the races, and is almost as fond of losing as of winning. This promising young gentleman is two-and-twenty, and intends soon to go home and see the old country. He is quite complacent about it, and talks of "doing Europe" as he would of doing "Collins Street."

Let me, in conclusion, add only that Mr. Smooth has not a very strong sense of moral responsibility; for though he would not willingly do a dishonourable action, he is so impressed with the virtue of success, that a "smart" scoundrel is, in his eyes, a far more worthy

125

being than an honest dunderhead. He is making money, however, and has no reason to be otherwise just now than honest. His station is fitted with the latest improvements. His prize cattle are fattened on prize principles. His sheep are washed with hot water, and his paddocks are sown with English grass. He has not arrived at the glory of his next neighbour, the Hon. Tom Holles Street, younger son of the Marquis of Portman Square, who was educated at Oxford and Cirencester, and has taken up squatting on scientific principles. The Hon. Tom washes his sheep in an American dip at the rate of two hundred a minute, drafts cattle in lavender gloves, has nearly perfected a shearing machine, quotes Æschylus to his overseer, prohibits all swearing, except on Sundays, and has named his working-bullocks after the most distinguished of the early Christians. The Hon. Tom belongs to a later phase of development, and our young friend is far behind *him* in civilisation; but Dudley Smooth stands out in alarming contrast to poor, honest, simple-minded Robin Ruff.

THE FUTURE AUSTRALIAN RACE.

OUR ANCESTORS

THERE has been much vaguely talked and written about the Coming Man. There is certainly no doubt but that in a few years the inhabitants of the colony of Australasia will differ materially in their mental and physical characteristics from ourselves. Let us consider for a few moments why and in what probable respect this difference will occur.

The tendency of that abolition of boundaries which men call civilisation is to destroy individuality. The more railways, ships, wars, and international gatherings we have, the easier is it for men to change skies, to change food, to intermarry, to beget children from strange loins. The "type"—that is to say, the incarnated result of food, education, and climate—is lost. Men rolled together by the waves of social progress lose their angles and become smooth, round, differing in size only ; as differ, and remain similar, the stones of the sea beach. The effect of the increase of ease in the means of locomotion has been making itself apparent for the last three hundred years. With the discovery of the Americas there came upon all nations a sort of spirit of freedom and a desire for change. Though the terms "Greek" and "Roman" had been held to signify two distinct and certain forms of physiognomy, yet, in the feudal towns of *moyen age* Europe, were priest-artists who revived the one, and stern Crusaders who re-begat the other. The Moors brought the eagle beak of the East into Arabian Spain ; and the fair-haired Northmen, precursors of Columbus, sailing to the site of Boston city, bid their savage virtues live again in their descendant redskin warriors. The only "types" which have come down to predecessors of Columbus as unaltered, say the archæologists and the naturalists, are those of the Copt, the Ass, and the Hyæna. The Chaldean is much the same as he was pictured on the Ninevite marbles 3000 years ago, but in 1600 years the Egyptian has had far less change than the average face of the dweller by the Mediterranean knew during the three hundred years between the death of Phidias and the placing of the Castellani sarcophagus in the British Museum.

As for England, variation in national physiognomy is so astounding that one is tempted to suspect the representation as untrustworthy. Yet Holbein, Vandyke, Reynolds and Romney were fully competent to represent what they saw, and we are forced to admit that, from the chivalresque attitudes of Vandyke, through the sedate romance of Reynolds, to the grosser intelligence of Romney, and up again to the spiritual brightness of Richmond, the changes are true, though sudden. When we say of a portrait, "What an old-fashioned air," we are really saying, "That is the grandfather's face come back again." Even in the rudest times, and under the most unfavourable conditions, those who drew the human face did their best to copy the faces of their neighbours. An Egyptian artist never presented a fair-haired or round-eyed face as his type of beauty. An English manuscript-illuminator made his saints and virgins always delicate and blue-eyed. Through the clumsy handling of the monkish painters, we can still understand that our ancestors had, for the most part, rolling eyes, fleshy noses, larger at the tip than the bridge, long upper lips, strong chins, and coarse jaws. The long, symmetrical, oval face, with its arched eyebrows and melancholy air, has, in these days, disappeared. The Norman type is becoming absorbed. The face is square. The Danish eagle-beak—the characteristic of the predatory race—sinks down and broadens into the sensual and cogitative proboscis of the ruminating animal. Those stern eyes which glowered in the semi-darkness of a down-drawn visor have evanished. The cheeks, no longer pressed forward by the locked helmet plates, relieve the mouth and raise the corners of the lips. The nation, recovered from the Wars of the Roses, seems to breathe freely. A chastened air of spirituality is cast over the brows, and the features appear moulded by serious thoughts and high emotions. The liberal patronage which the Tudors bestowed upon art culminated with the arrival of Holbein in England, and from that date we can examine at our leisure the gradual collection and assimilation of those features which make up the "English Face."

Let us turn to the Royal portraits, as they are produced for us by photography, and understand how it comes that at masquerades and on the stage the modern countenance looks so obtrusively out of place. The type of his nation during his life was Henry the Eighth, and Holbein's picture of him does more than Froude's whole history to show us his real character. Broad, burly, somewhat sullenly he stands, his feet wide apart, his hands thrust into his belt, and his eyes looking straight at you ; his lips are full, sensual, firmly shut ; his nose broad and clubbed, with heavy wrinkles at the brows, his eyes crow-footed, and his ears widely opened. The expression is that of the elephant—great sagacity, little refinement, strong will, and courage dauntless to resist. Anne of Cleves, who simpers beside him, is a long-chinned, big-eyed, narrow-browed creature, perfectly placid and wholly uninteresting.

But when we come to Anne Boleyn, Jane Seymour, Kate Howard, and Parr, we see the vivacity which was to thrill the next generation already stirring. Anne Boleyn is plump, voluptuous, but of high courage and temper. But for the full jowl the face would be refined and daring. Seymour has an intelligent, earnest, and thoughtful face ; Howard a sly, sensual, and self-restrained one ; Parr has the forehead of an artist, and the mouth of a wit. Intelligence gleams from each head. In the next generation the coarseness of lip and jaw vanish. Mary has no sexuality save that which springs from disease. Her pressed, vinegar lips, the lower one almost split, the wide nostrils, and the prominent cheek bones, give ample assurance that the broad lips, the high brow, and the somewhat æsthetic weakness of her husband, could never match her temper. Elizabeth's fine and haughty face comes like a burst of sunshine among these gloomy intellects. Who is accountable for that aquiline nose, and that firm, sweetly-moulded chin of Louis de Hervè's picture? Anne Boleyn perhaps alone could tell. Elizabeth's nose is a revelation in national physiognomy.

The club nose was the characteristic of the age. Louis XII. had it, so had the noble, serious face of the Duke of Suffolk, so had Dorset, Jane Grey, James IV., Francis II., Mary of Guise; the beautiful, intellectual face of Guilford Dudley would be nearly Greek but for this trait. Elizabeth and her rival, Mary of Scots, were almost alone in exception. Wère not the supposition too fanciful, one might imagine that they escaped from the influence of parental impress, and that their minds moulded their features wholly. The heads of both women are keen with intelligence. There is not a trace of the sensual weakness or the sensual strength of the last generation. An age of Spensers, Wriotheslevs, and Raleighs was at hand. Women began to rule, not through the flesh, as in the days of chivalry and lust, but through the spirit. Elizabeth and Mary were alike in one regard. They were both incapable of loving, and both for the same reason. They never met a master, or at least one who cared to master them. Elizabeth was too contemptuous to surrender, Mary too confident to keep. One scorned to admit a lover, the other disdained to obey him. The keynote of passion struck by these two women vibrated through Britain. Men became adorers, poets, adventurers to win the one; murderers, rebels, plotters, martyrs, to secure a lasting claim upon the other. What result had this state of things in moulding the fleshy masks which these daring and impetuous spirits wore? Let us see.

The portrait of Spenser shows us a haggard-eyed, eager-browed and disappointed man. From the eagerness, the disappointment, came the banishment of the world, the turning to nature, the yearning for the good—the Faery Queene. Sir Nicholas Poyntz has a long, curling upper-lip and no chin; Babington is an ardent visionary; Drake has soft, curling hair, a streaming silk beard, a full face, and a look of deep melancholy. A beautiful miniature of Barbor (who, by the death of Mary, was delivered from the stake) is a most noticeable face. Nothing of the former generation but the firm jaw remains. The nose describes a waved line, the lips are keen and close, the forehead broad and slightly retreating, the eyes large, well opened, and at once sad and scornful. When we compare these faces with those of the Duc d'Anjou, cold, cruel, and selfish; Henry Valois, weak, mean, and treacherous; the Duc de Guise, violent and conceited, we begin to understand how England succeeded in creating a literature and reforming a religion. The only French face which presents strongly the characteristics of the English one of 1500-1600 is that of Coligni, the Admiral of France, murdered at the Huguenot massacre. The type of the intellect which was foreshadowing the reign of the Grand

Monarque is to be seen in the wonderful and beautiful face of the infamous and delightful Catherine de Medicis.

Out of this melancholy and thoughtful splendour what came. Take the portrait of William Lenthall, Speaker of the Rump Parliament, on the one hand; and Charles the First, when Prince of Wales, on the other. Charles is a young man of high brow, secretive mouth, heavy nose, and a head remarkable for its narrowness. There can be no question that the spirit which animates such features is at once irresolute, rash, and untrustworthy. Lenthall is sour, grim, and bitterly in earnest. The relentless mouth, with its snag-tooth, the pinched nostrils, the long, sloping nose, the eyes scaled like those of a snake, present a type of extravagant melancholy even more detestable than that of the English king. Between these extremes, however, there is a whole gamut of notes. Cavaliers and Roundheads were both gallant fellows, and if some portion of the dash and fire of the old barons held the one, the grave and serious air of the thinking thrall gave solidity to the courage of the other. The square brows, serious eyes, and stern air of the daughter of Sir Richard Stewart is preserved in the rugged and thoughtful face of her son, Oliver Cromwell.

With the restoration came the reaction. Black-browed hysterical-lipped Charles loved pleasure, and gathered round him wits and rakes. Have not all the portraits of this Court the same air? Make allowance for the similarity of costume, for the fact that the artist, having to paint every woman half naked, endowed each with the same redundant bosom and flowing hair, and we shall yet be forced to admit that all the "beauties" are very stupid, sleepy-eyed, over-fed persons; in their "fitness" resembling Dudu, but though "large, languishing and lazy," yet by no means of a "beauty that would drive you crazy." The men are better. Rochester and Sedley had brains enough to have made them great men; but the large mouths and bald temples show that the curse of the age was upon them and that they were too lazy to be virtuous. Across the Channel, however, men of the world enjoyed life still. The Court of Louis le Grand was crowded with men of genius, and the best of much that was good in a society which existed on a quagmire, looks out of the serene and religious eyes of the second wife of Louis Quatorze, Francoise D'Aubignè, Madame de Maintenon. There was no woman in England equal in sense and wit to the widow of Scarron, but there was also no one equal in boldness and villainy to Frances Howard, the poisoner of Sir Thomas Overbury.

During the next century the increase of the means of living gave a solidity to the jaw, and banished the wrinkling lines of thought around the eyes. There arose a race of refined Elizabethans. The English face in the days of Anne was the face of indolent greatness. The very vices of the age were those which sprang from a disdain of consequences. Men, lived, made love, fought, drank, got into debt, or died in a stately manner, doing out of sheer indolence all those things which the train of the French Regent—his clever, pimpled, careless face is the mirror of his age—did in laborious pursuit of pleasure. The strain of French vivacity yet lingering in the airs which blew over the kingdom, gave us eager, impulsive Pope; genial, careless Steele; brought us, by force of its example, the bitterness of Swift; the salacious humour of Sterne; nay, even the jovial tenderness of Goldsmith; while the backbone of " old English manners " (as eating, drinking, and healthful profligacy were termed) saved the nation from ruin in the general overturn of the long-threatened French Revolution.

From this period the country of English physiognomy lies straight before us, with finger-posts on either side. Gainsborough, Reynolds, and Lawrence have reproduced our ancestors in their habits as they lived; Hogarth, Rowlandson, and Gilray have taught us how to recognise them, Lavater how to talk with them. These men and women were our immediate forbears, and yet we are no more like them as a race than they were like the men and women of the Puritan days, than the Puritans were like the Elizabethans, or than the heroes of the Armada and the Spanish main resembled the feudal barons or the knights of chivalry.

With this much of introduction, let us proceed from the accession of George I., and note the causes which have continued to produce those nondescript physiognomies which we meet in our daily walk. We are all familiar with the terms—" An Elizabethan face," " a Puritan face," " a face for hair powder," " a nineteenth century face." We know still better the expressions—" An Oriental face," " an Italian face," " an English face." Let us endeavour to understand what these terms mean. Let us see why, in a few years, we may talk of an Australian face, and what that face may be like.

OURSELVES.

WHEN we look at those portraits of gentlemen in white wigs, and ladies in short-waisted dresses, which adorn the walls of some few houses in the colonies, and are reproduced by the score in Wardour Street, for the benefit of modern gentleman who are desirous of begetting ancestors, we are struck with one peculiarity—the fulness of the jowl. In the portraits of notable men this peculiarity is almost exaggerated into a defect. Johnson, Goldsmith, Garrick even, had it. It is one of the signs of the times, and stamps a man as belonging to the Georgian era—to the days of Hogarth's *Beer Street*, Smollett's *Feast after the Manner of the Ancients*, and Gilray's *Evacuation of Malta*. What is the cause of big jowls, full temples, and bull necks? What, in fact, is the cause of the Georgian face? Simple excess of aliment. The men of 1720 to 1795 were gross feeders. The Germans are notorious crammers. It is their capacity for gorging which is the measure of their power. They are a race of strong-willed men—men combative and masterful. Experience shows that hollow-templed men are poets, philosophers, and essayists. *Facts* show that the wits who were supplanted by the strong thinkers of the Hanoverian invasion *were* exactly such hollow-templed fellows. From the instant the Germans poured into England—from that instant began the reign of full feeding and of drink.

Not to confine ourselves to the respective duration of the uninsurable lives of Kings, let us consider, as from a height of observation, the British people from Hogarth to Gilray. Their recorded lives are records of alimentary excess. *The Gate of Calais* is a jest at the sparse feeding of the French nation, and is remarkable as a proof that Hogarth, who may be justly considered a type of the middle-class Englishmen of that day, had no notion of nutriment save in the shape of lumps of cooked flesh. His Frenchmen are represented as having become lanterns upon a diet of rich soups, and his English as having been reared into grand adiposity by the mastification of beef-shins and collops of veals. In *Beer Street and Gin Lane* we see the same theory expressed. The drinkers of gin are squalid, haggard and thin. Men kill themselves; women drop their children over area railings; corpses are thrust into coffin-shells. All is hideous and terrifying. The beer-drinkers are presented, not as well-contented home-keeping persons, but as boozers, fat, swollen with malt, fermenting with new yeast, rudely amorous, bestially desirous of all sensual gratification. This full-up-to-the-throat sort of happiness was really what was enjoyed at the time. In *Midnight Conversation*, hot punch in huge bowls lends zest to song. In the *Rake's Progress* the hero is dyspeptically insane. In *Marriage à la mode*, a cur, half-starved, leaps on the table to seize a bone. In the *Four Stages of Cruelty* the good boy offers his cake to save the life of the tortured dog. Everywhere intrude shapes and forms of eating. In *Midnight and Noon*, the girl whom the black boy is kissing, carries a huge pie. In the *Industrious Apprentice* a whole row of Aldermen are seen, with napkins swathed under their fat chaps, gnawing bones. In the *Election Dinner* the prevailing taste for gorging and guzzling may be said to have reached its height. One man has burst his waist belt. One pours wine over his friend's head. The *disjecta membra* of the feast lie around, as are scattered the fragments of a carcase torn by dogs. The host is dying of a surfeit. Oyster-shells literally pile the tables. Tobacco-smoke completes what gluttony began, and burdened stomachs kick against their load.

Let the reader bethink himself of the incessant device employed by the novelists of the Georgian era to produce an *embroglio*. What is the excuse for Mr. Tom Jones, Mr. Joseph Andrews, or Mr. Peregrine Pickle leaving his chamber in the inn? A modern writer, true to modern facts, would insinuate sleeplessness, a desire to smoke and so soothe the too active brain, fear for his own or his horse's safety—a thousand other matters turning upon mental exercise. Nothing of this sort occurs to the heroes of Fielding or of Smollett. They go to bed and sleep soundly, but are awakened by the effects of their gluttony. "Joseph, in whose bowels the roasted pork was still sticking," and "Jones, who began to feel the effects of the punch, combined with the too hearty supper which he ate," rise from their beds and, returning, blunder into different chambers. The device seems so easy that we are convinced it is natural. The men of that time did habitually that which men of our time do but seldom—they over-ate themselves. The caricatures of Gilray and Rowlandson are full of allusions to this practice. To put out of mind those grosser jests with which the student of caricature history must be of necessity familiar, we can remember the *Orgies of the P— of W—l—s*, and that recurring decimal in the humorous sum the *Household Economy of Farmer George*.

The example of riotous living set by the Regent and his friends was, however, an example tempered in some degree by taste. Escaped from the insularity of her moral position, England contrived to get into her cooks' heads some notions beyond roast beef, even though she was compelled to achieve the task by conquering the nations who understood the art of living. During the reign of H.B. we notice that the faces depicted are less gross than of yore. Lord Althorp is a heavy jowled man, to be sure, but the rising curve of little Lord John's nose had already risen above the horizon, and the Iron Duke brings back the severest Roman physiognomy. Though the sensual lip, the wrinkled throat, and the retreating forehead were not to be eliminated for a generation, we see clearly, in the first pages of the struggling *Punch*, that the English national face has undergone a change. It has become lighter and more keen. Science advances, restrictions upon trade are removed, men no longer embittered by fierce party struggles, turn their attention to money-making. Victoria reigns. The husband of the Sovereign is a man of wide sympathy and philosophic mind. Under his auspices philanthropy becomes fashionable. Universal peace brings attempts at improvement, engineering schemes are projected, industrial social exhibitions held. The picture has another side. The importance of trade is absurdly magnified. To die "rich" is considered to be worth the cost of living an unhealthy and dishonest life. Speculation—which hardens the eye, and wears the strained muscles always engaged in concealing the expression of natural emotion—is rife. Ruin, rapid and total, overtakes many. Genteel Poverty asserts a physiognomy of its own, at once humble and haughty, timid and stubborn. There rises out of this ruin, and this competition, a creature who is known as "Brummagem"—a man who is neither very rich, nor very clever, nor very well-behaved, but who pretends to be all three. *Videri quam esse* is the motto of smart brokers, sharp traders, and those who thrive by dexterity in avoiding legal offence. In the midst of this—when Tennyson, the hollow-templed, high-nosed, haughty poet, is writing "Maud" to urge the

> Smooth-faced, snub-nosed rogues
> To leap from counter and till—

war bursts, and England regenerates herself in the Crimea, and is fierily baptized in Indian plains. From the men of those latter days —from the men of the *last* half of this century, springs the Australian race. The gold discoveries attracted to this hemisphere some of the best nerve-power of England.

K 133

Already there existed in the Australias much sturdy Anglo-Saxon stuff. The officers and soldiers who, with their families, constituted the free population of early colonial days, were men of courage and daring. Many of the voluntary immigrants were at least equal to the best middle-class Englishman, while the banished population over which such men as Fyans and Therry ruled, had at least the merit of being eminent in their several capacities, even though their capacities had been misapplied. Among the convicts were many men of great courage, great strength, great powers of brain, and in many instances of astonishing talents for mechanics and the fine arts. It is only reasonable to expect that the children of such parents, transplanted to another atmosphere, dieted upon new foods, and restrained in their prime of life from sensual excess, should be at least *remarkable*.

But criminality is not reproductive. Being as abnormal a condition as skill in painting or playing is an abnormal condition, it cannot flourish beyond its generation. The genius of the thief buds, blossoms, and dies as surely as does the genius of the artist. But for immigration the convict continent would have been depeopled. Immigration ensued, and what an immigration! The best bone and sinew of Cornwall, the best muscle of Yorkshire, the keenest brains of Cockneydom—Bathurst, Ballarat, Bendigo, had them all. With them came also the daring spendthrift, the young cavalry officer who had lived too fast for the Jews, the younger son who had outrun his income. Barristers of good family and small practice, surgeons having all the Dublin Dissector in their heads and all the hospital experience of Paris in their hands, met each other over a windlass at Bathurst, or in a drive at Ballarat. If there was plenty of muscle in the new land, there was no lack of blood. Put aside prejudice and look at the Bench, the Bar, and the Church of this great continent. Look at the schools, libraries, and botanic gardens of Australia. Read the accounts of the boat races, the cricket matches, and say if our youth are not manly. Listen to the plaudits which greet a finished actor or a finely-gifted singer, and confess also that we have some taste and culture. Go into those parts of the country where the canker of trade has not yet penetrated, and mark the free hospitality, the generous kindness, the honest welcome which shall greet you. Sail up Sydney Harbour, ride over a Queensland plain, watch the gathering of an Adelaide harvest, or mingle with the orderly crowd which throngs to a Melbourne Cup-race, and deny, if you can, that there is here the making of a great nation. You do not deny it; but——. But what?

"There are many factors in the sum of a nation's greatness—Religion, Polity, Commerce."

Granted; but these are controllable. There is only one influence which we cannot escape, though we may modify it, and that is the influence of Physical Laws. Let us consider what climate the Australian nation will live in, and what food it will be prone to eat, and having arrived at a distinct conclusion upon those two points, we can predict, with positive certainty, their religion, their polity, their commerce, and their appearance. You stare? Attend for a moment, and you will see that a proposition of Euclid is not clearer.

OUR CHILDREN

THE quality of a race of beings is determined by two things: food and climate. The measure of that quality is the measure of the success in the race's incessant struggle to wrest nature to its own advantage. The history of a nation is the history of the influence of nature modified by man, and of man modified by the influence of nature. The highest practical civilisations have been those in which man came off victor in the contest, and employed the wind to drive his ships, the heat to work his engines, the cataract to turn his mills. The lowest, those in which nature reduced men to the condition of brutes—eating, drinking and feeding. Given the price of the cheapest food in the country, and the average registration of the thermometer, and it is easy to return a fair general estimate of the national characteristics. I say a general estimate, because other causes—the height of mountains, the width of rivers, the vicinity of volcanoes, etc., induce particular results. But the intelligent mind, possessed of information on the two points of food and climate can confidently sum up, first, the bodily vigour; second, the mental vigour; third, the religion; fourth, the political constitution of a nation.

Before speculating on future events, let us apply our test to history. The climate of Egypt is hot and moist, the inundation of the Nile renders the soil wonderfully fertile, and food is extremely cheap and easily obtained. The climate of India is hot, and the inhabitants live for the most part on rice, which is cheap and usually obtained in abundance. The climate of Mexico is hot. Indian corn, which formed the staple of the food of the inhabitants, is astonishingly prolific and consequently cheap. Now, cheap food means in all cases cheap marriage, or in other words rapid reproduction of the species. A hot climate means small expense in house-building, clothing, or furniture. A man sells his labour to meet his requirements, and in a hot country his requirements are few. In a hot country, therefore, wages are low, and the rapid increase of population renders human life of little value. The difference between the labourer and the employer of labour, then, is great, and from this difference comes tyranny on the one side and slavery on the other. The rich grow richer and the poor poorer. Wealth means leisure, and leisure means luxury and learning. Consequently we should expect to find that a nation living under these conditions would present the following characteristics :—A poor and enslaved peasantry, a rich and luxurious aristocracy, who cultivate great learning and some taste for art.

Now, this condition answers precisely to the condition in which Anthony found Egypt, Warren Hastings found India, and Cortez found Mexico. In each place the nobles lived in incredible luxury and the poor in incredible misery. The learning of each nation was the marvel of its successors. The expenditure of human life in each was terrible. Human beings were not only sacrificed in thousands for the building of the gigantic temples common to each country, but absolutely slaughtered like sheep to celebrate the triumphs of a conqueror, or appease the anger of a god. It is remarkable that the religion of each nation was bloodthirsty and full of terror. Siva the destroyer, Tyhon the Betrayer, Kitzpolchi, God of the Smoking Hearts, alike demanded offerings of blood and tears. It is quite easy to account for this. Each nation grew up among scenes of natural grandeur, and a witness to the almost daily performance of the most majestic operations of nature. The hurricane, the storm, the simoom, the flood, the earthquake—all were familiar to their minds, and poets were created by the influence of the scenery which they described. Men having, by the expenditure of their own blood, modified nature with aqueducts, canals and roads, nature modified their struggles for freedom by the imposition of a terrible superstition which darkened all their days.

It is an absolute fact that religion is, in all cases a matter of diet and climate. The Greek, with pure air, light soil, and placid scenery, invented an exquisite anthropomorphism, in which he deified all his own attributes. The Egyptian, the Mexican, and the dweller by the Ganges invented a cruel and monstrous creed of torture and death. The influence of climate was so strong upon the ancient Jews that they were perpetually relapsing from Theism into the congenial cruelties of Moloch and Astarte. Remove them into another country, and history has no record of a people—save, perhaps, the modern Pagans of our Universities—more devotedly attached to the purest form of intelligent adoration of the Almighty. The Christian faith, transported to the Libyan deserts, or the rocks of Spain, became burdened with horrors, and oppressed with saint-worship. The ferocious African's Mumbo Jumbo, the West Indian's Debbel-debbel, are merely the products of climate and the result of a dietary scale. Cabanis says that religious emotion is secreted by the smaller intestines. Men "think they are pious when they are only bilious." Men who habitually eat non-nitrogenous substances and pay little attention to the state of their bowels are always prone to gloomy piety. This is the reason why Scotchmen and women are usually inclined to religion.

Now let us consider what climate and food will do for Australians.

In the first place, we must remember that the Australasian nation will have an empire of many climates, for it will range from Singapore and Malacca in the north, to New Zealand in the south. All varieties of temperature will be traversed by the railroad traveller of 1977. The enormous area of Australia, that circle whose circumference is the sea, and whose centre is a desert, is a strong reason against federation. It is more than likely that what should be the Australian Empire will be cut in half by a line drawn through the centre of the continent. All above this line—Queensland and the Malaccas, New Guinea, and the parts adjacent—will evolve a luxurious and stupendous civilisation only removed from that of Egypt and Mexico by the measure of the remembrance of European democracy. All beneath this line will be a Republic, having the mean climate, and, in consequence, the development of Greece. The intellectual capital of this Republic will be Victoria. The fashionable and luxurious capital on the shore of Sydney Harbour. The governing capital in New Zealand.

The inhabitants of this Republic are easily described. The soil is for the most part deficient in lime, hence the bones of the autochthones will be long and soft. The boys will be tall and slender like cornstalks. It will be rare to find girls with white and sound teeth. A small pelvis is the natural result of small bones, and a small pelvis means a sickly mother and stunted children. Bad teeth mean bad digestion, and bad digestion means melancholy. The Australians will be a fretful, clever, perverse, irritable race. The climate breeds a desire for out-of-door exercise. Men will transact their business under verandahs, and make appointments at the corners of streets. The evening stroll will be an institution. Fashion and wealth will seek to display themselves out of doors. Hence domesticity will be put away. The " hearth " of the Northerner, the "fireside" of Burns' Cottar, will be unknown. The boys, brought up outside their homes' four walls, will easily learn to roam, and as they conquer difficulties for themselves will learn to care little for their parents. The Australasians will be selfish, self-reliant, ready in resource, prone to wander, caring little for home ties. Mercenary marriage will be frequent, and the hotel system of America will be much favoured. The Australasians will be large meat-eaters, and meat-eaters require more stimulants than vegetarians. The present custom of drinking alcohol to excess—favoured alike by dietary scale and by carnivorous practices—will continue. All carnivora are rash, gloomy, given to violences. Vegetarians live at a lower level of health, but are calmer and happier. Red radicals are for the most part meat-eaters. A vegetarian—Shelley *exceptio quæ probat regulam* —is a Conservative. Fish eaters are invariably moderate Whigs. The Australasians will be content with nothing short of a turbulent democracy.

There is plenty of oxygen in Australian air, and our Australasians will have capacious chests also—*cæteris paribus*, large nostrils. The climate is unfavourable to the development of a strumous diathesis ; therefore, we cannot expect men of genius unless we beget them by frequent intermarriage. Genius is to the physiologist but another form of scrofula, and to call a man a poet is to physiologically insult the mother who bore him. When Mr. Edmund Yates termed one of his acquaintances a " scrofulous Scotch poet," he intended to be personal. He was merely tautological. It may be accepted as an axiom that there has never existed a man of genius who was not strumous. Take the list from Julius Cæsar to Napoleon, or from Job to Keats, and point out one great *mind* that existed in a non-strumous body. The Australasians will be freed from the highest burden of intellectual development.

For their faces. The sun beating on the face closes the eyes, puckers the cheeks, and contracts the muscles of the orbit. Our children will have deep-set eyes with overhanging brows; the lower eyelid will not melt into the cheek, but will stand out *en profile*, clear and well-defined. This, though it may add to character, takes away from beauty. There will be necessarily a strong development of the line leading from nostril to mouth. The curve between the centre of the upper lip and the angle of the mouth will be intensified; hence, the upper lip will be shortened, and the whole mouth made fleshy and sensual. The custom of meat-eating will square the jaw, and render the hair coarse but plentiful. The Australasian will be a square-headed, masterful man, with full temples, plenty of beard, a keen eye, a stern and yet sensual mouth. His teeth will be bad, and his lungs good. He will suffer from liver disease, and become prematurely bald—average duration of life in the unmarried, fifty-nine; in the married, sixty-five and a decimal.

The conclusion of all this is, therefore, that in another hundred years the average Australasian will be a tall, coarse, strong-jawed, greedy, pushing, talented man, excelling in swimming and horsemanship. His religion will be a form of Presbyterianism; his national policy a democracy tempered by the rate of exchange. His wife will be a thin, narrow woman, very fond of dress and idleness, caring little for her children, but without sufficient brain-power to sin with zest. In five hundred years, unless recruited from foreign nations, the breed will be wholly extinct; but in that five hundred years it will have changed the face of Nature, and swallowed up all our contemporary civilisation. It is, however—perhaps fortunately—impossible that we shall live to see this stupendous climax.

ASK FOR
Victoria Brewery

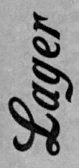

Lager *Bier.*

Guaranteed Absolutely Pure,
And free from Chemicals of any kind.

The Only Genuine LAGER BIER
Manufactured in the Colonies

S. BOND,
CYCLE ENGINEER
(17 Years' Experience),
94 LITTLE COLLINS STREET.

BUILDER OF FIRST GRADE AND UP-TO-DATE CYCLES,
FOR GENTLEMEN, LADIES AND CHILDREN.
Specialty: All Classes of Repairs at Reasonable Rates.

Best Materials and First-Class Workmanship Guaranteed.   Machines built from 17lbs. weight.
Inventions worked out ; strict Secrecy Guaranteed.   Parts Made to Order.

HERR HANS RASSMUSSEN,
The Celebrated Danish Botanist, Sole Proprietor of the Purely

HERBAL ALFALINE REMEDIES,

Which have become the most popular BLOOD AND NERVE REMEDIES, not only throughout the Australasian Colonies, but throughout the World, and which have given general satisfaction to the Australian public for over ten years, as proved by the thousands of unsolicited Testimonials received by the proprietor.

Send for his Free Book, "THE NATURAL DOCTOR" which contains a great deal of very useful information, and valuable hints concerning the Cure of Blood and Nervous Diseases, together with a list of the ALFALINE REMEDIES and numerous Testimonials, which will prove the great virtues of the ALFALINE HERBAL REMEDIES.

Head Office—547 GEORGE STREET, SYDNEY, N.S.W.

Letters to the Head Office may also be addressed simply thus :—
"PROPRIETOR, Box 208, General Post Office, SYDNEY."

INTERCOLONIAL BRANCHES—VICTORIA—150 Bourke-st., Melbourne. QUEENSLAND—160 Queen-st. Brisbane. SOUTH AUSTRALIA—154 Rundle-st., Adelaide. NEW ZEALAND—91 Lambton Quay, Wellington. WEST AUSTRALIA—Central Buildings, corner of Hay and William-sts., Perth.
Branches and Agencies throughout AFRICA, AMERICA, ASIA and EUROPE.

I.

iii.

A PROGRESSIVE AUSTRALASIAN INSTITUTION.

THE CITIZENS'
Life Assurance Company Limited.

(BRANCHES AND AGENCIES IN ALL THE COLONIES).

SOME CLAIMS on Policies within the last 12 months paid by the Citizen's Life Assurance Company Limited

INDUSTRIAL BRANCH.

No. of Policy.	Initials of Assured.	District.	Amount Paid to Coy. in Premiums.	Amount of Policy Paid by Coy.
443,974	P. H.	Brunswick	£1 15 0	£25 0 0
461,346	H. C. G. S.	Eldorado	0 7 0	12 10 0
428,256 } 457,665 }	R. T. L.	North Melbourne ...	3 6 0	37 13 0
453,152	M. W....	Broadford	1 4 0	12 18 0
426,497	J. S.	Bendigo	1 14 8	25 4 0
469,103	W. P.	South Melbourne. ...	0 8 0	10 8 6
437,254	W. A.	Kangaroo Flat ...	2 6 0	31 4 0
431,366	E. P.	Yarraville	2 18 4	50 0 0
362,997 } 472,358 }	J. S.	Brunswick	1 7 0	22 7 0
437,131	W. S. D.	Narandera	2 6 8	43 15 0
464,338	E. E. S.	Ballarat	0 7 0	13 19 0
438,233	B. M. S.	Carlton	2 8 0	26 10 0
471,328	G. J. R. S.	Richmond	0 2 0	10 0 0

ORDINARY BRANCH.

No. of Policy.	Initials of Assured.	District.	Amount Paid to Coy. in Premiums.	Amount of Policy Paid by Coy.
7,323	G. M. H.	Bairnsdale	£12 13 4	£500 0 0
5,009	T. W. H.	Prahran	34 1 3	500 0 0
7,553	H. S. I.	South Melbourne ...	9 1 8	100 0 0
4,115	J. S.	North Melbourne ...	42 17 6	500 0 0
4,564	W. T. M.	Ballarat	19 18 0	200 0 0
10,120	E. R.	South Yarra	6 0 8	182 16 6
3,069	H. J. M.	Kerang	36 15 0	221 0 0
3,608	E. C.	St. Kilda	21 13 4	109 0 0
3,581	J. R. N.	Balwyn	48 15 0	322 10 0

Last year **4631** Claims, similar to the above, were promptly paid, being an average of nearly 15 for every working day.

The *Commercial World*, London, one of the highest authorities on insurance matters, in commenting on a recent balance-sheet of this Company, made the following significant remarks:—"Without fear of contradiction, we re-assert that results such as are here indicated by the Citizens' Company have never been approached in this or, we believe, any other country." The *North British Economist*, the *Bankers' Magazine*, and the *Insurance Journal* speak in equally congratulatory terms.

The career of the Citizen's Life Assurance Company has been one of uninterrupted prosperity.

It has now more Policyholders in Australasia than any other Life Assurance Company or Society.

Its splendid Industrial Branch organisation enables it to transact Ordinary Life Assurance business at a low rate of cost, thereby ensuring Liberal Annual Bonus Accumulations to its Ordinary Branch Policyholders.

Full particulars as to rates of Premiums, &c., can be had on application to any of the Company's numerous Agents, or to—

W. N. DEWAR, F.S.S.,
Resident Secretary.

Citizens' Buildings,
163 Queen St., Melbourne.

v.

vii.

CRAWFORD & CO.,

WHOLESALE AND FAMILY DRAPERS,

Importers, Manufacturers,

Have Large and Choicely Assorted Stocks of

Manchester Goods	Millinery
Dress Goods	Laces and Ribbons
Silks	Underwear
Mantles	Hosiery
Costumes	Boots and Shoes
Furs	Men's Boys' and Youths' Clothing
Haberdashery	Umbrellas
Carpets, &c.	Linoleums, &c.

Patterns forwarded Post Free to any Address in the Colonies.

THE PUBLIC SUPPLIED DIRECT AT WHOLESALE PRICES.

The Modern Family Warehouse,

250 & 252 FLINDERS ST., MELBOURNE.

Established 1853.

Telephone 912.

HERBERT KING,

Furnishing Undertaker,

HEAD OFFICE: LENNOX ST., RICHMOND.

157 Swan St., East Richmond.   Burwood Rd., Hawthorn.

Nicholson Street, Footscray,

Malvern Branch, Glenferrie Road, Malvern. Telephone 39.

xlii.

xlv

W. MENTIPLAY & SON,

AUSTRALIAN BOTANIC INSTITUTE,

188 Bourke St. East, Melbourne.

WE CURE Hydatids without operation, Erysipelas, Blood Poisoning, Eczema, Barbers' Itch, Liver and Kidney Complaints, Indigestion, Scurvy, Bad Legs, Nervous Debility, Bright's Disease, Gravel, Worms, Marasmus, and all other Diseases, when all other Remedies Fail.

The following are a few Testimonials out of the many thousands in hand :

BLOOD POISONING.

DEAR SIR,—I have much pleasure in thanking you for curing my leg of Blood Poisoning. As you are aware I came to you from Gippsland, and had been under treatment by three different Doctors, and none of them could do me any good. One of them thought it was Erysipelas, and the others thought the bone was diseased, and wanted me to have it scraped, and when you told me it was Blood Poisoned and you could cure it in a few days, I thought it impossible to cure it in such a short time, as I had then been laid up for five (5) months, and had medical attendance all the time, which cost me a good many pounds.

My foot is now as well as ever it was and I am thankful to you for it, and for any further information about it inquire at 157 Graham Street, Port Melbourne.

I remain, yours sincerely,
JAMES DUNCAN.

CHRONIC ECZEMA.

DEAR SIR,—I am sure you will be pleased to hear I am like a new man to-day. The Pills have done me so much good. I think you ought to publish them far and wide. I believe I told you I had been taking all kinds of Doctors' medicines for about fourteen (14) years, and I received no benefit from them. I do honestly say that a few doses of your Pills have done me more good than all the Doctor's medicines, and I must say I have every confidence you will cure me and prove that you can cure Chronic Eczema of 14 years' standing.

I remain, yours very truly,
JOHN WILSON, Briagolong, Gippsland,

THRUSH and MARASMUS.

Grant Street, West Brunswick.

DEAR SIR,—Allow me to express my gratitude to you and publicly thank you for saving the life of my little daughter, aged 3 weeks, who suffered shortly after birth from that terrible scourge to children, Thrush. At your advice we gave the little mite your Marasmus Pills (6 per day) and after the first day she began to recover, and in ten (10) days was perfectly free from the complaint. I only bought one box, for which I paid 3/6, and if it had been £3 I would have paid it cheerfully.

I am, etc., H. CAMERON.

HYDATIDS.

DEAR SIR,—I am very pleased to acknowledge with gratitude the wonderful cure you performed on my wife after 14 years, and who had been under treatment by six Doctors, who came to the conclusion she had a tumour. Being advised to see you, and after your examination, you told her it was no tumour but Hydatids, for which you treated her successfully. She is now enjoying good health and has been ever since. I am, etc ,
J. ANDERSON, 234 Burnley Street, Richmond.

DISEASE OF THE KIDNEYS.

Leceister Street, Carlton.

DEAR SIR,—Having suffered through Disease of the Kidneys I was recommended to try your Kidney Pills. I found three (3) boxes to cure me, and I can highly recommend them to anyone suffering from the same complaint. Do with this as you think fit. THOMAS WILKINS.

When you are‾‾‾‾

FURNISHING

GIVE

H. Ackman & Co.,

243=247 Smith Street,

‾‾‾Fitzroy, Melbourne,

A CALL.

Houses Furnished Throughout

OR ANY SINGLE ARTICLE

FOR

CASH OR WEEKLY INSTALMENTS.

Their Prices are moderate, and civility and attention is the order of the day.

Non-Purchasers are invited to inspect their extensive Show-rooms at any time.

John McIntyre & Co., Glasgow, N.B.,

Established 1790.

DISTILLERS

OF

"LIQUER"

Glenlivet Whisky. Guaranteed 10 Years Old.

"ERA"

Glenlivet Whisky. Guaranteed 5 Years Old.

"FERNDALE"

Islay Whisky. Guaranteed 5 Years Old.

"LOCHABER"

Campbelltown Whisky. Guaranteed 5 Years Old.

Buyers will find these Whiskies the Purest in the Market.

If you have any difficulty in getting supplies of the above, please communicate immediately with the Distillers' Sole Representative in Australia, Tasmania, and New Zealand—

DONALD MUNRO,

The Exchange, Melbourne.

John Adamson,

Wholesale and Retail

✳ GROCER ✳

AND

PROVISION MERCHANT,

133 Brunswick Street,

◁ FITZROY, ▷

AND CORNER OF

Lee Street & Canning Street,

◁ CARLTON. ▷

xxlii.

CPSIA information can be obtained at www.ICGtesting.com
Printed in the USA
LVOW112211120312

272723LV00014B/153/P

9 781146 297776